Roy Thompson

Saturation
Evangelism

Saturation
Evangelism

GEORGE W. PETERS

ZONDERVAN PUBLISHING HOUSE
Grand Rapids, Michigan

SATURATION EVANGELISM
© 1970 by Zondervan Publishing House
Grand Rapids, Michigan

Library of Congress Catalog Card Number 74-106433

CONTENTS

Introduction

PART ONE—DEFINITIONS 9
1. The Centrality and Motivation of Evangelism 11
2. The Unique Message of Evangelism 13
3. The Unique Method of Evangelism 18
4. The Unique Messenger of Evangelism 21
5. Summary: The Supreme Mission of the Church 25
6. Saturation Evangelism—Its Historical Antecedents . . . 27
7. The Biblical Basis of Saturation Evangelism 30
8. The Characteristics of Saturation Evangelism 37
   Footnotes for Part One 48

PART TWO—EVANGELISM-IN-DEPTH AND NEW LIFE FOR ALL . 49
9. The Inception and Philosophy of Evangelism-in-Depth . . 51
10. The Program, Organization and Objections of Evangelism-
    in-Depth 55
11. The Record of Evangelism-in-Depth 58
12. The Ideals and Practice of Evangelism-in-Depth 63
13. Evaluation of Evangelism-in-Depth 67
14. Evangelism-in-Depth and Church Growth 72
15. Evangelism-in-Depth and Perennial Evangelism 78
16. Summary and Recommendations 82
17. The Birth of New Life For All 87
18. The Principles and Objectives of New Life For All . . . 92
19. The Purpose, Plan and Organization of New Life For All . 96
20. How New Life For All Works 101
21. Factors in the Success of New Life For All 110
22. Results of New Life For All 115
23. Points of Weakness of New Life For All 124
24. Lessons Learned From Evangelism-in-Depth and New Life
    For All 127
    Footnotes for Part Two 142

PART THREE—HOUSEHOLD EVANGELISM AND GROUP MOVEMENTS 145

25. Biblical and Missionary Perspectives on Household Evangelism 147
26. Principles of Household Evangelism 160
27. Group Evangelism 168
28. Determining Principles 182
29. Gospel Saturation 188
30. Cultural Adaptation 193
31. Mobilization and Training of Believers 200
32. Ten Steps to Group Evangelism 206
33. Dangers and Advantages of Group Evangelism 215
    Footnotes for Part Three 221
    Summary 222
    General Bibliography 224

INTRODUCTION

IN 1966 I BEGAN A STUDY of the various patterns and movements of evangelism around the world. The work was hastened and expanded when I was requested by the executives of the Evangelical Foreign Missions Association and the Interdenominational Foreign Mission Association to prepare several evaluations for the joint executives' retreat of the two bodies at Winona Lake, Indiana, September, 1968. They wanted me to include studies of Evangelism-in-Depth, sponsored by the Latin America Mission; New Life For All, conducted by the evangelical churches and missions of Nigeria; similar crusades being conducted by Overseas Crusades, the Southern Baptists, and the Assemblies of God; and the last nationwide evangelistic endeavor of the Korean churches.

Soon it became evident that the assignment was too comprehensive to be completed in one year. I decided, therefore, to survey some movements for general information and study others in depth. I concentrated on Evangelism-in-Depth and New Life For All, the two most dynamic programs of saturation evangelism. While Evangelism-in-Depth has been extensively publicized and is consequently well-known, that is not so with New Life For All. The latter movement has been too modest about its contributions and accomplishments. It deserves more publicity. Students and leaders of saturation evangelism would do well to study both movements before they tailor a program for their own countries.

In both cases I was privileged to do field studies. For Evangelism-in-Depth I was also able to secure the records of the last ten years of nearly one thousand churches in six different countries, as well as some one hundred and fifty personal evaluations from church and mission leaders who had participated in the program.

In studying New Life For All I worked in the field, where I gathered sufficient information for an evaluation. I was also privileged to obtain the records of hundreds of churches.

The report of my studies, the findings and conclusions are found in the 1968 Mission Executives' Retreat Report of the Evangelical Foreign Missions Association and the Interdenominational Foreign Missions Association (pp. 95-166). They are included in this book with some modification, expansions and illustrations.

The missionary and office personnel of both movements were most gracious, cooperative and helpful. Indeed, they were more anxious to learn of their own weaknesses than to hear of their credit and praise. My gratitude as well as congratulations go to these devoted people.

The additional movements mentioned above were surveyed from literature and personal interviews. A paper on "Evangelism in Biblical Perspective" was prepared and presented as foundational.

These studies eventually developed into the present volume on saturation evangelism. It is my deepest conviction that saturation evangelism rightly conceived, carefully organized, wisely supervised, and energetically executed under the direction of the Holy Spirit can revolutionize modern evangelism. It could result in the total evangelism of our generation. It embodies more biblical principles and comes nearer in practice and purpose to the New Testament than any pattern of evangelism that has been advanced heretofore. It deserves our closest study and our prayerful and sacrificial support.

PART ONE —

DEFINITIONS

BEFORE EXAMINING AND EVALUATING the current expressions of saturation evangelism around the world, it is necessary to lay the proper foundations by way of basic definitions.

First, we want to look at the subject of evangelism from the perspective of the Bible. What is the definition of evangelism in the biblical sense? In this section we will explore the centrality and motivation of evangelism, and the message, method and messenger of evangelism.

Second, we want carefully to define what we mean by saturation evangelism. This will include its historical antecedents, its biblical basis, and its major characteristics as it is practiced today.

Chapter 1

THE CENTRALITY AND MOTIVATION OF EVANGELISM

EVANGELISM IS NOT EXCLUSIVELY a New Testament concept. It has a history antedating the New Testament, but only there does it develop fully and deeply. In its Greek form "evangelism" is closely related to "gospel." In the New Testament it arises out of the nature of the Gospel, which came to mankind in Jesus Christ and which announces to the world the great redemptive acts of God in His Son, our Savior and Lord.

Since the New Testament is the infallible record of the redemptive purpose and acts of God in Christ, it is our authority, starting point and pattern in evangelism. Apart from the acts of God and the record of them in the New Testament, there would be no Christian evangelism. That is why we must start there, if we are to proceed in the right direction.

THE CENTRALITY OF EVANGELISM IN THE NEW TESTAMENT

Neither Christ nor Paul are ever called an evangelist, yet both were evangelists par excellence. They were in the true sense gospellers, announcers of the good tidings of God, for that is what evangelism means. A study of the New Testament words "gospel" and "evangelize" — *euaggelion* and *euaggelidzo*—shows the central place evangelism held in the ministries of Christ and Paul.

There are one hundred and twenty-seven references to these two words in the New Testament. The method of evangelism is expressed by the word "evangelize," often translated "preach the Gospel." Christ told the multitude that He must *evangelize* the other cities also by bringing them the message of the kingdom (Luke 4:43). He could not concern Himself with only one locality or one company of people.

Twenty-three times Paul spoke of his ministry as *evangelizing*. In comparison, he referred to it as preaching only eighteen times. Explicitly he declared: "Christ sent me not to baptize, but to preach the gospel [evangelize]" (I Cor. 1:17a). Paul was supremely an evangelist, an exponent of the Gospel of Christ, the Lord.

The patterns of Christ and Paul are stamped upon the New Testament; evangelism became the major characteristic of the New Testament thrust. Upward in worship and outward in evangelism are the two major movements of Christianity; expansion and enlargement belong to its very nature.

MOTIVATION IN EVANGELISM

Evangelism is not a natural phenomenon. It becomes *natural* only when the Gospel of God is personally known, believed and obeyed, and when the Holy Spirit has unhindered control of the Christian. The external command to evangelize and the inner motivation combine so that obedience and compassion flow together to form a spiritual dynamic. The Word of God and the Holy Spirit merge to become the motivation and dynamic in evangelism.

We may, therefore, speak of motivation as obedience to the command of God and obedience to the inner direction of the Holy Spirit. Such is the ideal of the New Testament.

However, Christians who are not living on this ideal level are not exempt from the responsibility of evangelism. In no uncertain terms Christ commanded us to herald the good tidings to every creature (Mark 16:15, 16). Paul seemingly felt the full weight of the divine obligation when he said: "For if I preach the gospel, that gives me no ground for boasting. For necessity is laid upon me. Woe to me if I do not preach the gospel!" (I Cor. 9:16, RSV).

The Holy Spirit of Pentecost, the need of the world, commitment to the mind and concern of Christ, zeal for the honor of his Lord, obedience to his command, a sense of divine stewardship, devotion to his call and calling as an apostle, and the love of Christ combined in Paul to fill him with motivation and courage in evangelism.

Chapter 2

THE UNIQUE MESSAGE OF EVANGELISM

THE BIBLICAL MEANING of evangelism is best understood by looking at the three New Testament words that directly relate to it.

1. The word for "gospel," literally *evangel,* means "good news." It is found seventy-six times in the New Testament. The Anglo-Saxon form of it was God-spell, that is God-story, indicating that the Gospel concerns the great acts of God.

2. The verb *evangelize* means "to bring," or "to announce," or "to proclaim good news." It appears fifty-one times in the New Testament.

3. The word *evangelist* describes the person involved in telling the good news. It occurs only three times. However, the functions of the evangelist were included in the word "apostle," though that does not exhaust the latter term.

The New Testament presents the message, the method and the messenger of evangelism.

Evangelism is the announcement of a unique message. It concerns itself primarily with the proclamation of the Gospel of God, the redemptive act of God in Christ Jesus. It is not a general proclamation of the Word of God. It does not necessarily deal with the whole counsel of God. It is not a polemic, program of indoctrination, a series of evidences. While it does not by-pass the church and membership, it does not concern itself with particular church doctrines, policies and emphases. It is the announcement of good news to a world alienated from God, bound in sin, and under a sentence of condemnation.

The word gospel may have a broad, general meaning and refer to the message of the New Testament as a whole. Such, no doubt, is the meaning of Mark 1:1, where it is said that this is the beginning of the Gospel of Jesus Christ. In a similar manner, Paul speaks of the Gospel in general terms on numerous occasions (compare Galatians 1).

There is, however, a specialized sense in which the message is "the Gospel." This is clearly enunciated by Paul in I Corinthians 15:1-4. This is the basic kerygma of Paul, the bare Gospel, the hearthrob of God's saving deed in Christ:

1. Christ died for our sins according to the Scriptures;
2. Christ was buried — a proof of His actual death;
3. Christ rose again the third day according to the Scriptures.

It should be noted that this is a declaration—Christ died; a confirmation—according to the Scriptures; and an exposition—for our sins. The death-resurrection of Christ is more than history. It is history according to the declared purpose of God, which constitutes the redemptive event of God. Here God deals effectively with sin. Without the death-resurrection event not even Christ would be a Savior.

The Christ of death-resurrection became the pivot of New Testament gospel declaration. Everything else relating to the Gospel revolves around the focus. The Gospel has not been preached until Christ's substitutionary death on the cross and His victorious resurrection from the death have been proclaimed. This is in keeping with the words of Christ: "Thus it is written, that the Christ should suffer and on the third day rise from the dead, and that repentance and forgiveness of sins should be preached in his name to all nations" (Luke 24:46, 47, RSV).

Paul enunciated the Gospel in Romans 1:1-6. The Gospel of God centers in His Son Jesus Christ—His incarnation, His death, His resurrection—that He as the source of all grace might be preached among all nations for obedience of faith. The Son of God is not merely the bearer of the Gospel, nor merely the incarnation and demonstration of the Gospel; He is its substance and its essence, especially in the two supreme facts of His person, His incarnation and His death-resurrection.

If the preaching of the Gospel in evangelism is encumbered with too much doctrine and ethics, the central act of the Gospel will be beclouded and the sinner will be confused. Simplicity and directness of presentation are, therefore, greatly to be appreciated.

William Barclay leads us into the history, meaning and usage of the word. Says he:

> The word *euaggelion* means "gospel" or "good news," and when we come to study it we are of necessity at the very heart and centre of the Christian faith. The word *euaggelion* is so specifically and characteristically a Christian word that it has not a long history outside the NT. In classical Greek it has three meanings. (i) Originally it meant "the reward given to a messenger for bringing good tidings." It is so used in the Septuagint in II Sam. 4:10. (ii) It went on to mean "the sacrifices made to the gods when such good tidings were received." (iii) Not in classical Greek at all, but in late hellenistic Greek it comes to mean "the good tidings themselves" (I Sam. 31:9), the good tidings of "the birth of a child" (Jer. 20:15), and sometimes simply of tidings of any kind.
>
> In the Septuagint it has two usages which are faint foretastes of its NT use. (i) In the Psalms, the corresponding verb is used of telling forth the righteousness and the saving power of God (Ps. 40:10; 96:2).

(ii) In Isaiah it is used of the glad tidings of the coming of God's anointed one to His people (Isa. 40:9; 52:7). In the papyri, both noun and verb are very rare. The verb (*euaggelizesthai*) is used of a slave coming with news of a general's victory, and the noun (*euaggelion*) is used in an inscription which says that the birthday of the Roman Emperor Augustus was the beginning of good tidings for the world. But it is when we come to the NT that *euaggelion* becomes a tremendous word.[1]

I hesitate to follow Dr. C. H. Dodd slavishly in his detailed interpretation of the New Testament. However, the principle of two distinct emphases in the New Testament that he advocates in *The Apostolic Preaching and its Development* seems to me sound.

There is a distinction in the preaching of the *kerygma*—God's acts in Christ for the salvation of men—on the one hand, and the *didache*—the ethical ideal for corporal church life and individual behavior—on the other. This principle seems borne out by a comparison of apostolic preaching in the book of Acts and the instructions in the epistles. The former shows the horizontal expansion of the church through evangelism, the church facing the world with the good news; the latter point to the deepening and follow-up work in the churches, the Christianization of the church.

From the doctrinal point of view, the book of Acts seems so simple, almost superficial. Yet, it has a clear enunciation of the kerygma, the Gospel of God. Very little "teaching" is found in it. It is a book of evangelism and missions.

The Bible, however, sets the Gospel of God into a specific frame of reference. The *leitmotif* of the Old Testament is ethical monotheism. God is good and holy, so holy that He cannot behold iniquity. Sin is personal transgression and brings guilt and defilement to the degree that it separates God and man. Man is condemned as a sinner from the presence of God. Ethical monotheism makes sin more than a human weakness, a fault due to environment. It makes sin as that which justly deserves death.

Ethical monotheism makes the cross necessary; it gives the cross soteriological meaning and significance. A right concept of ethical monotheism, therefore, is an essential prerequisite to feel the need for the Gospel of God. A right and deep concept of sin does not spring from hammering on sin, but from a right concept of God. The emphasis in evangelism, therefore, is not primarily on the sins of the people, but on their concept of God.

Man's concept of God is all-determining. It dominates and determines the course of his attitudes and appetites. It makes him into a sinner and into a saint. It causes him either to flee God or to draw near to God.

This is a key to much ineffective presentation of the Gospel. There is little significance in preaching the cross where there is not a sense of guilt and condemnation. The latter, however, finds its source and enforcement in ethical monotheism.

It is essential to distinguish *evangelism* both from making disciples and the *Christianization* of the church, and from the work of civilization. We acknowledge all three as part of God's order and all three must be cared for. The mandates of God relative to them are clear and emphatic. However, evangelism is a Christian specialization. Even though it cannot be separated organically from the other aspects, it should be distinguished from them in emphasis and practice.

Such a distinction, if clearly kept in mind and conscientiously adhered to, would help us in several ways:

1. It would clarify and crystalize the message of evangelism.
2. It would give a clear focus and single thrust to a program of evangelism.
3. It would create a basis for wider cooperation in a strategy and program of evangelism. We should be able to cooperate in evangelism with all those who hold to the evangel as God's only way of salvation, even though we differ in other doctrines, church policy, and emphasis.

THE SALVATION OF GOD FOR MAN

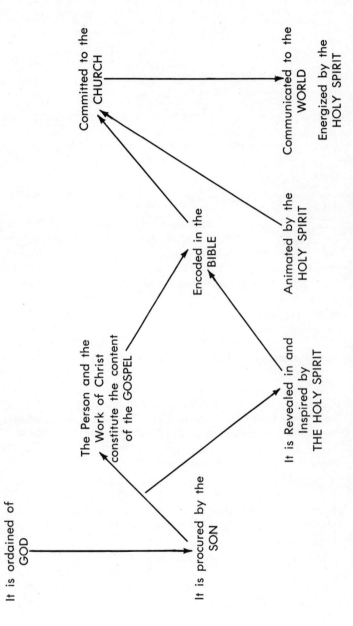

It is ordained of GOD

The Person and the Work of Christ constitute the content of the GOSPEL

It is procured by the SON

Encoded in the BIBLE

It is Revealed in and Inspired by THE HOLY SPIRIT

Committed to the CHURCH

Communicated to the WORLD

Energized by the HOLY SPIRIT

Animated by the HOLY SPIRIT

In the proclamation of the Gospel God does not by-pass Christ, the Bible nor the church, if the latter is defined according to the New Testament and performs her function according to the New Testament.

Chapter 3

THE UNIQUE METHOD OF EVANGELISM

EVANGELISM IS BOUND TO A UNIQUE AND SINGULAR METHOD. To evangelize means "to announce," "to proclaim," "to tell forth," "to bring good news." Whether this happens through personal and informal witnessing, group dialogue, drama, or formal proclamation is of minor importance.

The Scriptures present various patterns of communicating the message of Christ to people.

1. The person-to-person method so well illustrated in the ministry of Christ and in the book of Acts. There is Christ's meeting with John and Andrew (John 1:35-40); His discussion with Nicodemus (John 3:1-21); His conversation with the Samaritan woman at Jacob's well (John 4:5-25); His restoring visit with Peter (John 21:15-22). This method was followed by Philip in his unique meeting with the Ethiopian eunuch (Acts 8:26-38); and somewhat later by Ananias as he assisted Paul in his crisis experience (Acts 9:10-19). These, no doubt, are only some of many similar incidents recorded to illustrate a principle and method of gospel communication.

2. The group method, or household evangelism, as illustrated in the numerous home services and ministries Christ conducted up and down the villages of Galilee. This method is further illustrated in the experience of Peter in the home of Cornelius (Acts 10:24-48). The many household conversions recorded by Paul were the results of similar services.

3. The informal and public proclamation of the Gospel, as so richly practiced by Christ in Galilee and Judea, and later by Peter at Pentecost and the days following. Paul preaching in the market places and on Mars Hill followed the same method (Acts 2:1-40; 17:17-31).

4. The proclamation of the message in the form of formal Bible readings and expositions, dialogues and disputations, reasoning and persuading, as Paul practiced it at numerous occasions in the synagogues of the dispersion (Acts 9:22-29; 17:2, 10, 11, 17; 18:4, 5).

5. The rebuking and compelling historic and polemic messages of Peter (Acts 3; 4); Stephen (Acts 6; 7); Paul (Acts 13; 22; 23).

6. The persuasive, factual and experiential apologetic type of presentation of the truth as illustrated by Paul in his message to Agrippa in Acts 26 and referred to in Galatians 3:1.

It is well to note that the method of presentation is not the determining factor. The important fact is that no evangelism has happened until the good news has been *told*. The presence of the Christian and the humblest and most helpful service of a Christian in itself is not evangelism. This may prepare the way for effective evangelism. But presence in itself is not sufficient.

What if Jesus had silently walked the paths of Galilee or the streets of Jerusalem? If He had only demonstrated the love of God and the compassion of His own heart, but had never proclaimed and expounded the motive, meaning and purpose of His life, service, death, and resurrection? If He had never informed us of the nature and mind of God?

To the contrary, Mark 1:14 says, "Jesus came . . . preaching the gospel of God" (RSV). This became the primary note of His ministry. Indeed, He was a miracle-worker, He was a life-transformer. But He was first and foremost a proclaimer of the good news of God. Jesus attached priority to His preaching ministry. And, having practiced it Himself, He so commanded His disciples. Therefore, Mark tells us: "They went forth, and preached every where" (Mark 16:20). The book of Acts is the evidence and the result of the apostles' obedience.

Again, imagine Paul living in Antioch, Corinth, Ephesus, and Rome, being satisfied that his presence was all that was required of him. He never would have written his letters because he would not have founded churches. While presence in the true sense is important, it is not sufficient in itself. "It pleased God by the foolishness of preaching [proclamation] to save them that believe" (I Cor. 1:21).

Evangelism does not take place until the good news has been orally, intelligently and understandingly communicated. Presence is never a substitute for proclamation.

The tremendous pressure for social action is well-known and generally felt. There is a crying need for social action and much room for it. But it most certainly is not a substitute for proclamation. It never has been and it never will be.

Far be it from me to minimize Christian responsibility in civil and social life. I am deeply conscious of the responsibility of the church toward its members and community. Social responsibility is rooted in the Bible and social action has its place. However, this is not the same as evangelism.

Social action seldom aids evangelism. It more often confuses the message, nature and purpose of evangelism. Evangelism is a specialized

Christian ministry, called into being by divine ordination to perform a singular task, the proclamation of the good news of God. Evangelism organizations are circumscribed by divine assignment to a unique and special ministry, a special thrust. Evangelism, the proclamation of the good news of God, must remain their central mission, lest they betray their calling.

This is in perfect keeping with the commands of Christ as given to the Twelve in Matthew 10:1, 5-8; the Seventy in Luke 10:1-20; the Twelve in Matthew 28:18-20; Mark 16:15, 16; Luke 24:45-48; John 20:21-23. In every case proclamation, the preaching of the Gospel, is central.

Such proclamation is not that of a man who is neutral toward the good news he announces. As a herald, he proclaims the message with authority. As an evangelist he announces it with warmth, enthusiasm, urgency and persuasiveness. Paul says that he beseeches and persuades people (II Cor. 5:11, 20). The degree of his enthusiasm and sincerity is well seen in his message before King Agrippa, who on hearing the persuasive voice and piercing message of Paul, cried out: "Paul, you are mad; your great learning is turning you mad" (Acts 26:24, RSV).

Christ commissioned us to invite and to compel people to come in. There is an urgency in the motivation and tone of the announcer of the good news that arrests and attracts, draws and compels the listener. It is an encounter of men for decision, not only to listen and to consider. Evangelism never leaves man neutral; it compels him to take a position for or against Christ. It definitely aims at conversion to Christ, though not necessarily at proselytism in the popular sense of the term. It is an announcement of momentous significance that may spell life or death, happiness or misery, heaven or doom. Nothing less is true evangelism.

Chapter 4

THE UNIQUE MESSENGER OF EVANGELISM

EVANGELISM MUST BE DONE BY A MEDIATORIAL MESSENGER. The principle of mediatorship runs through the entire Bible. It is one of the fundamental principles of divine revelation. In the procurement of salvation it began in Genesis 3:15. It remained foundational until it culminated in Christ, the Lamb of God (I Tim. 2:5).

The principle of mediatorship in the proclamation of salvation began in Genesis 12 with the call of Abraham. A new dispensation in the order of God's way of operation was ushered in. Heretofore, God had spoken to mankind as a whole. In Genesis 1–11 there is no unique nation nor a special priesthood. Neither is there a peculiar people to whom God is revealing Himself in a special way. His revelation was to the totality of mankind. No special channel of revelation is known to us.

In Genesis 12 there is a new departure, a new beginning. Israel, in the person of Abraham, became the mediator between God and the nations of mankind and remained so throughout the history of the Old Testament. Israel was specifically called to be a kingdom of priests and a nation of witnesses.

We know of no special revelation throughout all nations of the world that equals or even compares to the revelation graciously and sovereignly granted to Israel. Of course, such revelation was not given exclusively *for* Israel, even though it was given *to* Israel. It was for the world. But it was granted to Israel as God's mediatorial people. Israel was God's channel and God's servant. (Compare Gen. 12:1-4; Ex. 19:1-6; Isa. 43:10, 12, 21; 44:8.)

As far as I am able to discover from the Bible, the principle of mediatorship still prevails. Today the church is God's mediatorial agency, not in salvation but in the proclamation of it. Thus, the divine order for our age in relation to salvation is: God in Christ reconciling the world; God in Christ reaching out toward the world in salvation through the Holy Spirit, who resides in the church by means of the written Word of God.

This principle of mediatorship in communication is well illustrated in three successive chapters and three impressive events in the book of Acts. In chapter eight the Ethiopian eunuch is on his way to Ethiopia from Jerusalem. He was deeply absorbed in his search for an answer for his crying heart. He had turned to the right source and to the right portion in the book. Yet, a Philip was needed to communicate the gospel message and consummate the experience.

In chapter nine Saul was met by his Lord. He was granted a most glorious vision and heard the voice of the Master. But only as Ananias ministered to him did the "scales" drop from his eyes, his vision was restored, and he got his commission.

In chapter ten God-fearing Cornelius was praying for right and direction. His prayer was heard and he was assured of an answer. But such answer was mediated by a man who had to be brought in from a distance, who had to cross cultural and religious lines, overcome serious personal religious barriers, and communicate the gospel message.

Where the Word and/or the church are not present in proclamation, the Holy Spirit does not unilaterally and sovereignly work out the salvation in Christ in the biblical and spiritual sense of the word, offering forgiveness of sin, regenerating men, constituting them into sons of God and qualifying them for the kingdom of God. This is one of the deepest and most overwhelming divine imperatives of biblical evangelism.

Accepting the biblical principle of mediatorship in the procurement of salvation and also its proclamation, we need to delineate the agency more precisely.

The word "evangelist" has a specialized meaning in the three references in the New Testament (Acts 21:8; Eph. 4:11; II Tim. 4:5). It refers to an office and specialized function in the church of Jesus Christ. God calls out men and bestows upon them uniquely the gift of an evangelist, if the word is taken in its biblical significance.

In the Bible, the evangelist is comparable to today's foreign missionary. He is the messenger of the church in a non-Christian world. He is a pioneer in Christian ministries, seeking to win people to Christ and bind them together in a congregation. He is followed by the teacher-missionary, who assists in establishing the church.

According to Acts, the persecuted members of the church engaged extensively in evangelizing (Acts 8:4; 11:19, 20). The Greek words tell us that they evangelized and/or spoke the word, indicating the informal communication of the message of salvation.

The Gospel of Jesus Christ is not committed to individual men and offices as such but to the church. The church is the body of Christ; the church is the temple of God; the church is built upon the foundation of the apostles and prophets; the church is the pillar and ground of the truth (Eph. 1:23; 2:20; I Tim. 3:15).

The church is in the line of apostolic succession, not some office or officebearer. The office and officebearer receive their significance, authority and value from the church, not vice-versa. The church is God's authoritative, responsible and mediatorial agency and creation.

I emphasize this for two reasons. First, to correct the sense of independence of some evangelists and evangelistic organizations. They must keep in mind that they are God's agencies only as part of the church of Jesus Christ, the body of Christ, and the temple of God. The church never exists for the evangelist or the evangelistic organization. The reverse is always true. It is well to keep in mind that we as individuals are never the whole, nor can an organization claim primacy. Such prerogatives belong to the church of Jesus Christ under its Head, the Lord Himself.

Of course, you are entitled to raise the troubling yet realistic questions: What if the church fails? What if the church does not sense the urgency? What if the church loses its divine message of evangelism? These are not hypothetical questions. Such situations do arise.

There is, however, a second and much deeper reason for the emphasis upon the church as God's mediatorial agency. Current literature on mission, missions and evangelism is filled with the idea of God's mission in the world. There is much truth in such ideas, and yet they are being unscripturally interpreted and applied. Much light is needed in this area. Confusion prevails at present.

Can anyone doubt that God is operating in this world? Is it not His creation? Has He ever completely abandoned the world? Has He abdicated as Lord of Lords and King of Kings? Has He become untrue as Creator and Sustainer? Is He not the sovereign Lord working out His plan and purpose with man and in spite of man? Why then question the direct mission of God in the world? Is He not the God of history?

First, we must point to a biblical paradox. The Bible makes it clear that God is both working in the world as well as against the world. God is both the Redeemer of the world and the Judge of the world. His judgments may come in the form of special and destructive events, or in the withholding of peace, prosperity and other necessities required for advancement and welfare. Only the illumination of the Holy Spirit can enable us to distinguish within this paradox. Here a spiritual mind is absolutely necessary.

Second, we must point to the biblical teaching that God's direct activities in the world are limited in quality. Certainly God is at work everywhere, but it cannot be said that He is at work in everything.

No doubt, God, the Holy Spirit, because of His creation-relationship and because of His omnipresence in the world, is at work in the world. But what is the quality of the work He is accomplishing?

Three things seem to be evident from the Bible and biblical history:

(1) The Holy Spirit resists and controls evil in history to the degree that it cannot completely overwhelm mankind, His church and the people of Israel (Isa. 59:3-19; II Thess. 2:6, 7; John 1:10, RSV). This is also evident from the judgments upon the nations as recorded in the Old Testament. (2) The Holy Spirit also encourages and stimulates general good for mankind (Matt. 5:44-48). Humanistic endeavors and philanthropy are not evils in themselves. Properly applied and motivated, they are good and serve for the betterment of mankind. They become evil when they lose their moral nature, or when they become substitutes for man's religion or build the glory of man. (3) The Holy Spirit also broods over mankind and preserves it in a salvable condition (Gen. 6:3; Job 32:8, RSV; John 1:9). Thus, man remains psychologically within the realm and in the condition of salvation. Also, the Holy Spirit operates sovereignly and mysteriously to prepare individual hearts and communities in a unique manner for the Gospel of Jesus Christ, creating providentially and mysteriously a "fulness of time," or, in our phraseology, high potential areas. In all these areas there is a direct activity of God through the Holy Spirit in the world without the mediation of His people.

However, we do not find in the Bible that God is working out His salvation in a restricted sense of the word in a similar manner. In this realm there is an essential difference. In salvation the principle of mediatorship prevails. This holds true in the procurement of salvation as well as in the proclamation of it. In its procurement Christ is the sole and sufficient Mediator. In its proclamation the Holy Spirit operates through the revealed Word and the church (I Pet. 1:22, 23; Jas. 1:18; Tit. 3:4, 5). Thus, the urgency of evangelism.

Chapter 5

SUMMARY: THE SUPREME MISSION OF THE CHURCH

IN THE LIGHT OF THE TOTALITY of revelation, evangelism is the central thrust of the Bible. God is minded to make Himself known and to have the good news of the salvation in His Son communicated to all mankind. For this purpose He encoded His message in the Bible by revelation and inspiration of the Holy Spirit in an infallible manner. For this purpose He also called out in the Old Testament the people of Israel and in the New Testament the church of God. These are not institutions in themselves nor for themselves. They are institutions by the sovereign calling of God and for the purpose of His glory. This glory, however, manifests itself chiefly in the good news of the salvation in Christ Jesus, His Son, the only Savior and Lord. Toward this end the chief energies of the Holy Spirit operate. Herein lies the supreme mission of the church.

The supreme mission of the church is missions—the sending forth of heralds to announce the good news of God. From missions to mission sounds rational, but from mission to missions is revelational. The urgent mission of the church remains missions as long as there are people without the Gospel.

Well does Phillips Brooks declare: "It is the sincere and deep conviction of my soul when I declare that if the Christian faith does not culminate and complete itself in the effort to make Christ known to all the world, that faith appears to me a thoroughly unreal and insignificant thing, destitute of power for the single life and incapable of being convincingly proved to be true." [1]

Equally true is the observation of Dr. Robson when he says: "At present the life of many congregations is sterilized by its self-centered character. The world-wide duty of the congregation is relegated to a secondary place and the congregation is proportionately nonefficient for the chief purpose of the church. What is needed is that all its endeavors should be so ordered as to subserve and culminate in world-wide service." [2]

World evangelism is not an elective in Christianity that we may choose to do or not. It is rooted and grounded in eternal verities. In the words of Dr. R. E. Speer: "These grounds are in the very being and thought of God, in the character of Christianity, in the aim and purpose of the Christian Church, and in the nature of humanity, its unity, and its needs. . . ."

25

And again: ". . . It is the very being and character of God that the deepest ground of the missionary enterprise is to be found. We cannot think of God except in terms which necessitate the missionary idea." [3]

Evangelism originated in the heart of God by purposing the Gospel, by sending His Son to become the content of the Gospel, by sending the Holy Spirit to magnify the Gospel and by creating the church to live and proclaim the Gospel in the energy, power and conviction of the Holy Spirit. Let us keep our perspective within the framework of biblical revelation. Here are the absolute perspectives and divine priorities. As we permit ourselves to be shifted away from them, we lose not only our divinely-ordained purpose, but also our Christian meaning and the deepest blessings from the heart of God.

Chapter 6

SATURATION EVANGELISM —
ITS HISTORICAL ANTECEDENTS

TODAY, AS NEVER BEFORE, various strands and dynamic factors in evangelism are being blended and unified into a functional structuralism. This type of evangelism is making an impact upon countries and continents in a way not true since the days of the apostles.

There is no general agreement on the designation of this pattern of evangelism. The earliest name for it seems to have been saturation evangelism, and thus we have used it as the generic designation. And it is indeed saturation evangelism, if considered from a certain perspective of the purpose to be achieved. It is also spoken of as mobilization evangelism, if viewed from the standpoint of methodology. The former speaks more of the function, while the latter emphasizes the structure.

The pattern is also thought of as depth evangelism and is known in large parts of the world as Evangelism-in-Depth. It is such if contemplated from the position of the deeper penetration and permeation of the believers with the Gospel of Jesus Christ, and their conformity to the purpose and program of God in Christian living and evangelizing as members of their own local churches. This, too, bespeaks purpose and function.

I have chosen to use the designation saturation evangelism because it well describes the total program of the movement and keeps me from being partial to any one of the designations and the patterns as they are operating at present.

To this species of saturation evangelism belong such movements as Evangelism-in-Depth in Latin America; New Life For All in Africa; Christ for All in the Congo; the National Evangelistic Campaign—Win Thirty Million to Christ in Korea; Mobilization Evangelism in Japan; Evangelical Advance in Honduras; Campana Nacional de Evangelism in Guatemala; and other similar movements.

Saturation evangelism is becoming a world phenomenon as never before, and we do well to acquaint ourselves with the movements. Before we study some of them, however, let us look at some historical antecedents and the biblical basis of saturation evangelism.

While saturation evangelism as a unique type and emphasis of evangelism has come to the forefront in our days, it is by no means new. The sixteenth-century biblical Anabaptists knew something about the total mobilization of all believers and their means. They required every baptismal candidate to commit himself and all his goods to the cause of the Lord and gospel propagation.

As early as 20 August 1527 a synod was held in Augsburg, attended by more than sixty Anabaptist leaders, to design a grand strategy of evangelism. Their aim was to bring the Gospel to all of Europe. Teams of evangelists were assigned to various areas and all believers were to have a vital and personal part in penetrating Europe with the Gospel.

This was a comprehensive plan of saturation evangelism. Only the combined swords of Roman Catholics and Protestants were able to stop them in this great and noble undertaking; most of the strategists died as martyrs within a few years. Thus the conference became known as the "Martyr's Synod." Europe had refused one of the most precious opportunities to hear the Gospel.

A similar opportunity came in the nineteenth century, though not as extensive and widespread. Writing of the rapid spread of the Baptists on the continent in the nineteenth and early part of the twentieth centuries, Adolf Keller says:

> In the year of Waterloo, 1815, there was no Baptist Church to be found in the whole of Europe, but by the year 1850 there were about 4,000 church members. By 1900 the number had increased to approximately 220,000. For the present day [1927] no exact figures can be had, . . . though there is reason to believe that it would raise the number of Baptists to considerably above two millions. This advance of a single denomination on the Continent within three generations [1834-1927] may be partly attributed to what has been a *working principle* of the Continental Baptists from the outset: *"Every member a missionary."* [1] (Italics mine.)

In recent years literature has appeared that speaks of "Revolutionary New Testament Christianity" in evangelism. Writes Charles W. Kingsley:

> During an encouraging all-day men's retreat, when men with their pastors and church leaders dared face their barrenness and accepted the challenge of the theme of growth, "Double in a Decade," a burdened Canadian layman stood to his feet and cried, "But under our present methods it took us over a half century to double. What are we going to do differently that will cause this growth?"
>
> This is a good question. It calls for a drastic reorganization, a revolution of our thinking, our motives, our program.
>
> Our evangelistic strategy of "building-centered evangelism" and "enlistment evangelism" falls far short of the New Testament. Both of these concepts have one glaring flaw that hinders our church from ever becoming the instrument of the Great Commission.

Gene Edwards said, "The flaw is this: The only people who can be won to Christ by these two methods are those who will deliberately get up, get dressed, go down to the auditorium, and willingly expose themselves to the preaching of the Word. Most people will not do this! Today our *church building* concept of evangelism is the greatest single hindrance to world evangelization — not because we have the church buildings, but because we have failed to get out of them."

In many new communities across our nation, we have built new physical structures without building New Testament outreach. Imagine a farmer building a barn in a new field and expecting the barn to harvest the crop.

"We must get the right perspective," Edwards exhorts. "Realize that evangelism is not to be centered inside but outside the church building. Church is not a place to bring the converts into. It is a battle station to send Christians out from!" [2]

Upon this analysis, Kingsley presents a diagram that visualizes the lesson of "reversing the arrows" from an inviting church to an invading church, a church that does not depend upon people coming into the church building to be evangelized. Rather, it prepares its members in the church building to go forth into the community and win people for the Lord just where they are. Church centripetalism is to be converted into church centrifugalism.

In the same book Kingsley presents a thirteen weeks' program for the local church for penetration and saturation evangelism of the local community.

The Southern Baptists have been known for their evangelism zeal and emphasis as well as their extensive campaigns. The Reverend Waylon B. Moore published an article in the *Baptist Standard* in March, 1960, which is noteworthy both for its content as well as its title. Seemingly unaware of an incipient, dynamic movement by the name, he published an article entitled: "Evangelism in Depth." The basic thesis of the article deals with principles and methods on building quality membership, which he equates with Christian discipleship. This in turn equals evangelizing agents used by the Holy Spirit in winning people for the Lord and making them into disciples of dynamic quality.

He speaks of: "Conserving the Results," "Methods Used by Paul," "Multiplying the Messengers," and "Deepening the Spiritual Life." He concludes his article with the following words: "Such evangelism in depth is the need today; it means multiplication of disciples to the glory of God." [3] The title as well as the principles unfolded in this article will arrest the attention of many. Is it a coincidence that the words "evangelism in depth" should have lived in the minds of Waylon B. Moore in Fort Worth and Dr. R. Kenneth Strachan in San Jose, Costa Rica?

Chapter 7

THE BIBLICAL BASIS OF SATURATION EVANGELISM

WE NEED NOT AGAIN ESTABLISH the biblical priority of evangelism in the church's ministries. We have spoken of evangelism as being central in Scripture and as being the horizontal thrust of the New Testament. Evangelism as such has never been disputed. Only the questions of the meaning, nature and methods of evangelism have been discussed with considerable disagreement.

SATURATION EVANGELISM AS A NEW TESTAMENT IDEAL

The words saturation evangelism are not found in the New Testament, but neither are personal evangelism, visitation evangelism, church evangelism, camp evangelism, mass evangelism. The emphasis is upon evangelism. Saturation evangelism, however, can be well illustrated.

The city council reported that the apostles had *filled* Jerusalem with their doctrine (Acts 5:28). Luke writes that "the churches throughout *all* Judea and Galilee and Samaria" had rest and were edified. Again, *"All* that dwelt at Lydda and Saron saw him [Aeneas] and turned to the Lord." Also, *all* Joppa was informed of the gospel (Acts 9:31, 35, 42).

This type of saturation evangelism reaped much fruit. Myriads (Greek N.T.) of Jews (tens of thousands) turned to the Lord (Acts 21:20).

Similar were the reports on Antioch in Pisidia and Ephesus. Of the former city and area it is said that "the word of the Lord was published throughout *all* the region" (Acts 13:49). In Luke's record on Ephesus we read: "So that *all* they which dwelt in Asia heard the word of the Lord Jesus, both Jews and Greeks (Acts 19:10).

The most comprehensive report on saturation evangelism came from the pen of Paul. He wrote that "from Jerusalem and round about unto Illyricum, I have *fully* preached the gospel of Christ. Yea so have I strived to preach the gospel [evangelize], not where Christ was named . . . But now having no more place in these parts . . ." (Romans 15: 19, 20, 23).

This is saturation evangelism, evangelizing every creature, making it possible for all to hear and to know the good news from heaven. This is the ideal of the New Testament. There must be presentation, penetration and saturation before confrontation can take place. This is biblical evangelism. The question remains: How is this seemingly insurmountable task to be accomplished? We all believe this to be the will of God. But how can it be done? The answer lies in total mobilization.

SATURATION EVANGELISM AND THE MOBILIZATION OF ALL BELIEVERS

Mobilization of all believers in evangelizing is not only a serious and practical question; it is foremost a theological concern. Has God actually willed that every believer become an active evangelizing agent, or is it sufficient to be only a supporting evangelizing standby? Are there not many different gifts of the Spirit and assignments according to these gifts? Is it the design of God that every believer personally participate in the evangelizing process of the world? If so, what is his part? How is he to be involved?

The answers to these questions can be given by another question: Is every believer really a priest of God? Do we realistically and not only ideally and theoretically believe in the universal priesthood of all believers? It is time that we put some realism into our idealism.

I speak of the believers as evangelizing agents or instruments. I have avoided the words witness and evangelist. The latter is used only three times in the New Testament and seems to describe an official function because of a special gift from the Lord. The word witness is most frequently used in the gospel of John and the book of Acts; it seems to relate rather closely to personal knowledge of the historical person and events of Christ, at least much more so than to Christian experience in general.

Of the early Christians it is recorded that *they evangelized* (Acts 8:4; 11:20), or *spoke the word* (Acts 11:19), that is, they were engaged in speaking to others about the good news of God in Christ Jesus with the intention of informing and persuading them. This was not their command, this was the outflow of their lives. Evangelism was not staged or programmed. It happened. It was a spontaneous sharing with others of the good news of the discovered salvation in Christ Jesus, the Lord.

Evangelizing is more than speaking about personal experience. Evangelizing means first and foremost to explain the Gospel to others and persuade them to accept the precious gift of God by believing in Jesus Christ. This is what happened in the early church. To this all Christians are called and for it all are endowed by the Holy Spirit.

DYNAMIC TENSION

We need to explore the secret behind this spontaneous yet dynamic movement in the church of the apostles. To say that spontaneous evangelism was the glorious afterglow of Pentecost is to oversimplify the case. This would ignore some very basic factors and principles of the Scriptures.

Evangelism is not an afterglow of an experience, no matter how glorious the experience may be. It is the ever-increasing glow of an ever-maturing life in Christ; it becomes the full business of a full-grown man in Christ.

A certain degree of maturation precedes mobilization for evangelization, as is clearly evident from the book of Acts. Only paralysis in personal and spiritual growth impairs the motivation and the desire to evangelize. The desire may also be choked with ecclesiastical structuralism, if such dominates dynamic, spiritual functionalism; or by ministerial professionalism which overshadows and overwhelms New Testament perspectives of the Christian calling.

The theological key to this marvelous phenomenon in the church in Acts lies in the continuous experience of obeying imperatives in the Great Commission of our Lord: make disciples and preach the Gospel to every creature. Here is a divine and creative tension.

MAKE DISCIPLES

Our Lord commanded His disciples to disciple all nations, or to make disciples (Matt. 28:18-20). In this He had set the pattern. Christ was supremely a disciple-maker during His ministry. Elsewhere we expound His pedagogy in making disciples, as well as the concepts He sought to engrave upon their souls.

Jesus made the Twelve first into disciples before He made them into apostles. Followship preceded apostleship. Learning preceded teaching. Having made them into disciples and constituted them into apostles, He commanded them to go forth and make disciples. This could easily have absorbed all their efforts, as it seems to have done in the first five chapters of Acts.

In chapter six "creative tensions" arise. The apostles were compelled by pressure to set priorities for their ministries (Acts 6:4). Not a severing of ministries and fellowship, but a division of labor was initiated that continued to develop in the New Testament to strengthen the base to make disciples.

TO EVERY CREATURE

There is, however, the other imperative in the Great Commission. Its emphasis is upon world evangelism, the heralding of the Gospel to every creature. It is stressed in Mark 16:15, 16; Luke 24:47; Acts 1:8; and especially in the command to Paul in Acts 26:16-18.

There is no question that world evangelism is the will of God and the design of the New Testament. Thus a tension is set up between the time-absorbing, individual, personal care needed for the deepening of the spiritual life of the believer — the making of disciples on the one hand—and the imperative, inner Spirit-motivation of world evangelism willed by the Father, commanded by the Son, and directed by the Spirit on the other (John 16:8, 11; 12:32).

Such tension is not a contradiction, but the divine pressure that releases within believers their best. This tension finds its focus, intensity and solution in the church as an organism and as an institution. The church is God's creation for both of the above purposes—the making of disciples and the evangelization of the world. This is portrayed in the book of Acts and propositionally stated by Paul in Ephesians 4: 11-16.

The resolving of the tension is observable in the gradualism found in the book of Acts. Nothing is said of an evangelizing church or evangelizing believers in the first several chapters. The apostles were the main, if not exclusive, instruments of the Holy Spirit. They preached, taught, prayed, suffered, served. Little is said about the activities of the believers. Two most significant facts about them are recorded. First, they were under the instruction of the apostles. Second, they were in fellowship in larger and smaller groups.

"They met constantly to hear the apostles teach" (Acts 2:42, NEB). "Daily in the temple, and in every house, they [the apostles] ceased not to teach and preach Jesus Christ" (Acts 5:42).

As the apostles had been under the teaching and molding influence of the Master to be made into disciples, so the first believers remained under the teaching influence of the apostles. They, too, were being molded into disciples by the example and words of those whom the Lord Himself had shaped. Only after this had been accomplished to a certain degree did the Lord permit them to be scattered.

As they were being scattered they evangelized others with the blessed Gospel they had experienced and learned from the apostles. They were not untrained laymen going about without a clear gospel message. They had been well-established in the doctrines of the apostles. Neither were they moving about as mere individuals. Temple fellowship had bound them together into a larger spiritual unit and built into them a sense of belonging. House-to-house fellowship had formed them into small, dynamic groups or teams. They went about in teams and evangelized.

This procedure needs to be recognized as a most dynamic principle and needs to be revived and retintroduced into our churches. There is nothing as dynamic as group dynamics, and no evangelism is more dynamic than evangelism by teams. The early believers had been made into disciples by the teaching and personal impact of the apostles, and in the fellowship of the church. Only thus did they become evangelizing agents.

In relation to evangelism we need to note here a most important principle. While they were learning and were being molded *in* the church, they had to evangelize *outside* of the church. They were being scattered abroad. The apostolic church did not evangelize by inviting people to attend a church. The believers took the Gospel with them into the world. Thus, while evangelism was being done *by* the church, it was not done *in* the church. The believers (the church) had to fan out and invade the world in order to evangelize. This is the pattern of the book of Acts in its horizontal expansion.

Similar to this is what Paul wrote in Ephesians 4:11-16. This is the classic passage on the inner ministries of the church. Though Paul does not use the word disciple, he speaks of the believers becoming full-grown men, established in doctrine, speaking the truth in love, performing their part in the body of believers.

The church is God's institution to indoctrinate, establish, nurture, discipline and mold believers. All this is to be done in order to equip the saints for service. The question, however, arises: Whom are they to serve?

Paul does not spell it out in so many words in this passage, but the church of Ephesians 1-3 most certainly finds herself in the environment of the world in chapters 4-6. This is her walk and her warfare. This is her service.

Within the church every believer is made and molded that he might serve outside of the church in an attractive and effective manner. The believer's missionary and evangelizing assignment in the world is evident. It must be kept in mind that the epistles of Paul are his serious attempt to "make disciples" by written word, in order that the church might serve her God-appointed purpose—to shine as light in the world and to hold forth the Word of life. The believer's missionary and evangelizing purpose is evident in most of Paul's epistles.

That they actually served such a purpose is evident from the words of Paul in I Thessalonians 1:6-10 and Romans 1:8. Dr. Adolf Harnack, who has researched the early centuries of the Christian era most diligently, informs us: "We may take it as an assured fact that the mere existence and persistent activity of the individual Christian communities did more than anything else to bring about the extension of the Christian religion." [1]

The church is God's instrument to mobilize, discipline and equip God's saints that they might perform nobly in the world the task of evangelizing. Only thus will the church fulfill her purpose. Only thus will the tension between the two imperatives in the Great Commission be resolved. Only thus will the world be evangelized. Such is the biblical basis of total mobilization and total evangelism.

The fact that the church of Jesus Christ as a local body of believers is God's instrument in evangelism leads to the important question whether saturation evangelism must be carried on as a united crusade enlisting as many churches as possible; whether it could be a simultaneous undertaking of all churches, or whether it is most successfully conducted on a denominational level. The advantages and disadvantages of such proceedings could be argued at great length practically and theologically. The fact, however, which I do uphold is that *all* churches must engage in evangelism if they are to be New Testament churches, and if saturation evangelism is to be thorough and complete.

The church is the body of Jesus Christ, the body he loved and for which He shed His blood to purchase it. His concern reaches down to every true member, mature or immature, pure in doctrine or held captive by some erroneous or perverted views, ideal in conduct or falling short of such an ideal. He desires their welfare, correction, restoration, maturation, equipment, fellowship and service.

This is clearly evident from His consistent call to repentance to five of the seven churches in Revelation 2 and 3. These churches were in a rather pitiful condition, plagued by error in doctrine and practice. Sin and false teachings had crept in. Yet Christ speaks of them as churches and symbolizes them in the golden candlestand. Certainly most of them would not have passed our tests for "association membership." Yet Christ walks in the midst of them, judges them, and calls upon them to repent. He delights to see them purified, restored, mobilized, trained and used.

It is not primarily a question of my cooperation and affiliation with other churches and denominations, but basically my attitude and relationship to them. Do I love whom Christ loves? Do I share in the concern of Christ for His body and for every member in His body? Is my presence and attitude a help or an offense to His children, and to the local church that is at least in part a manifestation of His church?

It behooves us to walk softly, speak tenderly and act lovingly within the household of God. We cannot remain indifferent toward churches that are failing the Lord in the most sacred trust He has committed to the churches. These churches are not helped by our criticism or condemnation. Help must come on a higher level and in a more Christian way. They need to be revived and restored. They must be mobilized in evangelism if they are to be healed, and if saturation evangelism is to become a full reality.

Conclusion

We conclude that saturation evangelism is a biblical ideal and pattern. Whether present-day patterns have discovered the full dynamics of biblical saturation evangelism is a matter of study and investigation, and the answer will become more apparent as we present them.

It is a matter of deep gratitude to God, however, that He has revived the pattern again and is making it a world-wide phenomenon.

Chapter 8

THE CHARACTERISTICS OF SATURATION EVANGELISM

SATURATION EVANGELISM as a world phenomenon takes on various forms and appearances. This is natural. This is the way it ought to be. The cultures of the world differ in their focus and configuration; the psychologies of the people are not alike. The patterns of life differ and the tastes and likes vary. The outer phenomenon is conditioned by the cultural milieu and psychological mood. Thus it is natural that evangelism in different cultures will assume different patterns. The same method that may be very effective in one culture may not be attractive nor effective in another culture.

Undergirding saturation evangelism, however, is a certain uniformity of principles that makes for common characteristics. This commonness is noted by Max Warren as he writes about the East African Revival. Says he: "The Revival . . . is a movement within the Church over wide areas of East Africa. . . . and in all these places there is a recognizable kinship established through a common pattern of development. This is not to say that the Revival has been forced into a common mold. There are in fact considerable local differences in its manifestations. These local characteristics have been derived from local history and from the interaction of local personalities.

"It is of considerable spiritual significance that in each area there was in the providence of God a local preparation for the Revival, something quite unco-ordinated by man. The kinship which is none the less real is primarily due to the impress of the one Holy Spirit. Other factors, as we shall see, have contributed to this kinship, but the initiative has lain not with man but with God." [1] (Italics mine.)

Similar words must be written into the history of saturation evangelism. Sovereignly the Holy Spirit has been moving, especially in the areas of the younger churches, preparing men, churches and fields for a revival of the soundest principles in evangelism and for a great ingathering of people into the kingdom of God.

Graciously and almost simultaneously the Holy Spirit moved upon men and women in various continents to think seriously, deeply, biblically and disturbingly about the unfinished task of world evangelism. The circumstances and inner experiences varied.

In one case a man experienced frustrations and a sense of failure in the task of reaching not only masses but countries for the Lord; in

another there were inner tensions and disruptions, defeats and tragedies
in the churches, the stirring reminder of great and healing movements
in the past, and the tremendous challenge of the present; or it was the
gnawing awareness of the unfinished work and the depressing consciousness that the present pace and methods were not adequate to accomplish the task; again, it was the burden of an unfinished task in the
mission field in the presence of ebbing health and a forced early return to America, with no prospect of returning to the work again.

Such tensions, however, were wholesome and creative, whether they
were experienced in San Jose, Costa Rica; Kagoro, Nigeria; Seoul,
Korea; Hyderabad, India, or places in the United States. It is almost
impossible to establish with certainty who borrowed from whom and
what. Either the diffusion of principles and patterns was very rapid,
and much borrowing was unconscious, since many ideas were floating
around, published here and there in periodicals; or, similar patterns
sprung up simultaneously because of the similarities of needs, times,
circumstances and experiences. Documents and dates definitely point
in the direction of the latter.

It is evident that all master builders absorbed two common sources.
They all drank deeply from the book of Acts, and in their hearts re-
lived the experiences of the apostolic church which became their ideal
and inspiration. And, they drew heavily from the writings of Roland
Allen. These two objective sources, plus the immediate impact and
impress of the same Holy Spirit created a commonness that seems
much like sameness and duplication.

Such a phenomenon, however, is not strange for the student of cultural movements, nor should it seem strange to the believer in the
sovereign Holy Spirit. To claim originality for one and to make all
other movements only adaptations cannot be substantiated by the facts
recorded and thus far uncovered. Neither does such a claim give
adequate honor to the sovereign, omnipresent, all-wise Holy Spirit,
the administrator and inspirer of all mission activities.

We are safest in attributing all credit and honor to the Holy Spirit,
Himself, who led different men and women in different parts of the
world in a similar manner, though all these men and women freely
acknowledge adopting and adapting patterns from various sources, and
gladly give credit to whom credit is due.

The designations attached to these movements may not be as
original as they seem to us at this moment. It is well-known that New
Life For All is a Nigerian adaptation of New Life For You, the
Southern Baptist slogan for their Japan crusade in 1963. R. Kenneth
Strachan and Waylon B. Moore could have borrowed the significant
designation, Evangelism-in-Depth, from a common source.

The final and decisive question is not one of origin and originality, but one of successive adaptation and effective promotion. Here lies the real test of efficiency and ingenuity.

The common characteristics and qualities of saturation evangelism need careful presentation and definition. They constitute the qualitative distinctives of this pattern of evangelism and should be disseminated with vigor and freshness.

QUALITATIVE DISTINCTIVES OF SATURATION EVANGELISM

Saturation evangelism claims to be different. It contends to be an "opposite" to traditional evangelism, a revolutionary departure from former practices. It is not an innovation but a transformation, a return to the New Testament. What then, are some of these distinctives?

1. *Saturation evangelism aims at gospel saturation of the community and country, and also of the believers and churches.* It presents the Gospel in spoken and written form to every people of the land, to every strata of society, to every home and individual. It is a serious attempt to saturate the land with the good news of God, overlooking no area and no community. It is an in-depth evangelism program literally attempting to fulfill the command of Christ to preach the Gospel to every creature.

In order to achieve maximum presentation of the Gospel, saturation evangelism proceeds in an orderly way. It carefully studies the spiritual needs, designs a strategy, sets a time schedule, marshals all available resources, mobilizes all obtainable means, every medium, every Christian agency, explores various approaches, and opens numerous channels in an all-out effort to make known the Gospel of God. Creativity and courage must mark the movement if success is to be assured.

Every conceivable type of evangelism is employed—personal evangelism, house-to-house visitation, prayer, open air, team witness, child, youth, women, student, factory, literature, newspaper, poster, film, radio and television evangelism, church campaigns, united area campaigns, preferably in larger cities and public places such as stadiums, and if feasible a united national campaign in the capital city of the country. The latter two campaigns are usually publicly dramatized by large parades of masses of evangelicals who declare their faith and courage in this manner and attract multitudes to the rallies. Such parades have brought much praise to the evangelicals for orderliness in their march, while at the same time they have testified to the essential unity of the Christian community and have been a public witness to the common faith of much of evangelicalism.

A serious attempt is made to permeate and saturate the land with the Gospel of the Lord Jesus Christ. Whether such saturation can actually be done in such a limited time is a matter of debate. The program often resembles more a heavy shower than a steady, soaking rain; perhaps as much water runs off as penetrates. The fact remains, however, that a strenuous effort is put forth to make the Gospel known and available to every creature. This intention of the heart is praiseworthy. Often it bears much fruit.

2. *Saturation evangelism makes a strenuous attempt to reverse an age-old practice in evangelism, best described as church centripetalism, and transform it into dynamic, evangelistic centrifugalism.* Traditional evangelism has become structured as to time, place and personnel. Somehow the sentiment prevails among most church people that only at times of church-sponsored evangelistic programs are church members to be seriously concerned and engaged in doing a part in bringing people under the sound of the Gospel. Seemingly, only at times of evangelism programs in the church do Christians become involved in the evangelistic activities of the church and manifest their interest in bringing people to the church to be evangelized. Structured church evangelism holds the members captive as to time of evangelism.

Again, it has become the cultural and habitual practice of the Western churches to confine evangelism to the church as a place and building. People must come to church to hear the Gospel and become Christians. To many people it seems almost sacrilegious to think of religious services outside of the confines of the church building. Such may even be the sentiment of the true children of God. Evangelism is bound to bricks, mortar and a place. Our church building-centered evangelism is a major snare to our effectiveness in winning people for Christ. No less is the dependence upon the evangelist. People will wait for the evangelist to come so they can invite their neighbors and friends to "come and hear the Gospel."

Centrifugalism in saturation evangelism seeks to reverse this traditional pattern and sentiment, which hangs over the church like a paralyzing cloud of heresy. A radical realignment is instituted. Saturation evangelism initiates a drastic rearrangement of forces, a radical redirection of thinking, motives, procedure and strategy.

Mobilization for evangelization becomes a dynamic slogan—a reconception of the way of evangelism gradually takes place. Christians are taught to think of evangelism not in terms of church structure, program, place, time or building. Saturation evangelism mobilizes and trains every believer available to become an active and effective evangelizer for Christ, to go and tell the people the Gospel just where they are, and win them to Christ. The slogan — total mobilization equals total evangelization — is taken seriously and carried forward systematically, effectively, and according to a precise calendar and strategy. The enlishment and involvement of every believer in evangelism and the practice of evangelism outside the confines of the church building at the heart of the movement, with each one receiving a specific responsibility and assignment. Because of this emphasis and practice, it is often spoken of as mobilization evangelism.

While Christians are true to the church as a place of worship, edification, spiritual nurture, mobilization and equipment, they fan out for evangelism outside of the structure and locale of the church. They confront people with the Gospel and win them to the Lord. Only after they have made their commitment to the Lord are converts introduced to the church as a true spiritual home. The major effort of evangelism is done *by* the church but not *in* the church; by *all* members and not only by a professional man or team. This, no doubt, is the biblical order and pattern.

It is evident that if this world is to be evangelized, it will have to happen outside of the church buildings. The world is the field and not the church building. We must win the people in the world in which they find themselves, if they are ever to enjoy the salvation of God and become members of the church of Jesus Christ.

This practice does not eliminate the evangelist in the biblical sense of the word. He has his place in the economy of God. However, the evangelist according to the New Testament hardly fits into the ministry of the church as it is organized today. Probably the foreign missionary or frontier preacher who enters hitherto unevangelized fields fits more the New Testament pattern of the evangelist.

3. *Saturation evangelism follows a predetermined and coordinated schedule of simultaneous activities throughout all cooperating churches.* This makes for unity of spirit and depth of impact. It begins with series of meetings for purposes of organization, orientation, and inspiration to set the overall stage for the thrust. Next comes the time of intensive instruction in retreats for pastors and leading laymen. These in turn carry these instructions into the local churches, where men and women are being mobilized and equipped for evangelism.

   At the same time prayer groups are initiated and multiplied to undergird the movement and to become prayer evangelism cells. The records of the latter are perhaps the most encouraging and significant phenomenon in the history of the church at present. Thousands of such cells continue for years to follow.

When the program of instruction is completed, the program of evangelism is launched in an orderly and progressive manner, continuing over a number of months and employing the numerous patterns and approaches listed above. Coordination and cooperation make the impact of this program like a mighty army marching through the land. A small minority, united and coordinated, can become a tremendous influence for good in a land of opposing or neutral majorities.

4. *Saturation evangelism earnestly endeavors to enlist in the movement as many churches, missions, and denominations as will cooperate in an evangelical and evangelistic program in order to express the unity of the body of Christ.* This unity strengthens the cause of evangelism, involves and trains as many people as make themselves available, and creates the greatest possible impact upon the churches and communities.

The aspect of cooperation has been more critically observed and evaluated than any other phase of saturation evangelism. It is a matter of legitimate concern. The Christian church is composed of various shades of theology and practice. While these need not lead to the exclusion of each other, they often develop into unfriendly and even antagonistic attitudes and positions.

Some churches, of course, harbor serious errors and even apostasy. These have crept in unawares and are tolerated, even protected and propagated in some churches. The crises in theology will continue and will intensify in the years to come. More than ever biblical and spiritual discernment is required to walk circumspectly and wisely, especially in the lands of the younger churches where there are more babes in Christ than fathers and mothers in Christ to nurture and guide them.

On the other hand, it remains a fact of history that few sins have clung to the Christian church more strongly and have impeded its progress more severely than theological and ecclesiastical factionalism and separatism (to be distinguished from biblical separation). By this we mean the harsh and unchristian criticism of one body of believers toward the faults and limitations of others, the unloving boycotting and ostracism of believers who have fallen into error or who are held captive by some strange and peculiar doctrines and phenomena. It is seldom recognized that noncooperation and nonalignment with God's people may under some circumstances be as sinful as cooperation might be.

We appreciate the attitude of the Evangelical Foreign Missions Association, and the guidelines member missions have accepted to give direction in the matter of cooperative evangelism. These guidelines may not be to the liking of all concerned, but they are a serious attempt to find a way between indiscriminate cooperation and absolute separatism. The document is entitled, "Guidelines for All Those Involved in Cooperative Mass Evangelism."

The first section expresses the organization's attitude and concern in matters of mission-church relationships, relays words of appreciation for work that is being done, and encourages the missions to proceed in the blessings of the Lord and unity of God's people.

Section two presents several pertinent observations that lead up to the suggestions which form the major part of the document, and from which we quote several parts that may clarify our position:

Suggestions

1. These are days of superficial and fuzzy theological thinking. Biblical terms which are precious and meaningful to us take on different interpretations in the hearts and minds of those of liberal and neo-orthodox persuasion. We strongly believe that the doctrine of the Scriptures, including their divine inspiration, is basic to all other doctrines and one that is being subjected to heavy attack by ecumenical theologians. Because of this, we strongly urge you to have a minimum doctrinal statement as a basis for sponsorship of any of your campaigns. It would seem that this statement should be believed and signed by all who serve in places of leadership in any campaign, either national or local.

2. We would point out what seems to be a difference between sponsorship and endorsement. We feel that sponsorship implies participation at the planning and leadership level and that this can be controlled by your evangelistic team through the use of a doctrinal statement and a careful selection of men, following patient and adequate consultations with *known* evangelicals in the area where the campaign is to be held. We feel that this point is extremely important when your advance men *first* go in to consult missionaries and national Christians on the planning of a campaign or conference.

   Endorsement, on the other hand, cannot be controlled by you and is certainly to be encouraged on the part of all organizations in an effort to secure as large an attendance as possible by people belonging to the endorsing groups.

3. Our next concern relates to those who are used on the platform during a campaign or conference. Inviting participation in a public way implies to uninformed and spiritually undiscerning people, endorsement (or at least approval) of the men being used. Our suggestion that only known evangelical men be used does not mean that they must be members of evangelical organizations, but that they be solidly evangelical in their personal relationship to Christ.

You might be interested to know that one world organization has had for some years the policy that there could be cooperation only with other Christian bodies that are true to the statement of faith of the particular organization. It was also agreed that each autonomous group within the organization would maintain its testimony "by only inviting to its platform speakers who accept the statement of faith" of the organization.[2]

The question of cooperation vs. noncooperation will continue to vex the various bodies within the Christian church. It is seldom recognized that separatism is a matter of degrees. All Christians believe in separation at a certain point. To define that point no absolute has been discovered. To find a solution, therefore, that will satisfy and please all is hopeless. Not even Christ could satisfy all. Peter would never have entered the home of Cornelius had he listened to a committee in Jerusalem. And Paul would not have become the world missionary that he became, had he waited upon the counsel of the mother church of Jerusalem. Separatism has been a serious force in the Christian church from the very beginning.

On the other hand, the Bible takes an unbending attitude toward false doctrines and apostates, and commands the people of God to separate from them and have no fellowship with them. This, too, is a serious matter. Let no one belittle the sin of compromise and confusion in the name of Christian charity, or for the expediency of greater impact upon the community in evangelism or any other purpose and cause. While Christ is not divided, He does divide.

In the situation of such biblical tensions, we must appeal to Christian charity, tolerance and patience. Keep in mind that it may be as sinful for me to judge my brother for his relationship and cooperation as it is for him to draw on the net with a man of a position and persuasion strange to me and that seems in conflict with the Bible as far as I understand it.

The Bible teaches both aspects and keeps them in beautiful balance. Therefore, it behooves me to walk and work in the Spirit and personally stand before God, while at the same time I trust my brother that he, too, stands before God under the guidance of the Holy Spirit. Christian charity and brotherly confidence will go a long way in helping us to live in the peace of God.

ADDITIONAL QUALITIES

There are certain additional qualities that are definitely a part of the plan and program of saturation evangelism. These may be thought of as evangelism-in-depth and the creation of a self-image in the churches.

Evangelism-in-Depth

The mobilization of the believers for evangelism is accompanied by a training program that aims at a deeper penetration and permeation of the participants with the Gospel of Jesus Christ. Many of the enlistees have a superficial knowledge of Christianity from the experiential and doctrinal points of view. Much surface evangelism has resulted in a widespread and easy "believism." Many other believers have remained practically untouched by the Word of God. While we have increased the quantity of church membership, the quality has suffered severely.

We caution, however, not to attribute the lack of quality to the increase in quantity. Such deficiency is due to a lack of teaching and a failure to disciple the converts. They need to be permeated with the message of God, become enlisted in the army of God, be encouraged to become involved in the mission of the church, accept a place of service to exercise their faith and obedience and mature in their faith. Only then will they become fruitful branches in the vine, glorify their Lord, and serve mankind in an acceptable manner.

There is a ministry in depth to be performed, which, if neglected, will prove disastrous to the church and the individual Christian. Believers must be discipled if they are not to become the baggage of the church and impair growth and a greater ministry. A disciple, however, does not just happen, does not just grow. There is a work in depth to be done. People must be taught. They must become involved in Christian ministries. They must learn to accept responsibilities, bear burdens, fill positions and discharge obligations. All believers must be transformed into active, sanctified disciples by a program of gospel permeation and saturation and enlistment in the evangelizing outreach of the church.

In order to accomplish this, saturation evangelism consciously and deliberately adds an in-depth dimension to its program, an aspect that traditional evangelism has practically overlooked and which is more or less incidental to traditional evangelism. Saturation evangelism seeks to evangelize the evangelizer first of all. This in-depth dimension must not be underestimated nor minimized.

Such evangelism-in-depth is most significant for the individual believer, the church and the cause of the Lord. In fact, only as this aspect is achieved can saturation evangelism of the community and the country truly take place. Only to the degree that in-depth evangelism by training, involvement and experience of the Christians and churches is successful will evangelism continue in and through the church, expand in and about the church. Only then will the program become a perennial and spontaneous movement within the church. Such evangelism-in-depth is the crying need of the church, and only thus can world evangelism be accomplished. Only as we produce quality membership can we expect to grow normally, steadily and healthily.

Because of this very significant in-depth dimension, saturation evangelism is also rightly known as evangelism in depth. Such indeed it is, or ought to be, if it is true to its goal and nature. To bring out this in-depth quality it has often been contrasted with in-breadth evangelism, or the traditional pattern of evangelism that aims mainly at outreach and is only secondarily an in- and downreach.

The Self-Image of the Churches

As we count the blessings of saturation evangelism, we come upon, what seems to me, one of the greatest contributions of the movement. This is an additional contribution that is so unique in the history of modern missions that it constitutes a major departure from the established and traditional missions, and becomes a breakthrough in modern missionary strategy. It signals the beginning of a new era in the evangelization of the world. It is the dawn of a new day in the lands of the younger churches.

Dr. Arthur Glasser speaks of "the sinful tangle of inertia that has delayed for so long the advance of the Gospel at home and overseas. This sinful tangle of inertia of modern missions has been the dependence of evangelism upon foreign agencies, personnel and finances to do the job in all the world. Little thought is given to the stockpile of hoarded natural and national resources of unused, unprepared, uncommitted manpower, hiding fearfully behind the walls of the church or mission compound, slowly but surely wasting away." [3] An erroneous idea of indigenous principles and indigenous churches, and a dichotomy of organizational structure has hindered us from really involving the national resources in a unified and integrated program of all-out evangelism.

Saturation evangelism movements have not yielded to the temptations of either a dichotomous organization, or fighting the spiritual battles of conquest with foreign resources. They have appealed directly to the national churches and have mobilized and trained the raw material to be used by God. This has brought inestimable blessings to the younger churches. It has awakened in them a new sense of dignity as churches of Christ, created a new sense of responsibility in national leadership, trained them in programming evangelism, and aroused a new and sanctified sense of self-reliance and independence in them. Numerous testimonies from pastors and laymen confirm the fact that for the first time it really dawned upon them that they were meant to do the job of evangelism in their lands. They realized that they were the evangelizing agencies of God, instead of merely holding the fort missionaries had won. They were challenged to act as responsible churches and were drawn away from their satellite mentality. Many churches have been put into orbit, as it were, to chart and to navigate an independent course not as satellites but as independent and responsible bodies.

For the first time in their history many were seriously challenged to become evangelizing centers and forces. This is a tremendous achievement. The mission situation will never again be the same where saturation evangelism programs have been successfully conducted. From the historical point of view this is of utmost significance. The churches have gained a self-image which, we hope, they will never surrender nor lose.

The missions should learn the important lesson and rethink and revamp their attitudes, approaches and training programs. Through practice and institutional training most missions have created in the mind and/or the subconsciousness of the nationals the impression that their ministry in the main is responsible for the care of the churches that have been established. The major training prepares them for pastoral work and church ministries.

Evangelism and church planting are on the periphery. The impression prevails that the mission is responsible for the evangelization of the country. Few pastors have learned to think of their churches as evangelizing agencies. They have assumed this to be the responsibility of the mission. This has come to us again and again from national pastors. This feeling was rooted even stronger in the minds of the laymen. Many of the members, especially men, were surprised when they were challenged to mobilize and accomplish that which they had expected to be the business of the mission.

May it please the Lord to sanctify, clarify, strengthen and build this self-image in the churches throughout the world. Let the church be the church wherever it is found, in whatever culture and whatever land, and serve the Lord aggressively in evangelism, that the task of bringing the Gospel to our generation may be accomplished speedily.

FOOTNOTES

PART ONE

CHAPTER 1

[1] *A New Testament Wordbook*, William Barclay (New York: Harper & Brothers, 1957), pp. 41, 42.

CHAPTER 5

[1] *Christianity and the Nations*, Phillips Brooks as quoted by Robert Speer (New York: Fleming H. Revell), p. 20.

[2] *The Primacy of the Missionary*, Dr. Robson as quoted by Archibald McLean (St. Louis: Christian Board of Publication), pp. 30, 31.

[3] Robert Speer, *Ibid.*, pp. 17, 18.

CHAPTER 6

[1] *Protestant Europe: Its Crisis and Outlook*, Adolf Keller and George Stewart (New York: George H. Doran Co.), p. 93.

[2] *Go!*, Charles Kingsley and George Delamarter (Grand Rapids: Zondervan Publishing House, 1966), p. 18.

[3] *Baptist Standard*, Waylon B. Moore (March, 1960).

CHAPTER 7

[1] Robert Speer, *Ibid.* (quote from Adolf Harnack), p. 21.

CHAPTER 8

[1] *Revival, An Enquiry*, Max Warren (London: SCM Press Ltd.), p. 38.

[2] Mimeographed material. Evangelical Foreign Missions Association, Washington, D.C.

[3] Mimeographed notes, Arthur Glasser.

PART TWO —

EVANGELISM-IN-DEPTH AND NEW LIFE FOR ALL

IN THIS SECTION, which comprises the bulk of our research, we want to examine carefully the two major patterns of saturation evangelism, known as Evangelism-in-Depth, primarily in Latin America, and New Life For All in Nigeria.

Our studies will include not only descriptive material about the purposes and objectives of these programs, and how they have been carried out, but also critical evaluations which we hope will serve to stimulate further thought and refinements.

Also, if research is to be practical for the missionary enterprise of the church, it must include recommendations. These we have fashioned under a separate chapter covering our studies of both Evangelism-in-Depth and New Life For All.

Chapter 9

THE INCEPTION AND PHILOSOPHY OF EVANGELISM-IN-DEPTH

EVANGELISM-IN-DEPTH is the designation of a program of gospel outreach sponsored by the Latin America Mission of San Jose, Costa Rica. It is a serious attempt to hasten the evangelization of Latin America by a reconception of the philosophy and methodology of evangelism, leading away from traditional campaign evangelism with the evangelist as central and bringing evangelism into conformity with idealized "apostolic patterns" of making known the Gospel of Jesus Christ.

Its focus is evangelism; its means, the mobilization of all believers; its scope, a country for Christ; its dynamic, multiplicity of prayer cells and dependence upon the Holy Spirit; its goal, the salvation of souls and the strengthening of local congregations.

Evangelism-in-Depth was born in the heart of a man whose life had been devoted to the evangelization of Latin America, Dr. R. Kenneth Strachan, missionary and general director (1950-1965) of the Latin America Mission. God endowed this man with unusual ability, energy, vision and wisdom. The future history of missions will place his name alongside such names as William Carey, J. Hudson Taylor, John L. Nevius and Roland Allen, as men who dared to depart from established ways of doing things. Such men projected new and dynamic ideas, ideas that history modified and cultures adapted, but which in their essential nature have remained unchanged and thus have greatly enriched and expedited the process of world evangelization.

As director and campaign evangelist of the Latin America Mission, Dr. Strachan acquainted himself well with the needs and possibilities of the countries of his adoption. A number of factors combined to make him a restless and diligent student of the programs of evangelism and lack of progress of evangelical Christianity. He studied the soaring figures of world population explosion, especially as they related to Latin America. He observed the rapid spread of Communism, Islam and such pseudo-Christian sects as Jehovah's Witnesses and the Latter-day Saints. He saw the renaissance and progress of Roman Catholicism, especially in Africa and Latin America. He noted the rapid progress of the Pentecostals in several countries in Latin America.

In contrast, he also observed the relatively complacent, introverted Protestant churches, the evangelicals included. They seemed to suf-

51

fer from a sort of deadness and paralysis. "We saw many congregations with tired, discouraged pastors, preaching trite sermons to members that were stuck to their seats. Week after week the same thing, and no appreciable growth." [1]

Discontent and fractionalism among the conservatives was evident in many places. Careful comparative studies convinced him that some basic presuppositions of evangelical missions were inadequate to complete the ministry of world evangelization. For instance, the assumption by many that if only enough missionaries could be recruited, the job could be completed. On the other hand, dependence too exclusively upon modern media and techniques of mass communication, such as radio, television, or even movies, visual aids, airplanes and literature. Though he fully recognized these media and techniques as a divine gift to our age, they could not be the final nor the main answer to the baffling problem of the unfinished task, any more than mass evangelism in campaigns could be, no matter how successful. A new approach to evangelism had to be found if the Great Commission was to be realized and the world was to hear the Gospel.

Dr. Strachan's fertile and creative mind was greatly stimulated by books like Roland Allen's *Missionary Methods: St. Paul's or Ours?* and *The Spontaneous Expansion of the Church;* Donald McGavran's *The Bridges of God;* Tom Allen's *The Face of My Parish;* Harry Boer's *That My House May Be Filled;* Hendrick Kraemer's *A Theology of the Laity,* and, from a secular viewpoint, Eric Hoffer's *The True Believer.*

Furthermore, his persistent and comparative study of certain dynamic and growing movements such as Communism, Jehovah's Witnesses and Pentecostalism (he could have added Soka Gakkai of Japan) and the work of the Assemblies of God in El Salvador proved extremely stimulating and helpful. He formulated his findings in the following words:

> So as we examined groups like these: one anti-Christian, the other pseudo-Christian, and the third Christian but not in the conventional pattern, we wondered just what was the secret of the success of each one. Was it their doctrine? That could not be, because each was preaching a different message. Was it their emphasis? Was it their method? Was it their organization? The answer did not seem to lie with any of these. Finally we came to recognize that in spite of their many differences in doctrine, organization, emphasis and practice, they were alike in only one thing — they had one thing in common and that was the secret of their success.
>
> What they had in common was this: their success in mobilizing their total constituency in continuous evangelistic action. And so we came to the conviction that the secret of expansion was to be found in this

thesis: that the successful expansion of any movement is in direct proportion to its success in mobilizing and occupying its total membership in constant propagation of its beliefs.[2]

Indeed, this is a great statement as far as it goes. It should be noted that this "Strachan theorem" is not a discovery of a principle in the true sense of the word, but rather a deduction and formulation of a principle practiced by groups antedating Evangelism-in-Depth by many years. It is therefore not original with the Latin America Mission. They learned and borrowed the principles from other movements, systematized, modified, enriched and adapted them. They undergirded them by an organizational structure; put feet under them within an evangelical interdenominational framework; and popularized them by practicing and preaching them without fear or apology and with wholehearted enthusiasm.

Such words do not detract from the greatness of the principles, nor from him who formulated them. They merely put the emphasis where the facts lie.

It is only to be regretted that Dr. Strachan stopped his search with the observation and formulation of this very significant principle, the "Strachan theorem." Had he continued his search, he could have found several other principles equally dynamic and significant to the one he formulated. Had he done so, he could have given to us a more complete and a more dynamic program of evangelism and church multiplication. However, as happens so often, overenthusiasm because of a discovery blinds a man to the even greater of which we see in part. As it was, however, he drew the conclusion: "This alone and nothing else is the key."[3] This has naturally narrowed the door considerably to additional and necessary essentials to make the movement all that it might have become. Its incompleteness will become evident in our evaluation and later presentation.

Once the conclusion of the principles had been phrased, the question of implementation arose on the horizon. About this he writes:

> As we mulled over the problem of an effective strategy for evangelizing the continent of Latin America, we knew we had to find some way of mobilizing the evangelical Christians in each republic and bringing them together in a plan of action that would unite their forces and make for the greatest impact. In the course of such thinking, certain basic considerations came to the fore:
>
> (1) Rather than think in terms of a continent, we ought to think in specific terms of national or regional territories.
> (2) In each country the key to total evangelization, we concluded, lay not with the foreign missionary organizations or even the

national ministers — important as both of these were — but with
the sum total of the Christian believers.

(3) This individual witness needed to be carried out both in everyday life and in special endeavor within the total witness of the
local Christian community.

(4) Another consideration that weighed greatly upon us was the
necessity of bringing together the different church bodies and
organizations in a united witness.

(5) Finally, it was our conviction that the individual activity of all
the believers and all the local churches and the cooperative efforts of the sum of the different churches had all to be related
to one overall plan and strategy that would aim at nothing less
than the total and effective evangelization of the territory selected.[4]

Evangelism-in-Depth has not found it necessary deliberately or consciously to depart from these basic formulations in its eight years of
practice (1960-68) and ten major campaigns: Nicaragua 1960; Costa
Rica 1961; Guatemala 1962; Honduras 1963-64; Venezuela 1964;
Bolivia 1965; Dominican Republic 1965; Peru 1967; Colombia 1968;
Appalachia 1968. The principles and formulations have stood the test
of time and have proven their value and workability.

Chapter 10

THE PROGRAM, ORGANIZATION AND OBJECTIVES OF EVANGELISM-IN-DEPTH

THE PROGRAM OF Evangelism-in-Depth follows in orderly sequence usually through one year. The flip chart presents the following program:

January	— Organize committees
	Start prayer cells
February	— Train leadership
March	— Train every Christian
April	
May	— Visitation
June	— Local Campaigns
July	— Special efforts
August	
September	— Regional Campaigns
October	
November	— National Campaign
December	— Follow-up

How nearly this follows to original design can be seen by comparing the chart with the following outline:

> . . . we drew up a tentative outline which involved the following stages:
> First of all, it seemed advisable to attempt to hold a special Conference for Christian Workers — missionaries, pastors, lay leaders and their wives. In the course of this Conference we felt that the first emphasis should be a waiting on the Lord in prayer and then secondly an attempt to convey to these Christian leaders a vision of the need in their country and an outline of the method and plan for meeting that need. And our prayer was that bringing together the leaders from all the different groups could accomplish this purpose.
> The second stage might be called one of mobilization. We felt that prayer groups should be organized throughout the country, as many prayer cells as possible, and that daily prayer should be going up from Christians everywhere to seek the Lord's blessing upon the effort. Then a training program should be organized in all the principal centers of the country for the purpose of preparing Christians for personal and visitation evangelism, and for active participation in the united crusades and in the follow-up which we would be holding throughout the country. We also wanted to stress house-to-house visitation, and we hoped that it would be possible to organize visitation work, starting

from the local churches and reaching the homes around each church.

Following this second stage, which was to last two to three months, we planned a series of united evangelistic crusades to be held in the strategic centers and cities of the chosen area. These would help bring Christians of many different groups and denominations together for united evangelistic action and also make it possible to bring the Gospel to the attention of the entire citizenry in the strongest possible way.

A fourth and final stage was one of follow-up, in which we would seek to encourage local churches to carry out their own evangelistic meetings, renew visitation work, and continue in the pattern of total purposeful witness and outreach that would result in constant growth and expansion.

The chief goals in this plan were: first to impart to the Christian community a new vision and desire for all-out evangelism; secondly to make an initial effort to get the Gospel out to towns and villages that had not yet been reached; and thirdly to leave behind a Christian Church that would engage in continuous evangelistic action. And the attainment of this last objective would be the real measure of success.[1]

The flip chart vividly presents the total program of Evangelism-in-Depth in three main divisions under: Presuppositions, Principles and Program.

The Presuppositions

The presuppositions, which are also thought of as attitudes, are stated in four propositions:
1. Abundant reaping requires abundant sowing.
2. Christians can and must work together in evangelism.
3. When Christians pool resources for evangelism God multiplies them.
4. A dedicated minority can make an impact on an entire nation.

The Principles

With the word *mobilization* being central, the principles read:
1. Mobilization of every Christian in witness.
2. Mobilization within the framework of the church.
3. Mobilization by local leadership.
4. Mobilization with global objectives.

The Program

The program calls for prayer, training, visitation, special efforts, evangelistic meetings—local church, district, national—continuation.

The total philosophy, principles and program are effectively presented in a chart of a suspension bridge. The principles of Evangelism-in-Depth are likened to the supporting towers of the bridge. The program may be compared to the traffic area. The presuppositions form the foundation stones of the bridge. Indeed, it is a fitting symbol of leading man safely from death to life, from darkness to light, from the kingdom of darkness into the kingdom of God's dear Son.

THE ORGANIZATION

Considerable attention is devoted to the development of an elaborate, comprehensive and efficient organization which spreads itself like a network over the entire country and integrates every phase of activity into a comprehensive and unified strategy, holding the movement together and advancing it from stage to stage and phase to phase according to a prearranged calendar, plan and program. This makes for order and unity, not always, however, for efficiency. It should be noted that all leading positions of the organization are filled by men—missionaries or nationals—of the sponsoring country.

THE OBJECTIVES

The objectives of Evangelism-in-Depth are clearly outlined in the official notebook prepared for a continental institute on Evangelism-in-Depth under "General Objectives and Particular Objectives." We quote its main points:

General Objectives

A. Total mobilization of the Christian community.
B. Total evangelization of a given area.

Particular Objectives

A. The awakening of pastors and missionary leaders to the potential that lies dormant within the local church, and a practical proof of what can be done when this potential is tapped.
B. The development of strong national leadership.
C. The development of a strong national church.
D. The evangelization of every stratum and facet of national life.

These are comprehensive and practical objectives and deserve careful scrutiny and evaluation.

Chapter 11

THE RECORD OF EVANGELISM-IN-DEPTH

THE RECORD OF Evangelism-in-Depth has been written in glowing reports. Numerous photographs and personal presentations have achieved world-wide publicity and fame for it. How much of this is due to the moment of time, relationships involved, a grand public relations machine, enthusiasm on behalf of those involved, or actual success achieved in the field only eternity will reveal. Perhaps all factors are contributing their share.

At present it is a world phenomenon. It has successfully survived attacks and criticism, even over the grave of its founder, Dr. Strachan, who died on 24 February 1965. However, he left a team behind, a group of men sold on the program, true to the Gospel, dedicated to God and the work, anxious to be a success for God. It has numerous ardent students, devoted disciples, dedicated supporters, and uncounted co-workers and admirers. The author is one who firmly believes in the principles upheld and advocated by Evangelism-in-Depth as far as they go. It has its determined opponents as well.

It has conducted a very profitable Congress on Evangelism-in-Depth in August of 1966 in San Jose, Costa Rica, with representatives from most republics of Latin America, and men from Asia, Africa and the United States as well. Teams have conducted workshops in Europe and Asia, making known the principles of Evangelism-in-Depth.

Considering Evangelism-in-Depth *quantitatively,* it has a tremendous record. Evangelism-in-Depth has successfully completed nine years of enthusiastic and fruitful ministries in nine Latin American Republics and one area in the United States. It has made an indelible impact upon nine Latin American Republics. Nine years of practice have given it an experienced team to inspire, guide, coordinate and integrate the work into a dynamic program.

It has discovered and called forth unknown and unnoticed national evangelists and challenged them to cultivate and use their talents for God by providing for them an opportunity to become engaged in evangelism.

Its massive training program has trained some eight thousand leaders and more than one hundred and forty thousand lay Christians. This cannot leave the respective countries without some positive and lasting impact.

Its year-long school of prayer, listing more than twenty-five thousand home cells, has taught countless Christians the value and practice of prayer.

The more than one million homes visited during the campaign year, and more than one hundred thousand professions of faith registered during that time, are evidences of great efforts, strong motivation, careful planning and bold reaping.

The *qualitative* contribution of Evangelism-in-Depth is no less significant than the quantitative. We agree with W. Dayton Roberts' reply to certain inadequate understandings of the objectives of Evangelism-in-Depth, which people take to be church growth solely in terms of membership additions. Says he:

> But immediate church growth is not the only positive result which should be expected from a large-scale Evangelism-in-Depth effort. The new spirit of faith, courage and optimism on the part of the Dominican people as they discovered that not even war or revolution could thwart God's evangelistic purpose through His church was exciting. This new zeal, this new enthusiasm, this new boldness to speak the Word of God, is difficult to measure, but it is one of the most significant products of an Evangelism-in-Depth effort.[1]

Again he writes:

> . . . the subtle but significant change toward which we are striving — a collective experience on the part of the whole body of Christ, wherein discouragement turns to hopefulness, negativism to optimism, indifference to aggressiveness, doubt to faith, and timidity to courage. The experience of Acts 4 is one of Evangelism-in-Depth's basic objectives, as by God's grace and the work of the Holy Spirit, are patterns of growth in the Christian community.[2]

There are qualitative contributions which cannot be measured by counts and figures, which add to the spirit of the church and which eventually will break forth in quantitative enlargements. While it is difficult to separate quality and quantity, God may see fit to time them separately. Here patience and wisdom of the saints are needed.

Such, then, is the record of Evangelism-in-Depth quantitatively and qualitatively. This record is upheld by men who have been closely associated with and deeply involved in Evangelism-in-Depth.

The Reverend Allen Thompson, general director of the West Indies Mission, former missionary to the Dominican Republic and national coordinator of Evangelism-in-Depth in that republic, writes:

> In 1939 the West Indies Mission began work in the Dominican Republic, a country which soon proved to be almost impenetrable to the Gospel. The 27 years of difficult sowing in tears yielded 15 con-

gregations and around 900 believers in Christ. In the year of evangelism just past, the reaping in joy has added to the WIM effort 2 churches, 8 additional preaching points, and approximately 700 new believers. What are the implications of this apparent success in an explosive, revolutionary environment?

The first implication is that here we see an illustration of the stage being set for spiritual awakening. In the plan of God for reaching a nation, time is an important factor. Missionary activity, political climate, national awareness — all are contributing elements in preparing a people for the time of spiritual sensitivity. The Dominican Republic is presently discovering her own potential as a nation, throwing off yokes of political and religious bondage, and opening her heart to the challenges of a new day. This hour is one of unprecedented receptivity to the Gospel.

There is a second implication: only as the church evaluates its methods will it be ready to meet the hour of opportunity with adequate impetus. This evaluation must be grounded on the fact that while the gospel message does not change, it demands the most appropriate means for its dissemination. These variables in methodology revolve around several biblical principles of evangelistic action.

First, evangelism must be rooted in the total experience and witness of each Christian. Therefore in our WIM work an effort was made to mobilize every one of the 900 believers. As a result, 164 prayer cells were organized, 430 graduated from our training course in evangelism, and 305 participated in house to house visitation.

Then, evangelism — to be successful — must give testimony to the unity of the body of Christ without compromise. In the Dominican Republic this principle was obeyed by laying down a clear doctrinal statement as the basis for cooperation in the evangelistic venture. Groups or individuals who could not subscribe to this statement did not take part and the result was a unity that was spiritual, not organizational, and gave witness to our oneness in Christ.

Evangelistic activities must be planned, coordinated, and implemented systematically to bring the greatest results. This we did through matching resources against the needs in the various phases of prayer, training, visitation, and campaign ministries.

A third implication would appear to be urgent: only as the church maintains the biblical attitude toward evangelism can its influence continue. In this campaign the spotlight was taken off the pulpit and focused on the pew — away from the evangelist and onto the believer. This emphasis must continue until it becomes part of the life of the church.

Already, evidences of this spirit are encouraging. Laymen in our churches for the first time are taking their place in leadership positions. Three fronts of evangelistic endeavor have been charted — by young people, men's groups, and women's organizations. Our hopes are high as we see the awakened church penetrate their society with the Gospel.[3]

The Reverend A. Merle Sluyter, field chairman of the Christian and Missionary Alliance Mission in Peru, writes:

Yesterday, August 18, 1968, along with a group of 70 young people from the main Alliance church in Lima, I visited a new group of believers in one of the heavily populated "barriadas" of Lima called Ermitano. This group of Christians has been brought into existence as a direct result of Evangelism-in-Depth. Two carloads and a large bus took the Alliance young people to Ermitano. But no sooner had we arrived on the scene, when two by two they fanned out to do house-to-house visitation and distribute tracts, like a small trained army. What thrilled my soul most was to see the enthusiasm with which these well-trained young people went unashamedly about their task, all returning to the place of meeting, testifying, singing and taking active part in the open-air service. Next Sunday we shall visit another new group in San Cosme, which also had its beginning during the year of evangelism.

Last evening in the main church several responded to the invitation and went forward for salvation. No sooner had they gone forward, when several young people accompanied them to deal with them individually, while the pastor and the visiting evangelist went to the door to shake hands with the crowd.

If Evangelism-in-Depth accomplished nothing else, it certainly started lay people working for the Lord. A couple of weeks ago I visited our far-flung work in the jungle area of Tingo Maria. In this region the president of the interdenominational Evangelism-in-Depth committee had been an Alliance missionary. The impact of this evangelistic drive was so outstanding, that it was plainly visible in this Youth Convention which I attended. Though the convention was held in an out-of-the-way place (one had to travel by bus or truck, dugout canoe and foot), some 150 young people attended, and were more interested in filling the program with Bible studies and discussion groups, than they were with sports. In this area, every church during the month of September will have an evangelistic campaign, and practically all of them will be under the leadership of trained lay people. Two new works have been brought into existence in the Tingo Maria region, and one of them invited the Youth Convention for March of 1969.

Thus, as a direct result of Evangelism-in-Depth, the C&MA has at least four new works: two in the jungle and two on the coast. Regions which have been slumbering in indifference, such as Huamalies and Dos de Mayo (in the high Sierra), have sprung back to life under lay leadership, as there are no full-time preachers nor pastors in these large areas.

Wherever Alliance churches went all-out for Evangelism-in-Depth, there the harvest was great. Some churches increased their number two or three times over. But I believe one of the most important results of the entire program has been the intensive and thorough training given to church members in the art of soul-winning and the duties and responsibilities of church members. Offerings have increased in most of the churches, souls have been converted, and the church has been activated.[4]

From pastors in other countries come similar positive reports about the values of Evangelism-in-Depth:

Guatemala: "During the course of the year we have accepted into the church approximately 65 new believers. All of this has been the result of the evangelistic activity of the church . . . The brethren have continued to be so enthusiastic and so well-prepared that they are constantly going everywhere to preach the gospel." [5] — *Jose R. Estrada, pastor, Southern Baptist Church, Puerto Barrios*

"This (new) congregation is the direct result of the evangelistic activity of the church during the course of the year. This is of course due in a great deal to E/D, which has unified the church and has launched it into a program of aggressive evangelism." [6] — *Edmundo Madrid, pastor, Friends Church, Zacapa*

"E/D has moved me to have a greater concern for sinners, and I observe the same feeling in the members of the church . . . In praying, in visitation, in the evangelistic campaigns, and even in our offerings, we have seen new prosperity, spiritual and material. These activities have also made a deep impression on the unbelieving community . . ." [7] —*Francisco Julian Tzunun, pastor, Primitive Methodist Church, Chichicastenango*

Peru: "Evangelism-in-Depth is of God . . . and God is mobilizing us. We have been sleeping and now we have awakened to a great revival. More than 18 young people have given their lives to Christ; the church is hungry for God. Before we had 60 members; now there are 150. We have 60 new converts and three new preaching points." [8] — *Arturo Paucar, Huancayo*

Colombia: "Our church has had many evangelistic campaigns, but this year we have seen far more of our congregation involved. There are 78 prayer cells and the majority of our members took the training classes. Some are still afraid to visit. Yet, 30 couples hold children's classes each Sunday afternoon, while another 90 members go out house to house, sharing their faith in Christ. We have visited about half of the 80,000 residents of Girardot, and plan to keep on until we have called in every home. Evangelism-in-Depth has awakened many in my church and has stimulated much interest in our city as well." [9] — *Aristobulo Porras, pastor, Presbyterian Church, Girardot*

Chapter 12

THE IDEALS AND PRACTICE OF EVANGELISM-IN-DEPTH

BEFORE WE EVALUATE Evangelism-in-Depth, it is well to state what it is ideally and as it is envisioned by its representatives and supporters, and then what it is practically, or what it has become on the battlefield of the world.

We consider several ideal projections, and self-evaluations as they appear in definitive descriptions of Evangelism-in-Depth.

The founder, the late Dr. R. Kenneth Strachan, clearly summarized his view on the program in the following words: "Evangelism-in-Depth has been hailed by some as a new strategy of evangelism. But in fact it involves nothing basically new. If there is anything different about it, it is perhaps the fact that it represents a formal effort to relate in a long-range program the best elements of personal witness and mass evangelism, integrated in the continuous testimony of the local church and linked to the total witness of the entire Body of Christ. It also involves a challenge to all Christian bodies to plan and carry out their respective evangelistic programs in a simultaneous, coordinated effort aimed at the ultimate goal that the Great Commission enjoins. To many individuals, moreover, it comes as a personal summons to take the Lord's command seriously and to adventure with other Christians in obedient involvement and witness in the world." [1]

Dr. John Stam, eminent theologian of the Latin America Mission, presents the following meaningful summary. "First, Evangelism-in-Depth has taken the biblical order and emphases on evangelism seriously in all their biblical radicalness. Secondly, the late Dr. Strachan, the founder of Evangelism-in-Depth, has taken that which is scattered throughout the Scriptures on evangelism and brought it together into a systematic whole. Thirdly, these truths and emphases were given legs in an organizational pattern and structure." [2]

The present director, the Reverend Ruben Lores, projects the following summary of the program and philosophy of Evangelism-in-Depth. Raising the question, "What is Evangelism-in-Depth?" he says:

> There are those who believe that Evangelism-in-Depth is merely a method, but it is much more than that. In the first place, in Evangelism-in-Depth not one but many methods are employed — all the known methods and those yet to be discovered. The guiding principle here is to match all resources with all opportunities and the needs. Evangelism-

in-Depth provides the organizational structure and the spiritual and psychological atmosphere necessary for the application of the principle.

But more than a methodological structure, more than a missionary strategy, Evangelism-in-Depth is the practical expression of a theological thought with respect to the inescapable consideration of the mission of the church in this world.

There is a theological base which serves as a hidden foundation of Evangelism-in-Depth, and which sustains the visible structure of the program.

Although here we will deal only with the theological base, in order to limit the subject matter and deepen our understanding of one area, I think it necessary to point out that Evangelism-in-Depth rests upon certain sociological and methodological principles which constitute an essential part of the ideological conception that supports it.

1. "The growth of any movement is in direct proportion to the success it obtains in the mobilization of the totality of its membership for the constant propagation of its beliefs" (Strachan).
2. A dedicated minority can make a decisive impact upon a neutral or disoriented majority.
3. In order to achieve a global objective, a systematic and co-ordinated plan is needed to train personnel in the use of the resources.
4. The communication of an ideology is achieved more adequately among people of the same culture.
5. The relevance and continuity of a movement depend upon the success obtained in developing autonomous leadership.

The theological foundation of Evangelism-in-Depth could be described as an ellipse whose two foci are the Great Commission of the church and the unity of the Body of Christ." [3]

W. Dayton Roberts, an associate director of the Latin America Mission, says: "Mobilization is the key word in Evangelism-in-Depth. In its simplest terms, it is an effort to mobilize every Christian believer—man, woman, child, illiterate, intellectual, new Christian and mature disciple—in an all-out witness to Jesus Christ." [4] Elsewhere he says: "In fact, Evangelism-in-Depth might as accurately be called simultaneous evangelism as cooperative evangelism." [5]

Yet again, he says: "Evangelism-in-Depth is a year-long school of evangelism, of which the training of leadership is a highly significant by-product." [6]

In the flip chart it is declared that Evangelism-in-Depth represents a conscientious attempt:

1. To mobilize all Christians in a nation or area;
2. To evangelize all the non-Christians of that area;
3. To reach them in all of their personal and social structures and relationships;

4. To reach them with the whole Gospel of Christ, announcing pre-eminently its simple kerygma (Christ died for our sins, was buried, rose, and is coming again);

5. To proclaim it in the context of its ethical implications and the same time give tangible expression to its social concern for the total welfare of those from whom response to the Gospel is sought. (The numbering is ours.)

Depth in Evangelism spells it out in these words: "Evangelism-in-Depth is not a catch phrase; it is not just a new program of evangelism; nor is it something to supplant other programs. Evangelism-in-Depth combines a philosophy of evangelism with a program of evangelistic activities, and an indispensable attitude which brings new hope for our evangelistic task." [7]

"*Depth* in evangelism — this is what we are all looking for, what we need in our evangelistic outreach . . . Depth is in contrast to that which is superficial, temporal and partial." [8]

Elsewhere, Evangelism-in-Depth is contrasted with evangelism in breadth, the latter referring to the traditional type and program of evangelism, the former indicating a radical departure from the traditional patterns and philosophy.

Dr. Leighton Ford, though not organizationally related to the movement, endorses it and describes it thus: "Evangelism-in-Depth is not mainly a program or a technique, nor is it a trademark with some magical power. Rather it is a mood, a spirit, a deep conviction born of the Holy Spirit in the hearts of men—men who are ruthlessly honest, who realize the failures of the church to keep up with the galloping birthrate of the world, but who are also realistic enough to know that if we take God at His word and are willing to reevaluate our methods in the light of the New Testament and the demands of the new day, we can confront our generation with the living Christ." [9]

An analysis of the above statements reveals the following factors in Evangelism-in-Depth:

Strachan

1. It represents a formal effort to relate in a long-range program the best elements of personal witness and mass evangelism.
2. It integrates the continuous testimony of the local church and links it to the total witness of the entire body of Christ.
3. It involves a challenge to all Christian bodies to plan and carry out their respective evangelistic programs in a simultaneous, coordinated effort.
4. It comes as a personal summons to many individuals to take

the Lord's command seriously and to adventure with other Christians in obedient involvement and witness in the world.

5. It is not a new strategy of evangelism nor does it involve anything basically new. Rather, it is a return to apostolic patterns of evangelism.

Lores

6. Evangelism-in-Depth is a methodological structure in which there is a combination of several methods.
7. It is a missionary strategy which involves the guiding principle to match all resources with all opportunities and needs.
8. It provides the organizational structure and the spiritual and psychological atmosphere necessary for the application of the principle.
9. It is solidly undergirded by theological, sociological and methodological principles.
10. Its theological foundation could be described as an ellipse whose two foci are the Great Commission of the church and the unity of the body of Christ.

Roberts

11. Mobilization is the key word in Evangelism-in-Depth.
12. It is simultaneous and cooperative evangelism.
13. It is a school of evangelism.
14. Evangelism-in-Depth combines a philosophy of evangelism, program of evangelistic activities, and an indispensable attitude.
15. Evangelism-in-Depth is a "depth" movement.
16. Evangelism-in-Depth is a radical departure from traditional patterns and philosophy in evangelism.

Ford

17. Evangelism-in-Depth is primarily a mood, a spirit, a conviction born of the Holy Spirit in the hearts of men.
18. It produces men of vision, valor, insight and effective evangelism.

Add to these eighteen factors the five from the flip chart and we have more than twenty ideals, characteristics and/or qualities of Evangelism-in-Depth. For sure, some are duplicating and others are canceling out each other, yet it would be difficult to find fault with any of these ideals. They are biblical. They are practical. I find no fault with the principles of the program. Of course, it must be admitted that many of these ideals and qualities are not unique to Evangelism-in-Depth. They could be found in other evangelistic and revival movements.

Chapter 13

EVALUATION OF EVANGELISM-IN-DEPTH

BEFORE WE CONTINUE with our practical analysis and evaluation, some general remarks become necessary, for every movement is made by history at the same time as it is making history. We thus look at Evangelism-in-Depth in the moment of time.

Evangelism-in-Depth was timed divinely. It could not have appeared at a more appropriate time and at a more strategic place than it did. We may say that it came in "the fulness of time" and into a "field white unto harvest." Such was Latin America. Any dynamic movement is bound to succeed on this continent. A number of factors combine to make for this timeliness.

The first factor is the new mood of evangelism. We have pointed out previously that a most remarkable revival of evangelism has taken place. Today proclamation evangelism as confrontation, infiltration and permeation is becoming one of the major trends of missions. Some mission fields give the impression of being one vast evangelistic campaign. Evangelists and evangelistic programs are evident everywhere. A mood of evangelism prevails among evangelicals in many mission fields. This is a divine phenomenon that no man can create. God in His grace does bestow it upon His people, no doubt to meet the needs of the world and in answer to sincere prayers.

In such a mood almost any systematic, enthusiastic and spiritually motivated program of evangelism will succeed. This is evident from the great campaigns of the Southern Baptists, the Good News Crusades of the Assemblies of God, the evangelistic efforts of Overseas Crusades, and the ministries of Bakht Singh of India and others, which equal in their success the immediate accomplishments of Evangelism-in-Depth, both in professions of faith and church membership additions. In fact, in the latter several exceed Evangelism-in-Depth. Thus I was amazed to read that the Assemblies of God after a campaign in Santos, Brazil, succeeded in winning for their churches more than 1,000 members and 1,800 professions of faith. We are experiencing a time when evangelism is a living and dynamic reality throughout the non-Western world.

It behooves us, therefore, to be careful and honest in projections and distinguish clearly between that which is common to all programs of evangelism and that which is unique to Evangelism-in-Depth. Most certainly there are some qualities and projections that are unique to the latter, provided it is a unique program.

A second factor that must be taken into consideration is the cultural situation in Latin America. It is evident that Latin America is in flux, in a cultural revolution. Upheaval, transition and transformation are evident in every area of life. A general revolution of a unique quality is taking place. The distintegration of old cultural patterns of life and institutions of society is proceeding with rapidity, without precedent and without order.

Roman Catholicism, having been an integral part of the old culture and the obedient servant if not the cohort of the establishment, reaps the disdain of the old order with the loss of prestige and authority. The church has lost her grip upon the people and the prisoners leap into freedom. The cement of cultural cohesion is loosening. Numerous factors are contributing toward an acceleration of changes.

The Reverend Joseph S. McCullough, speaking about the causes, says:

> I think there are a number of causes — humanly speaking of course. First, there is the social revolution created by people moving to cities to seek greater opportunities in life. People are uprooted, and cultural ties are broken as they move away from rural areas and their traditions. With urbanization, people find themselves in a new environment with new friends. They are free from former restraints. They are wide open to everything. They are seeking better things economically, educationally, socially, and in every other way. They are no longer satisfied with living under the limitations of the past.
>
> Also, in many areas of Latin America, the schools are running two sessions daily, and many, many folks attend evening school. They are investigating new ideologies and philosophies. Travel is common, and people are no longer isolated.
>
> Mass media can now be used effectively to reach the multitudes of Latin America. Up-to-date printing presses are turning out literature by the ton. Television probably reaches mainly the upper classes down there, but radio reaches all classes of society and is proving amazingly successful in evangelism.[1]

In the midst of all changes and uncertainties man craves for security, friendship and stability. Change being beyond their control, the masses follow any movement of promise and appreciate any sign of friendship.

The message of the Gospel, therefore, will prove attractive to any listener who can be arrested to listen long enough to hear the Word and see its relevance, provided it is preached as such and with enthusiasm. If in addition to the message genuine reality radiates from the speaker, the attraction increases and becomes a mighty power to draw men toward God, whether the presentation is made in the form of preaching, personal witnessing or conversation.

A third factor is the new attitude of the Roman Catholic Church.

Whether such attitude is genuine, strategic or temporary expediency, we must leave to history. The fact remains, however, that the face of Rome has changed. People are encouraged to read the Bible, are not forbidden to listen to Protestant preaching, and are admonished to be courteous and tolerant. The Roman Catholic Church is opening the floodgates through which the Gospel of Jesus Christ is permitted to enter.

This, of course, removes the fear from the hearts of multitudes and makes for wide and unhindered hearing of the Word. Since an atmosphere of liberty and tolerance prevails, people need not fear to respond to the Gospel. Ecclesiastical persecution and ostracism have been lifted. Thus the respondents increase in large numbers. This, however, does not necessarily also imply Protestant church growth in Latin America.

A fourth factor is the gradual permeation of Latin America with the gospel message, which pours into the continent from more than twenty missionary radio stations and numerous programs that are being aired over commercial stations. Television, too, is making its contribution. Literature and gospel recordings are making themselves felt. The combined impact of these efforts, plus the presence of missionaries and evangelical institutions, cannot be measured in facts and figures. However, it is qualitatively real.

Gospel response can be and should be expected from the combined forces of evangelicalism in Latin America. God assures us: "My word . . . shall not return unto me void, but it shall accomplish that which I please, and it shall prosper in the thing whereto I sent it" (Isa. 55:11).

A fifth factor is the improving intercontinental relationship between North and South America. This creates a new openness to ideas and ideals from the outside world, especially from North America. Latin America is moving toward full maturity, which naturally leads to greater openness, flexibility and tolerance.

All of these providential factors must be taken into consideration lest we credit human instruments, genius and a human pattern with honor which is due God alone.

It is into this moment of time that God has sovereignly and graciously placed Evangelism-in-Depth. This in turn was possible because a servant of His found time to study and search for a new way, was open to new insights, had the courage to chart a new course, challenge the established patterns as inadequate, and launch an improved program.

TOTAL AND COOPERATIVE MOBILIZATION

Evangelism-in-Depth seeks to mobilize the total *body of Christ* in a given country in the evangelistic thrust. The reasons for doing so have been defended from the theological and practical points of view. Sometimes such defense seemed to betray a mentality of belligerency and perhaps offended more than it defended. However, Evangelism-in-Depth has pointed to an important biblical doctrine and principle of operation. We need not restate the defenses here.

The effort of total and cooperative mobilization has been made difficult for at least four reasons:

First, intercommunication between the various groupings in the mission fields has never been an easy matter. Social distance and physical barriers have often stood in the way and comity has kept them somewhat isolated, each minding his own business and working his own area. This has become an attitude, a mentality.

Second, theological differences have separated liberals and conservatives, ecumenists and non-ecumenists, establishing two camps with fairly clear demarcations. These are now developing into separate national, continental and intercontinental organizations.

Third, denominational distinctives, emphases and programs have isolated people and churches, each following his own program, interests and advancing his own work. Instruction and at times pressures from at home have strengthened separateness.

Fourth, separatist tendencies in missionaries and separatist pressures from North America have projected themselves into the fields and influenced the operations in missions and the minds of nationals.

Because of these tendencies some mission fields presented a rather pathetic portrait of Protestant and even evangelical unity in Christ. United efforts and a unified strategy even among evangelicals were practically out of the question. They saw threats in cooperation and infringement upon their rights, individuality and uniqueness of missions.

The modern mission field resembled the statement of conditions in Israel in the Book of Judges: "In those days there was no king in Israel: every man did that which was right in his own eyes." This held true not only of individual missionaries but also of the various societies, of whom the individual missionary was a miniature representation. The last decade has tremendously altered the attitudes and situations, and hopes are filling the missionaries and churches. However, this is by no means uniform, universal, nor is it welcomed by all. Some feel justified to oppose it.

To understand the proceedings of Evangelism-in-Depth in the midst of such complexities and conflicts, we need to keep several facts in mind:

First, at no time or place has Evangelism-in-Depth insisted that all churches must cooperate or that all must be invited to do so. At the same time Evangelism-in-Depth has not yielded to narrow separatism.

Second, the decision as to who is eligible to cooperate is made by the missionaries and national churches of the country in which Evangelism-in-Depth is to be conducted. In the first few countries all who were members of the Evangelical Alliance of that country were invited. Later (Bolivia and after) a doctrinal statement accepted by the national sponsoring body determined eligibility.

Third, in no country has Evangelism-in-Depth succeeded in enlisting all churches and totally mobilizing the Protestant community. The success in involving churches has been phenomenal and has ranged from sixty-five to eighty-five percent. Up to seventy-five percent of the adult men of the cooperating churches have been mobilized and trained. The high percentage of involvement is due to the high percentage of evangelical missions in Latin America, to the evangelistic mood and the appeal Evangelism-in-Depth was able to make. In my studies I gave special attention to the effects of cooperation, since this has been a special concern for many. As a result of my inquiries I came up with the following results:

No pastor felt that he or his church has been hurt theologically, spiritually, or morally by such cooperation.

No pastor felt that his or his church's loyalty to his own denomination had been weakened.

No pastor felt that his or his church's attitude toward theological liberalism and the ecumenical movement had been weakened or otherwise affected.

Most pastors felt that their lives and ministries had been enriched by the fellowship and cooperation, and their churches had benefitted by it.

Most pastors felt that it had been one of the greatest things ever to happen in their community, and that it had been an impressive demonstration of evangelical unity in Christ and in the cause of evangelism.

Most pastors (more than ninety percent) would enthusiastically again enter such cooperation for a similar evangelistic thrust.

The question of cooperation needs serious and impassionate studies. Only the Holy Spirit knows when it is advisable and essential to success. It does not seem to be wise to make it a principle that must be adhered to. Neither is it Christian to reject it outright and withdraw from all cooperation. The Bible upholds both unity in the Spirit and cooperation in ministries but also separation and non-cooperation. It is impossible to make a general ruling on it.

Chapter 14

EVANGELISM-IN-DEPTH AND CHURCH GROWTH

As WE COME TO THIS SUBJECT we enter one of the most perplexing areas of studies.

Evangelism-in-Depth registers the following figures under professions of faith:

Nicaragua	— 2,604	Costa Rica	— 3,153
Guatemala	— 20,000	Venezuela	— 17,791
Bolivia	— 19,212	Dominican Rep.	— 11,800
Peru	— 25,000	Colombia	— 22,000

These are arresting figures. There is no real reason to doubt the correctness of the registration, especially as we compare the counts with the results accomplished in Latin America by other movements. Comparable figures are listed by the Assemblies of God, the Southern Baptists and Overseas Crusades after their campaigns. Latin America has areas and masses of people which constitute fields white unto harvest. We need to put in the sickle and claim multitudes for the Lord. There is good reason to accept these counts as authentic.

The legitimate question, however, arises: What do these figures show in relation to church growth? Does Evangelism-in-Depth enlarge and multiply churches? This we would naturally expect. However, from records and statistics available there is no appreciable, immediate and measurable acceleration in church growth evident in most churches of Costa Rica, Guatemala, Venezuela and Bolivia in the years following the campaigns, although some hitherto stagnant churches recorded an increased and more regular attendance of their members at services, and some isolated churches continue to advance in a stronger manner.

Of course, this does not conclusively prove that there was no increase in church growth during or following the years of Evangelism-in-Depth. The depressing fact exists that many of the missions and churches have no records to present. Many speak enthusiastically of great success, which may be factual.

Yet, they are unable to produce the objective evidence. Also, new groups may have sprung up, as actually has happened in Guatemala. These could possibly have siphoned considerable numbers of new converts and drawn away other members. This has happened among the Baptists in Brazil.

Some growth is recorded by some Venezuelan churches related to

72

The Evangelical Alliance Mission. Acceleration is reported by the Free Methodist Church of Dominican Republic, and by the Missionary Church Association of the same country. It must be stated, however, that this is not reflected in the annual statistics of these two churches. No acceleration is shown, nor increase noticeable.

The plateau in the records is explained to be the result of migrations and emigrations, stemming from the revolution and continued unrest. Because of these facts, no definite growth rate can be established on a scientific basis. The World Gospel Mission of Honduras also claims measureable increase in church growth, but again no records are produced to substantiate the claims. Only the basis of "testimony" and "guessing" remains. It is evident that great unevenness and indefiniteness exists in this most perplexing matter. It is distressing to the researcher.

There is another matter of importance relative to the above mentioned figures, as well as figures presented by other movements. In order to do justice to the course of history and church growth, it is not sufficient merely to list great figures and startling statistics. They do not in themselves speak either of the effectiveness or ineffectiveness of a program of evangelism or any other effort. They merely report happenings. We must inquire what the professions have been in the years preceding and the years following the special efforts, to make an accurate assessment of the statistical results of the movement.

For this purpose I began the studies with statistics of the year 1957 and carried them through the year 1967. Including the denominational records of their annual church growth, I accumulated the reports of nearly one thousand churches. Because many missions and churches do not keep accurate statistics, and because new groups are constantly being formed, the best records are only relative. However, they do reveal trends.

A comparative study of the statistics available indicates that the professions the years preceding Evangelism-in-Depth ranged from sixty-five to seventy-eight percent of the records of the Evangelism-in-Depth year. It is safe to assume that an average seventy-two percent professions would have been made without the Evangelism-in-Depth efforts, or that approximately twenty-eight percent of the above figures are the result of the Evangelism-in-Depth program. In several cases the years following the Evangelism-in-Depth thrust, professions and accessions were lagging behind the years preceding the program, indicating that the biological supply of converts and sympathizers of the evangelicals had been pushed forward by a year or two because of the intensive drive of the Evangelism-in-Depth year.

This seemingly affected from three to five percent. Accepting four as the average, we need to reduce the twenty-eight percent by this number. This leaves us with twenty-four percent net gain.

It would be more accurate to list the figures in the following manner:

		Professions	Net Gain Professions
Nicaragua	—	2,604	624
Guatemala	—	20,000	4,800
Bolivia	—	19,212	4,608
Peru	—	25,000	6,000
Costa Rica	—	3,153	756
Venezuela	—	17,791	4,280
Dominican Rep.	—	11,800	2,832
Colombia	—	22,000	

While this does reduce the above figures considerably, it leaves a good and healthy margin. Any movement that can show a net gain of ten to fifteen percent would be considered creditable, healthy and strong by any measures. No shadow falls upon Evangelism-in-Depth in producing professions of faith.

Our problem, however, arises when we are confronted by the baffling fact that a comparable rise in figures cannot be shown in church membership. The discovery of the fact that Evangelism-in-Depth seemingly does not result in substantial measurable church growth at first alarmed me; later it troubled me; and now it has grown into a deep and steady concern.

Possible Reasons for Church Growth Failure

I am unable to pinpoint the difficulty in dogmatic terms. I can only suggest some possible factors for this unwelcome fact which do not exonerate Evangelism-in-Depth completely, but which point in the direction of circumstances over which Evangelism-in-Depth has little or no control. The following factors loom up before me:

1. *An incomplete Christian experience.* By this I mean an experience which does not mature into spiritual regeneration. This may result from superficial assent to truth, confused motivation, or inadequate knowledge of the Gospel.

First, there is the possibility of explaining profession of faith in the broadest possible terms until it may mean no more than assent to the presented facts and truths. Counting all those who in some way assent to the message or testimony would rapidly increase the number of professions.

Second, there is the possibility of confused motivation. More likely than the former is the fact that while people are sincere in their response to an invitation, they are confused in their motivation. It may lead to a psychological or sociological experience without spiritual regeneration. Studies of this problem have led me to a broad classification of all respondents in Latin America. The "seekers," though all real potentials for the evangelical churches, divide themselves at the time of their response roughly into four classes:

(a) By their response to an invitation, some express a protest against their religion of the past. They are literal "protestants."

(b) Some feel a strong desire and urge for social and cultural identification with a strong and prominent personality, in this case with the evangelist. Personality cult is a live and dynamic issue in Latin America. It is not altogether evil, though it is full of dangers.

(c) Some respond because of a deep sense of incompleteness, need and emptiness in their lives. They do not have the light nor ability to analyze themselves and to identify their need. They merely sense a lack and seek peace, freedom, and forgiveness, though most of these concepts are unformulated. The burden of a guilty and condemning conscience and hunger of heart drive them on to seek reality.

(d) A fourth and by far the largest group, actually the vast majority, responds to the invitation because of a definite desire for a new life and salvation in Christ Jesus. Most of these people have become acquainted with the Gospel either by means of radio, Christian literature, or the testimony of some Christians, perhaps a Christian friend or relative. The Holy Spirit has used this meager knowledge to create a desire for salvation. As the gospel message reaches them they respond to the gracious invitation.

While the first three groups of "seekers" constitute potential converts, many, however, will be lost to the church unless sought and found out and dealt with personally. The fourth group constitutes the immediate converts.

Third, lack of adequate knowledge of the Gospel results in a preparation of the individual rather than in actual regeneration. Mere illumination and conviction are too often accepted as a profession of faith. Instead of seeing this as a state of readiness that needs to be exploited for the Gospel and brought to a sure conclusion, we declare the individual a Christian. Christian workers need to be prepared more fully to perform the greatest and most sacred, as well as the most responsible, ministry if they are to reap as well as to sow.

2. *An ill-prepared and irrelevant church.* Most churches are ill-prepared for the important ministry of follow-up and follow-through, which is one of the major keys in church growth after successful evan-

gelistic campaigns. The difficulties along this line are tremendous in Latin America. Neither are the churches prepared to care for a considerable influx of new and perhaps socially dislocated and dissociated people. The people remain outside and adrift. The lack of and/or failure in follow-up work is a major factor in the lack of church growth.

There is, however, a much more serious problem in winning people not only to the Lord but also to the church. The *structured church,* as shaped and formed through the past centuries in the West and transplanted into the mission fields only with slight modifications, seems antiquated and irrelevant to today's world. This is becoming one of the most alarming and at the same time most challenging phenomenon of Christian missions in numerous lands. In general there is a wide readiness to respond positively to the gospel message, and almost a comparable disdain for the church, except for Sunday morning fellowship and social get-togethers.

This seems to be due to sociology and psychology more than theology. It is an unconscious reaction. Some have lived too long in a highly structured ecclesiastical religion. They fear new enslavement. Others find religion the only avenue of escape from a tightly structured social and economic order and life in which they are forced to function as a cog in a wheel. They will not formally join a structured church to become merely another member.

We need to rethink our concept of the church. Are we dominated by structure or by functions? This is the crucial question we need to face in a realistic manner. Men are looking for dynamic functionalism; they abhor static structuralism even in its most majestic form.

3. *The type of evangelistic campaign.* I am aware of the emphasis of Evangelism-in-Depth on the local church. The principle is "mobilization within the framework of the local church," and "mobilization by local leadership." These are two important principles and emphases. Yet, there seems to be something built into the program of Evangelism-in-Depth that defeats the goal of the local church.

The Southern Baptists seemingly are more successful in channelling their converts into the local churches, and so are the Assemblies of God. Dr. Freeman, executive secretary for evangelism of the Texas Baptist Convention and an ardent promoter and participant of the great campaigns in Japan and Brazil, suggested that perhaps the order of campaigns had something to do with this issue. Instead of climaxing their series with a national campaign, they begin with such services and from here funnel people into the churches by culminating the drive with simultaneous campaigns in local churches. They are not building up but building down, not away but toward the local church.

Evangelism-in-Depth ought to study this and some related questions most diligently. The matter is too serious to dismiss as irrelevant. The shocking fact remains that the churches in general are not accelerating their growth rate. To console ourselves with the qualitative contribution that Evangelism-in-Depth makes without a comparable quantitative increase is to fall back into an old rut which says, "We are doing good work even though we are not growing."

4. *The new religious atmosphere in Latin America.* With the opposition of Rome diminishing, with the traditional stress of Catholicism upon prayer, and the new emphasis upon Bible reading, the development of home Bible discussion gatherings, the encouragement of fellowship groups, and the sponsoring of social reforms and benevolent programs, we may anticipate that fewer and fewer of the respondents to the Gospel will take upon themselves the cultural dislocation and social inconveniences caused by leaving the Roman Catholic Church and joining an evangelical body. They will see a possibility to survive spiritually by means of personal devotion, radio messages, Christian literature, and occasional church attendance.

All of the above factors must be taken into consideration before judgment is expressed over the disappointing fact that in spite of strenuous efforts, sacrifices and seeming success, general church growth is not being accelerated as we would hope and desire. Let us not point fingers at one another, but rather examine all factors and seek a solution to this crucial problem.

Chapter 15

EVANGELISM-IN-DEPTH AND PERENNIAL EVANGELISM

EVANGELISM-IN-DEPTH is a year-long school of evangelism, of which the training of leadership is a highly significant by-product. It is the sincere expectation of the sponsors of Evangelism-in-Depth that a mood of evangelism will be created in the participating churches by the experience, that the training of leaders and lay Christians will outlast the year and continue in the church as a pattern of life and dynamic function, that the new method and strategy will teach the church a new and more effective way to grow and multiply. It is intensely hoped that the end of the year will be the beginning of a new "way of life" for the participating missions, churches and denominations.

How well the churches learn the lessons depends upon such factors as readiness to learn, flexibility to change, determination to grow and multiply, cooperation to proceed as a unit.

That the year-long school of evangelism has not been in vain, and that some do learn, is evident from closer observations in several fields and missions.

The continued emphasis of Evangelism-in-Depth by the Free Methodists in the Dominican Republic is an example that the lessons can be learned. They credit this to the year's experience with Evangelism-in-Depth in 1965.

The Reverend Virgilio Zapata of Guatemala emphatically stated that without the lessons learned from the year-long experience with Evangelism-in-Depth in 1962 the 1968 "Campana Nacional de Evangelismo" in Guatemala would have been unthinkable. Their executives would not have been able to design such a grand scheme and strategy, nor would they have been able to secure the cooperation and support of some one thousand leaders and churches.

It is highly improbable that the successful crusades of the Central American Mission throughout Central America would have gained the impetus and structure without being stimulated by and having learned valuable lessons with and from Evangelism-in-Depth. The Honduras Mennonite Church is duplicating Evangelism-in-Depth and sponsoring the program under the name "Evangelical Advance." This is noble, indeed, and the choice of the name is very appropriate.

It is significant to note that some ninety-six percent of the national pastors interviewed or responding by mail are enthusiastic about the program. They express a readiness to plunge into a "repeat" of Evangelism-in-Depth. Some are earnestly praying for it. It has awakened at least an understanding and yearning for evangelism. This in itself is a tremendous contribution to missions and church growth. It may be the dawn of a new day. Perhaps Evangelism-in-Depth should think more seriously, concretely and creatively in terms of "repeats" in Latin America.

The gnawing question, however, persists: Why is Evangelism-in-Depth not transforming itself into a persistent movement? This is the phenomenon we have been anticipating, praying for and which is the goal of a successful year-long school of evangelism. I have no questions about the scripturalness of the principles of the program (as far as they go), the contemporaneousness of the patterns of the program, the soundness of methodology and means employed by the program, the sincerity of the motivation of the men engaged in the sponsorship of the program. However, I doubt the practicalness of and wisdom in the application of the principles in the program. Several inherent factors seem to militate against Evangelism-in-Depth becoming a perennial movement.

1. *It is too exhausting in its drive, demands and promotion.* It drains the emotional capacity of men to the last, without finding time, ways and means of replenishing them to the degree that people and churches remain fresh to the end. There is a certain "looking to the end."

This has been expressed too frequently by missionaries and pastors to be disregarded. While I do not advocate a leisurely type of evangelism (if there is such a thing), an overtaxing can become disruptive, discouraging and self-defeating. It seems to me from the life of Christ, the life of Paul and the teaching of the Scriptures as a whole, that a ministry in the Spirit and done according to the directions of the Spirit will refresh a man even though it may tire him. It will accelerate instead of exhaust him to the point of discontinuity.

While I am not charging that the work is being done in the flesh, I am drawing attention to the fact that it is so exhausting that relatively few are abiding in it. Well does the Reverend A. M. Sluyter summarize the experience:

> I believe the program as a whole not only brought souls into the church, but it stirred up the lay people to a ministry which had been sadly neglected. On the other hand, I also have the conviction that the program, like so many intensified programs, has its weaknesses. In the first place, the activity of the concentrated year of evangelism was so intense, that once it was all over, the congregation sat back and rested, glad for a breathing spell when there were not meetings going on every night. This, however, was no time to rest, as the follow-up

program, the visitation and revisitation of those interested in the Gospel, should have had priority. Much fruit was lost, due to the fact that the churches either had not prepared adequately for intensive follow-up work, or else were too tired or too busy to do much of it.[1]

2. *The role of outside coordinators creates a leadership vacuum after the campaign.* I fully realize the significance of coordinators if a work is to proceed in an orderly, systematic, persistent way, so that no man is to be overloaded, no man is to be overlooked, no area or sphere is to receive overemphasis, and none is to be neglected. No human organization can function properly and successfully without coordination. Also, counsel, advice, and help are needed in any program. Where else could we go than to the expert?

However, should the expert be an outsider, an import? Should he move in to initiate (not necessarily direct) the work, promote the work, and oversee the work? Is his presence the wisest and best arrangement? His moving out has created a vacuum which no country thus far has been able to fill. This has been substantiated by leaders from every country where Evangelism-in-Depth has operated. It is also the testimony of numerous pastors.

No general continuity can be found in the first seven countries. As the coordinator team moved out, Evangelism-in-Depth as such moved out. Only fragmentary and sporadic continuity can be located. The team makes for a campaign and underwrites the movement. Of course, the team is necessary because of inadequate indoctrination in the principles of Evangelism-in-Depth. Also the highly structured form of the program requires the coordination.

> Evangelism-in-Depth has a thorough biblical basis, therefore as early as 1966 EID promoters and advisers should have been in Colombia for a teaching ministry, imparting truth to the Colombian church and mission leaders. Since this was not done everyone was more conscious of the machine rather than the power behind it.[2]

3. *Closely associated with the presence of the coordinators is an air of messianic expectation.* The source of this is difficult to determine. I am not prepared to place the responsibility for this at the feet of the coordinators. To my knowledge they do not wish to be central nor conspicuous. The fact of messianic expectation however is very apparent. Somehow, revival and evangelism have ceased to be spontaneous in Latin America. They have become bound up with a name, a program and a team of men, the very factors Evangelism-in-Depth is seeking to undo. Thus, it is defeating the very foundations for continuation.

I fully realize the significance of "expectation" and I would be the last to discourage it. However, even expectation can become abnormal and lead to disillusionment, disappointment or abrupt conclusion. The last seems to become true in the Evangelism-in-Depth program in the majority of churches.

4. *The timing of the national campaign tends to deflate the overall work.* The national campaign is a significant event in the year-long program and in the life of the evangelicals of that country. The unity and strength which the procession portrays, the invitation which it extends to the city, and the opportunity which it affords to the community to hear the Gospel are of momentous importance. The impact is unparalleled; neither the evangelical community nor the city will ever have the same feelings and attitudes toward the Gospel and Protestantism.

Many souls, too, have been won for Christ in these campaigns. Newspapers, radio, and other media have assisted in making evangelicalism known, more popular, and more appreciated. Public applause has been heard for the orderliness of the Protestants. All this is for the good of the Gospel and the evangelical churches. I have no reservation about the national campaign as such.

My question revolves around the time of such a campaign. Is it wise that it constitutes the climax of the year-long program? Does such culmination not almost necessarily spell termination of the program? This, no doubt, is a deep and determining factor, no matter what the team of the experts may hope, say, or wish it to be.

Further careful studies are needed on how to arrest and eliminate this determining, subconscious feeling that this is the end of the program, without diminishing the enthusiasm for the evangelicals and the cause of the Gospel. As it stands at present the national campaign is a great conclusion and the termination of a program that is not expected to continue and become an integral and integrated part of the movement and life of the evangelical cause.

Chapter 16

SUMMARY AND RECOMMENDATIONS

PREVIOUSLY I QUOTED several definitive descriptions expressing the ideals of the founder and present sponsors of Evangelism-in-Depth. Theoretically, the present staff subscribes to the original ideals. Practically, however, there is considerable deviation.

Whether such deviation is the result of expediency, lack of vision and sharing of convictions, or the inability on the part of the sponsors and coordinators to communicate the ideals; or whether the pressure of time and circumstances, and the lack of ability on the part of the cooperating churches to grasp the principles of depth in contrast to breadth evangelism — whatever the reasons may be, the fact remains that Evangelism-in-Depth is falling somewhat short of and drifting away from its ideals.

As I see it:

1. Evangelism-in-Depth is a revivalistic program of great dimensions. It has served to awaken numerous churches and individual believers to a new spiritual vision and dynamic. This is the unanimous report of several hundred missionaries, national pastors and church leaders contacted either personally or by letter. This is a remarkable testimony of blessings.

2. It is a sowing program of unparalleled scope as the statistics of services, home visitations and literature distribution undisputably indicate. Churches need to be alerted to the fact that the reaping is to be continued and accelerated in the years following the year-long campaign. The main harvest follows the year-long program, which is at least as much sowing as reaping.

3. It is a training program of inestimable value to the churches and believers. To this almost all churches witness. The training, however, needs to be harnessed and advanced over a period of years following the campaign year.

4. It is a year-long school of prayer which needs to be encouraged, stimulated and continued, if the dynamics and zeal of the church are not to wane.

5. It is a radical attempt seriously and more fully to discover and practice the biblical concept of true discipleship and the priesthood of every believer in a unique perspective, by actually and

practically mobilizing and involving the individual in systematic and united prayer, Christian witness and evangelistic campaigns. Here, perhaps, is its deepest theological fulcrum. Because of this the writer felt perfectly at home in the principles of the movement from the beginning of his acquaintance, except for its emphasis upon organization. I have taught these principles for at least twenty years in my "Principles and Practice of Missions" classes. However, I have failed to focus on them. Neither did I see the value and strengh of organization and a pattern of implementation.

6. It is a focusing program, focusing the church upon the pressing need of fervent, perennial and all-out evangelism, and directing the attention and energy of the church upon the world instead of upon self. It gives to the church a true and biblical perspective and life projection, making evangelism by proclamation the primary concern and thrust of the church.

7. It is a technical program with a great deal of emphasis upon organization, cooperation, time schedule and strategy. While its technical aspect is perhaps one of its major sources of strength and appeal, it is also one of its major pitfalls which is keeping it from becoming perennial and transforming itself into an abiding movement. Here is an unresolved paradox, not necessarily an inherent conflict. However, as it is, it makes the impression that organization (which is its momentary strength), more than spiritual dynamics, sustains the movement in its year-long program.

RECOMMENDATIONS

In the light of my findings and recent research in dynamics of change, growth and group expansion, I venture to make specific recommendations to strengthen Evangelism-in-Depth.

These recommendations are not suggesting a complete remedy. They are tentative, limited, and are thought of as temporary bridges until Evangelism-in-Depth will find time to restructure its program and organization to embody more newly-discovered dynamic factors. With this in mind, I suggest:

1. That Evangelism-in-Depth seek to complement and balance its emphasis of guiding principles by adding to "total mobilization" the dynamic concepts of "relevance of message" and "cultural adaptation."

The latter two principles, if clearly defined, carefully designed and radically applied, are definitely of equal importance with the former principle, as most recent research has well-established. Such a threefold emphasis, though not a complete embodiment of the several dynamic factors of rapidly expanding movements, as I show later, should

serve to strengthen the program considerably and bring it more in line
with the New Testament, and thus make it more enduring in its effects.

2. That Evangelism-in-Depth add to its emphasis on every home,
village, town, city, strata and profession, the new dimension of entire
or total, especially as it relates to the home and family. It should major
on winning homes or families to Christ and to the church. Any movement within Christianity that is to succeed and make an enduring contribution and impact must major on households. This is God's basic
unit of operation.

Total evangelization should be at least as emphatic in the program
as total mobilization is. A specialist in household evangelism should
be sought, and workshops in this type of evangelism should be conducted throughout the country preparing for a program of Evangelism-
in-Depth on the level of families and communities.

3. That Evangelism-in-Depth pay closer attention to the distinctions
between confrontation evangelism, or evangelism for individual decision;
permeation evangelism, or evangelism as personal, family and group
saturation; and infiltration evangelism, or indirect evangelism, evangelism by Christian education and Christian fellowship. Confrontation
evangelism should be practiced with caution and in divine wisdom.
Confrontation evangelism should be carefully evaluated in the light of
permeation evangelism. Family and group decisions take time, but are
more wholesome, more fruitful and more enduring.

4. That Evangelism-in-Depth integrate a follow-up training program,
conduct intensive and extensive workshops in household Bible studies
during the last months of the campaign year, and train hundreds, perhaps thousands, of men and women for such Bible studies in order to
assist the new converts in their newly-found faith and help them permeate their own communities more fully with the Bible.

It may even be advisable to transform in part the prayer cells to
home Bible studies for the spiritual nurture of the new converts.

5. That Evangelism-in-Depth seriously rethink its program of training in order to build evangelism effectively and enduringly into the life
of the churches. In some way, perhaps even at an expensive way, the
impression that the program is terminal must be weakened and if possible completely erased. If evangelism is to become the way of life in
the churches, everything that lends support to the idea of termination
must be avoided and removed. In the light of this, the final, culminating national campaign and procession should be carefully restudied
and perhaps be rescheduled. Perhaps a more beneficial time could be
found.

We must eliminate from our thoughts and vocabulary the idea that
we are moving into a country to "complete the job" of evangelism in

one year. To the contrary, we ought to sell the idea of conducting a one-year training program, assisting the churches to reform and mobilize themselves to move ahead aggressively, cooperatively and coordinately to complete the job, either in a continued united effort or a prolonged coordinated movement. Evangelism-in-Depth should not be a one year's campaign, but a one year's preparation, mobilization and experimentation for a sustained movement to complete the evangelization of our generation.

6. That Evangelism-in-Depth lay hold of the fact that it must remain a growing movement, growing not only in expansion but above all growing in depth, that it might remain Evangelism-in-Depth. Newly-discovered dimensions must be welcomed and built into the program, even at the cost of completely restructuring the plan and configuration of the movement. Flexibility and creativity are essential to any movement that seeks to remain contemporary and dynamic.

New Life For All

GO AND TELL

"NOT BY MIGHT, NOR BY POWER,
BUT BY MY SPIRIT"

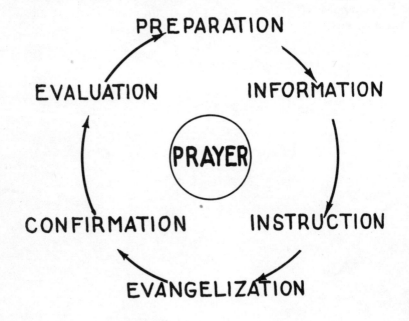

PREPARATION

EVALUATION

INFORMATION

PRAYER

CONFIRMATION

INSTRUCTION

EVANGELIZATION

VISIT EVERY HOME
SCHOOLS, SHOPS — LITERATURE
CRUSADES — GOSPEL TEAMS

TODAY IS THE DAY OF **SALVATION**

Chapter 17

THE BIRTH OF NEW LIFE FOR ALL

A VEILED WOMAN, the wife of a Muslim, stood behind the mud walls of her compound and listened attentively and nervously to a conversation just outside of her confines. The sound of the words, "new life for all," caught her attention. As this conversation went on, a crowd of spectators gathered. Soon she heard the music of a song; a message followed. Again and again the words "new life for all" were repeated.

Though she did not dare walk outside of her gate at daytime, the words, "new life for all," kept ringing in her ears; their meaning reached into the recesses of her heart. A longing was kindled and an overwhelming desire arose to know something about this new life for all.

When evening came and darkness settled upon the compound, she slipped out quietly. She approached a man on the street. "Can you inform me about the new life for all I heard a man talking about?" "Yes," was the kind reply, "I can tell you the story."

By means of a leaflet prepared by the New Life For All headquarters, he pointed out to her God's message about life and how to obtain this new life, life eternal, the very life from God. Having explained the way, he led the woman to his pastor, the same man who only a few hours before had stood at the wall of the compound to proclaim to the group of people God's gift and way of "new life for all."

As the two men of God in the pastor's home expounded the way once more, the same Holy Spirit who had created the desire in the heart of the woman, illuminated her heart to see God's gracious provision in His Son. As she related herself to the Son in simple faith, the miracle of regeneration took place and new life became her personal possession. The Holy Spirit, men of God, the Word of God and providence combined to make "new life for all" more than a slogan.

New Life For All is a dynamic movement of the Holy Spirit operating in Nigeria; it is rapidly spreading to other parts of Africa. This writing, however, is not a dramatic presentation of the movement, but rather an evaluative study. I do not claim infallibility in the evaluation, neither was it my intention to find the faults of the phenomenon. I earnestly looked for weaknesses in order to strengthen and not to criticize or destroy. With this in mind, I present its story and my findings.

New Life For All is an indigenous Nigerian evangelistic movement aiming to preach by united effort the Gospel of salvation in Jesus Christ to every creature, first in Nigeria and eventually in all of Africa. It was born in the heart of Rev. Gerald O. Swank, a missionary of the Sudan Interior Mission, at that time laboring in the Bible institute at Kagoro, Nigeria. The agonies of an unfinished task of evangelism in an area ripe for harvest, but without laborers to enter the fields and to garner in the sheaves, exercised his heart over a number of year. The burden of the uncompleted work was intensified by such statements of our Lord as, "Jesus saith unto them, My meat is to do the will of him that sent me, and to finish his work," and "I have finished the work which thou gavest me to do" (John 4:34; 17:4). Total evangelization of Nigeria became his consuming passion.

The crushing load was not lightened by the increasing conviction that the command of the Lord also assures the possibility of accomplishing the task. The anxieties of heart linked with an absolute certainty that total evangelism is the will of God urged him to find a way that would lead to the realization of the goal. Only gradually the burden of the unfinished job had given birth to the conviction of the possibility of the realization of the assignment. Even slower came the vision of a way that would resolve the burden, turn possibility into progressive realization, and lead to a triumph of the Gospel and the church of Jesus Christ unparalleled in Nigeria and, with few exceptions, in all of Africa.

The secret behind the movement is the gracious sovereign ministry of the Holy Spirit. It came by a rediscovery of some simple but basic scriptural principles of evangelism. These, however, demanded a drastic reconception of the method of evangelism, which gradually led to the development of a new pattern of evangelism. In the simplest manner, it may be stated in two basic formulas:

1. The total church worshiping must become the total church militant in Christian witnessing and evangelism. In the now familiar words: The total mobilization of the church and each local church must be achieved if the task of total evangelism is to be accomplished. Total evangelization of the lost requires total mobilization of the saved.

2. The practice of church centripetalism must be converted into the practice of evangelistic centrifugalism if success is to be assured and progress is to be accomplished. Church centripetalism refers to that traditional tendency to make the church as a place and building the center of its main activities and especially its evangelistic program. The people are asked, invited and urged to attend the services in the church building to hear the Gospel and become Christians. Church centripetalism is place and building oriented.

Evangelistic centrifugalism counteracts this traditional tendency and reverses the pattern. The church as a structure and place is the rallying point where the believers are mobilized and trained for effective ministries and then are sent out into the world to do the evangelizing. The believers fan out in small teams into the entire community to bring the Gospel into every home and, if possible, to every individual. The church must cease to live to herself. She must become an outgoing, aggressive body of living witnesses. Mission must be converted into militant missions. The church must be a going and sending church. The orders are to march into the world and possess it for the Lord.

These formulas were not handed down from heaven on tablets of stone. The inherent ideas were the result of years of study, prayer and observation. The method by which this ideal could be realized unfolded itself only gradually in the mind of Mr. Swank. In this his creative mind and fertile imagination were greatly stimulated and strengthened by reports on Evangelism-in-Depth published in various magazines, as well as a personal conference with W. Dayton Roberts of the Latin America Mission early in 1962.

The similarities between the two movements, which at several points almost seem like copied reproductions, must not be interpreted as conscious borrowing in total. Rather, they must in part be attributed to the sovereign and gracious ministry of the Holy Spirit. On this continent the Holy Spirit ministered to Kenneth Strachan and in Nigeria to Gerald O. Swank, though the latter willingly acknowledges great debt to the creative genius of the former in the structuring and patterning of New Life For All as it actually unfolded itself and now exists. The main principles of New Life For All, however, were formulated in the latter part of the 1950's before Evangelism-in-Depth had been launched as a program and was made known to the church at that time. New Life For All has been spoken of as an African Adaptation of Evangelism-in-Depth. It may seem as such to the superficial observer. In reality, however, it differs considerably in its basic philosophy as well as proceedings.

Upon his return to Nigeria in 1963 from a year's furlough, Mr. Swank found several strong and sympathetic supporters among the Sudan Interior Mission missionaries who had been reading with keen interest reports on Evangelism-in-Depth and its achievements in Latin America. Soon he had the opportunity to share his burden and vision, first with a group of missionaries of his own mission and later with the national pastor of the Evangelical Churches of West Africa (SIM related). A retreat was held on 20 June 1963 at which SIM was represented by six men and two women, and the ECWA churches by nine leaders. They heard Mr. Swank outline the possibilities of total evangelism.

While he found a most sympathetic hearing, real understanding and considerable enthusiasm for the program, it was felt wise that the mission and church should not attempt the program alone. A cooperative effort would strengthen the cause and bring added blessings to the joint body of churches in the geographical areas of the main thrust of the SIM and ECWA churches.

After considerable discussion concerning the churches to be included, the Rev. Mr. Gin moved that the churches which are a part of the Council of Evangelical Churches of Northern Nigeria (CECNN), the Assemblies of God and the Methodists should be invited. The motion was adopted unanimously. It was then suggested that all further discussions and plans should be suspended until a full committee could meet together. In this way, all concerned would join together in laying the first plans. This was unanimously agreed upon.

In consequence of the prevailing sentiment, a letter was issued by Mr. Kastner of SIM to the leadership of the missions and churches of the two provinces of Zaria and Plateau, inviting them to a meeting in Jos for 1 August 1963 to consider a plan of united effort for total evangelism of their mission areas. At this well-attended meeting both the challenge before them and confessions of failure were heard.

It had long been recognized by the representatives of missions and churches that while the Lord's command to preach the Gospel to every creature had been partially obeyed, not everyone in Nigeria, not even in the immediate mission territories, had yet heard the good news of the salvation in Christ. For this reason the following churches and missions decided to form an organization that would expedite this as quickly as possible:

> Anglican Church (Church Missionary Society representing the evangelical wing of Anglicanism)
> Nigerian Baptist Convention (Southern Baptists)
> Assemblies of God Church and Mission
> The Church of Christ in the Sudan (Sudan United Mission related)
> The Evangelical Churches of West Africa (SIM related)
> Methodist Church (British Methodists)
> Sudan Interior Mission
> Sudan United Mission
> United Missionary Church in Africa
> United Missionary Society

It must be emphasized here that the structure of New Life For All was local, and therefore cooperation was on the local church level rather than on the denominational or national level. It involved the churches of two provinces, though not all of the local churches co-operated.

The name New Life For All was not lightly chosen. While Evangelism-in-Depth was known and respected, it was held that the designation was not indigenous to Africa nor descriptive of the task envisioned. It was felt that the name of the movement must on the one hand avoid all offense, if possible, to those who were to be reached with the Gospel, such as the Muslims. On the other hand, it must have salvation meaning, express the concept of total evangelization, and at the same time arrest the attention of the non-Christian populace. Finally, the motto of the Baptist campaign in Japan was seized upon with a slight adaptation to conform to the goals of the movement. The slogan New Life For You was changed to New Life For All to become the name of the newly-born movement. The title has proven its value and appropriateness.

Chapter 18

THE PRINCIPLES AND OBJECTIVES OF NEW LIFE FOR ALL

THE BASIC PRINCIPLES were clearly formulated by Mr. Swank early in the history of the movement and were published in "Marvellous in Our Eyes," a pamphlet that permits us to look into the movement toward the end of the first year of its operation. Under the title, "To Every Creature," Mr. Swank states:

> Evangelism is not new! For many years, churches and missions have been carrying on the task. There has been fruit. Christians exist in considerable numbers, yet the task of total evangelization is not yet complete.
>
> At the same time consider the vast increases in population across the world. Consider too, the way in which the forces of communism have spread their evil influences. Islam, too, abounds with unprecedented vigor. The need of the hour is for the glorious Gospel of salvation by faith in Christ alone to be preached as He commanded . . . "to every creature," omitting none.
>
> Looking back over the New Life For All program in Nigeria, and judging by the churches' response to the challenge it has brought, we believe that certain basic principles have evolved which could well be put into practice not only in this country but across Africa, and even the world. These principles are utterly Scriptural, thoroughly evangelical and absolutely fundamental. They are as follows . . .

The Total Mobilization of All Believers

> As has already been said, the commission of the Lord Jesus is to preach the Gospel to "every creature." Some have been reached by those who have been faithful to the commission, but many even today have never heard the Gospel message. God desires that all born again Christians should witness to others their salvation in Christ. This is the responsibility of every believer.

The Church Is God's Instrument for Evangelism

> Total witness must be united witness on the part of all the Lord's people in any given area. Spasmodic unrelated evangelistic efforts will have their effect, but if the aim is total evangelization it must be thoroughly related through the existing churches. Here we have an already well-established body, ripe for revival by the Holy Spirit, a prepared instrument for the salvation of mankind. Remember! God has chosen that it is through the foolishness of preaching that men are saved.

Therefore until the church is fully active in evangelism this task will never be completed.

Total Evangelization Can Be the Only Aim

The world is crying out for new life. Thousands die daily in their sins. Thousands more live doomed lives without Christ. Children are being born into a situation as pagan as it was a thousand years ago, so far as spiritual values are concerned. How can we rest content in the light of such circumstances? As the Holy Spirit moves the church, so the Lord's people must reach out with the saving message to "every creature." A careful systematic program is needed to adequately cover an area with the Gospel. Every home, street, village, market, school, camp, town and city must be apportioned out and reached for Christ. Preparation by prayer and study must be thorough. Outreach must be well-planned. Effort must be untiring, enthusiastic, devoted if the final aim is to be achieved.

Christ said that His deep desire was to finish the work which the Father had given Him. He commanded His disciples to "lift up their eyes and look on the fields." That commission comes now to the church . . . "Go ye into all the world and preach the gospel to every creature."[1]

THE DOCTRINAL POSITION

Though NLFA functions on an interdenominational basis, the cardinal doctrines of the Christian faith are clearly spelled out in five brief but comprehensive statements. Every local church and mission declares itself not only for or against a certain method and movement, but also for or against a specific doctrinal position. The declaration of faith reads as follows:

New Life For All is interdenominational and evangelical, believing—

1. In one God, the Father, Son and Holy Spirit (Matt. 28:19).

2. In the divine authority and plenary inspiration of the Word of God as originally given (II Tim. 3:16).

3. In the fallen nature of man and his need of regeneration by the Holy Spirit through faith alone in Jesus Christ (Rom. 3:23; Tit. 3:5, 6).

4. In the virgin birth of Jesus Christ, His death and blood shed for our sins, His bodily resurrection from the dead for our justification, and in the expectation of His personal return to earth to reign in power and glory (Luke 1:26-35; I Cor. 15:3, 4; I Thess. 1:7, 8).

5. That it is the responsibility of all believers to bear witness of Christ to all men by a godly life and public testimony in the power and under the direction of the Holy Spirit (Acts 1:8; Matt. 5:16).[2]

NLFA entered upon its course as a united body of local churches with a clearly formulated evangelical doctrinal platform, a strong spiritual motivation from the Word of God, and with an unprecedented challenge and opportunity to get on with the job, to preach the Gospel to every creature and "to finish his work." It aspired to do this first within a specified geographical area for sound and legitimate reasons and, second, with the aspiration and anticipation to see the program expand over all of Nigeria and eventually engulf the whole continent of Africa.

The Objectives

The objectives of NLFA are clearly outlined under concern, formula and plan, guided by the motto of John 4:34-38, "To finish His work." We quote Mr. Swank as he presents the objectives in "Marvellous in Our Eyes."

1. *Our Concern:* In the light of Scripture and the primary place that evangelism must have in our churches, certainly there is a need for a complete program that will insure the proclamation of the Gospel to all people in a given area. There are several reasons which make this very urgent today:

   a. Failure of church members as witnesses.

   b. Inadequacy of our present program and methods.

   c. Population increase and indifference to the message of the Gospel.

   d. Character of this age in which the Bible, our faith in Christ, and our hope of heaven are being challenged.

   e. Church are often opposed to one another.

   f. Churches are facing inward rather than toward the fields.

   g. Increased opposition: Islam on the march, spread of sects, Marxist ideology.

   h. A slack attitude in many churches toward evangelism. Lack of vigorous young people who want to serve the Lord. Many feel that the job is done and there is no more challenge.

2. *Our Formula: Mobilization $\times$ Witness $=$ Evangelization.* For successful evangelism, the total membership of the church must be brought together for the purpose of continuous witnessing. This must be done in obedience of the Word of God and by the power and direction of the Holy Spirit. This was the practice of the first-century church. Is it possible to mobilize all Christians? How can it be done?

3. *Our Plan:*

   a. Every Christian without exception, according to his talents and circumstances, is called upon to be a witness for Christ. The first goal, even though the final result may fall short, is the mobilization of the total membership.

b. This personal witness must center in the fellowship of the local church. The church then begins to function as it should.

c. This personal and church witness must relate to the total witness of the entire Body of Christ. Therefore, in some practical way, without compromise, a living witness must be given to the unity of the Body of Christ. Since there is only one Lord and Saviour and only one Gospel, it is imperative that those who believe in Him should unite in their testimony to Him.

d. The witness of all must aim at nothing less than total and complete outreach. Therefore, we should think in terms of natural geographic or language areas. In this way we can face the problem of fulfilling our responsibility.[3]

Chapter 19

THE PURPOSE, PLAN AND ORGANIZATION OF
NEW LIFE FOR ALL

BEFORE NLFA ADVANCED ITS PLANS, it clarified the intended purpose of the movement both in negative as well as in positive terms. It was clearly stated what NLFA is not and what it is:

It is not a new missionary society or merely a mission project.

It is not a movement for church unity in the ecumenical sense.

It is not seeking to tell others how they ought to evangelize, implying that they do not know.

It is not to depend upon the program itself for success, but upon the Spirit of God who is the Lord of the harvest.

It was affirmed:

The movement is biblical, based on the Great Commission as recorded in Mark 16:15, 16, with emphasis upon every creature.

It is to be thoroughly indigenous. Missionary involvement is to be minimal. The real work of evangelism is to be done by Nigerians and the control to be placed in the hands of the local church.

It is to be simple and inexpensive. Literature will be used extensively and funds needed, but the use of expensive equipment will be discouraged.

It is to be a continuing movement. Long after the initial thrust is past, it is expected that the church will carry on the work of evangelism on its own.

Having clarified the purpose the joint council adopted a very simple but comprehensive plan embodied in three pregnant ideas:

1. To first prepare and equip all believers for an all-out effort in evangelism
2. To work only through the established churches and at their invitation
3. To work in a united effort to take the Gospel to every creature, leaving no one unreached.

It is significant to note that the idea of total mobilization for total evangelization laid hold of the representatives. To every creature could become a reality only if total enlistment could be achieved. The slogan "to every creature" had to be transformed into a correlated and inspiring passion if the goal was to be realized.

The aim to reach every creature with the Gospel of Christ was to be achieved through:

1. House-to-house visitation for the purpose of explaining the Gospel to each family.
2. Open-air evangelism to alert the crowds and present the good news to the masses in villages and cities.
3. Literature distribution of selected tracts and gospel portions, some of which were printed by New Life For All.
4. Local church conferences to preach the Gospel in a given community.
5. United evangelistic campaigns in stadiums to attract the crowds of larger cities.
6. Gospel teams composed of laymen to be sent to unreached areas, villages and tribes.
7. Radio programs broadcasting on as many stations as possible.[1]

Every member and means were to be utilized to reach every creature with the message of New Life For All. The plan was to be executed in an orderly and progressive way through six steps which are defined in the handbook as follows:[2]

1. *Preparation.* Church leaders must be brought together, committees formed, initial plans put into action, literature developed, a calendar of events laid out.

2. *Information.* This means bringing together the entire Christian leadership of a given area for a retreat to wait upon the Lord and to consider the evangelistic task before us.

3. *Instruction.* Believers to engage in weekly study classes in the handbook, learning how to help others find new life in Christ. At the same time prayer cells must be established everywhere.

4. *Evangelization.* Intensive efforts will be made, usually beginning in October and running on to March, to reach every soul for Christ. This will be done by house-to-house visitation, together with witnessing and literature distribution, etc. We want to combine all efforts in order to mobilize the greatest possible number of Christians. We want to make a strong impact upon the entire area. We want the Christians to embark upon a practice of continuous outreach and activity.

5. *Confirmation.* (Follow-up.) Going along with the evangelism must be a carefully planned and executed follow-up program, including instruction to new converts, organization of new congregations, and strengthening of friendship between local congregations.

6. *Evaluation.* This is looking back to see what real lasting results have been obtained The attendance at crusades and numbers of decisions, while encouraging, are not the final mark of success. But rather, success will have to be measured by the continued witness of Christians and churches.

Prayer is at the heart of these six steps. It is the lifeline by which all the work receives power. It is like the spindle upon which the whole wheel depends and turns.

Literature and radio. Working together at each step, one finds literature. The newspaper will keep all of us informed and working together. Radio will reach many homes and hearts impossible for us to enter.

Special Evangelism. Through the gospel teams unreached areas will hear. City crusades will make sure that our population centers are reached effectively.

The whole program is portrayed in the following chart:

THE ORGANIZATION

The overall program of New Life For All is directed from a central office with a general secretary who is responsible to the Executive Committee of New Life For All. This committee consists of representatives from church/mission organizations actively involved in New Life For All. Each organization appoints its own representative.

The detailed organization of a given territory engaged in New Life For All is set forth in the chart on the next page.

LOCAL CHURCHES

Every Area Needs:

1. Chairman
2. Treasurer
3. Secretary
4. Literature Distributor
5. Prayer Secretary
6. Organizer for Evangelism
7. Women's Representative
8. Schools Organizer
9. Instructor

Every Church Needs

1. Chairman
2. Literature Distributor
3. Prayer Secretary
4. Organizer for Evangelism
5. Women's Representative
6. Schools Organizer
7. Instructor

CHURCH COMMITTEE MEETS MONTHLY

2 Representatives from each Church (including leaders) go to Area Committee.

****

****

A City with more than one denomination becomes an area

A Training College may become an Area.

AREA COMMITTEE –

Sends 2 representatives to D.E.C.

CHURCHES AND MISSIONS IN N.L.F.A.

DISTRICT EXECUTIVE COMMITTEE

– consists of 2 representatives from each Area. This includes all denominations.

Note

1. Area may have about 10 centers of worship.
2. Area Committee meets every month.

THE SIX STEPS

NEW LIFE FOR ALL
GO AND TELL
"NOT BY MIGHT NOR BY POWER
BUT BY MY SPIRIT." Zechariah 4:6

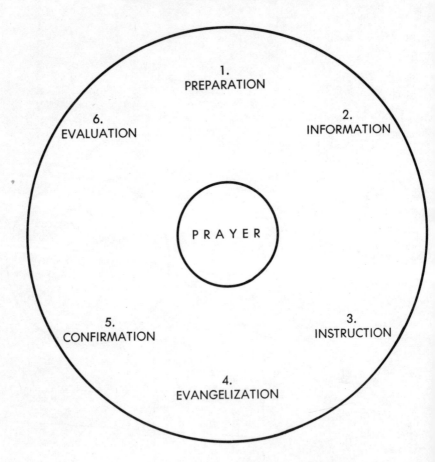

Visit every Home — School — Shop —
Market — Prison — Hospital
Use Literature — Gospel Records — Radio
Preach: Gospel Teams — City Crusades
Newspaper For Information

Chapter 20

HOW NEW LIFE FOR ALL WORKS

HAVING AGREED UPON THE purpose, plan and program, and having set out an organizational structure New Life For All began to work. Three factors present from the very beginning made New Life For All into a movement.

First, the implementation followed a carefully thought-out geographical strategy. It set its own geographical limitations. It was agreed to confine the program to the two provinces of Zaria and Plateau, though a number of the missions involved had extensive work beyond these provinces. Sound reason, therefore, directed the council to confine the work to a specific and limited geographical area. This was done for a number of reasons, including the following:

1. Historically Nigeria has been divided into North and South.
2. Ecclesiastically, there has been a marked division, the South being occupied principally by denominations, whereas the interdenominational faith missions have concentrated more on the North and these churches in general have worked together quite well.
3. The ethnic groupings of Nigeria were considered, deeming it advisable at first to concentrate on one, the Hausa-speaking people.

Besides these external factors, there were, however, some deeper reasons:

1. It was considered wise to use these two provinces somewhat as a pilot project to test theories and ideas, to mature, improve, and change the program or methodology where necessary in order to make the movement as effective and as indigenous as possible.
2. It was further felt that an in-depth program to reach every creature demanded the concentration of all available strength in a limited area at a given time, if the work was to be done by indigenous resources in men and finances.
3. Providence and prudence dictated the limitation and establishment of goals that were realistic and realizable.
4. It was fully expected that these efforts would prove their worth and that the program would become contagious and expand into the neighboring areas and provinces. Thus it would do several things:
   (a) It would keep the churches involved over a prolonged and indefinite period.

(b) It would enlarge by spontaneous expansion rather than by a huge organization that might degenerate into a machinery.

(c) It would provide time to dissipate prejudices in churches and men who were not so close to the center of the movement, but would watch the work from a distance and evaluate it for themselves. New Life For All would sell itself to the country and eventually to the countries round about. New Life For All would become an ongoing movement rather than a terminal program.

It may be said that these anticipations are becoming a reality.

The second factor in the implementation of New Life For All was a series of retreats for Christian workers.[1] All who wished to serve the Lord in NLFA were welcome to attend. The attendance at these retreats varied according to interest and Christian population within the district. In one center over seven hundred attended the evening meetings, which often were revivalistic in nature. Christians were challenged to put things right with the Lord in order to serve Him acceptably and effectively.

A total of eleven such retreats were conducted in the first months of 1964 and more than 1600 leaders came to receive spiritual refreshing, instruction and guidance about how to conduct a NLFA program in their areas.

Two vital pieces of information were given to those who attended the retreats. It was realized that the future of the venture depended upon the proper understanding of the principles of NLFA and the spirit of prayer that could be developed in the believers. The attendants were taught, first, how to begin and promote cottage prayer meetings and, second, how to establish instruction classes which would study the NLFA Handbook.

One of the staff members of NLFA, Mr. Harold Germaine, reports the following on one such conference:

> About 11 years ago God did the impossible in reviving the dry bones of the Angwa Takwa area about 125 miles southeast of Jos. As a result of those wonderful days, fruit is still being harvested.
>
> Similar Pentecostal blessings resulted in several other places. After ten years one wondered — will it ever happen again? It has!
>
> After seeing the blighted spiritual condition of Katanga, an area about 150 miles Northeast of Jos, in Nov. 1967, and hearing the reports of apostasy, we were challenged to return to try to help restore the years that the locusts had eaten. We suggested to their leaders that nothing short of eight days would bring down the needed blessing. After consultation they reported that their conference would be from Friday through Sunday. We flatly refused. So they quickly acquiesced

to a full week of meetings. This is a scriptural pattern. God required His people to meet three times a year in a week of fellowship.

For several months much prayer was offered in many places in the States, Canada, England, Nigeria and other points as well. God was pleased to answer.

Thus from the first service, when sin was defined and denounced, until the last, the power of the Lord was present. Blessings came about very quietly, naturally, methodically and scripturally. First, there was a volume of prayer ascending to God. Also, we involved local believers in extra sessions of prayer. On the first Sunday about eight of us met to pray at 6 A.M. Before the end of the week over 50 were coming at 4 A.M. Second, there was a fearless, faithful presentation of the Word, particularly exposing sin. Daily God's arrows found their mark. Third, a special day was set aside for fasting and prayer. This they had never done before. It gripped the hearts of the people. Fancy a prayer meeting nine hours long. Fourth, there was time for testimony, confession and song. One cannot go through such a week of four sessions a day without being greatly affected.

We wish you, the reader of these lines, could have been present at the day of prayer. We made it optional — sheep, however, need a shepherd. They followed! At 5 A.M. the church seating about 250 people or more was well-filled. From the outset we placed before the people ten reasons for unanswered prayer. They are not the usual dark, gross sins we hear and read about, but rather passed-over ones like murmuring. This and other exhortations struck deeply into their cold, hardened hearts.

Such a day is one not to be desired by the flesh. It is hard, tedious, tiring, and crucifying to the natural man. Young and older folk came. Mothers came with their babies. They stayed. They prayed. Some wept. They sang. We were there until 3 P.M. Following this it was a great sight to see that crowd of people divide into five groups and go out preaching and witnessing until sundown. They had nothing to eat or drink all day. One of the thrilling results of the day was that some for whom they had wept and prayed for by name came to Christ that afternoon. Friend, God lives! We saw Him at work!

Every night outdoors we showed filmstrips, "The Days Before the Flood," "Noah and the Ark," "The Three Hebrew Children," "Naaman, Saul and David," "The Miracles of Jesus," and "Christ's Trial and Death." This drew hundreds of people. Some were saved or restored every night.

Miracles were thrilling and faith fortifying. One night in full moonlight God sent a cloud bank to darken the sky so that people might better view the judgment and crucifixion of His Son through filmstrip. Again on the Sunday of the baptismal service, the Lord cooled the air and sent a cloudy formation to lessen the intense heat during our walk of over a mile to the water. One man estimated to be 100 years of age accepted Christ. "Now," he said, "I am ready to meet Jesus." One man prayed with strong crying and tears for his wife on the day of prayer. That afternoon she came to Christ. A school teacher, a former professing Christian, came to Christ with great brokenness, having been involved with Islam for eleven years. His wife, a Muslim, took Christ the same day. A blind boy, nine years old, having heard the Gospel only once or twice from us, came and said: "I want to accept Jesus as my Savior." We took him in hand and are making provision for him to go to the primary school for the blind. His name is Rabihu, a fine little fellow.

Seven young men testified in succession, "I give my life to Christ. I'm going to Bible School." Three others, including the above-mentioned teacher, gave their lives to go to Bible School. Another man gave his life to learn Braille. He has a blind son in Braille School. "Mr. Germaine," he said, "if I knew Braille, I could have a class of 30 right away." One of the seven young men was a boxer in his community for four years. He is a fine specimen of manhood. Now he is determined to fight the good fight of faith for Christ. Hallelujah! . . .

One is at a loss for words to write about such a week. One has to be there and live through it. Pastor Tambaya is like a man filled with new wine — the wine of the Holy Spirit . . .

We do not know the number of professions of faith at Katanga, nor the number of restorations, but there were several score. Perhaps someone is saying: "My, I wish that could happen in our church." It can! There is but one stipulation. Pay the price in time and obedience to God's Word.[2]

The third factor in the implementation was the readiness of the churches to respond to the challenge. This is proven by the fact that during the first year a total of seven thousand prayer groups met daily to intercede before God for the salvation of souls. The average attendance at these prayer cells is conservatively set at eight persons. Some fifty to sixty thousand believers met every day of the week to pray earnestly for revival and effective evangelism. The impact was astounding.

"I do not understand it," reported one worker, "I just begin to preach a simple message, and men and women burst into tears of sorrow for sin. This surely is the work of the Spirit of God."[3]

Such testimonies are numerous. Thirty thousand believers attended instruction classes, of whom twenty-four thousand completed the examination of the handbook. This is most remarkable for a community of Christians that totaled only twenty thousand baptized members. The completion of the handbook studies prepared the people for home visitation and personal evangelism.

GOSPEL TEAMS

A strong feature of NLFA was the gospel teams, groups of laymen from four to seven in number who visited unreached and unevangelized villages. These teams, made up on an interdenominational basis, received special instruction for their task and gave from two to four weeks' time (some up to three months) free for the ministry of the Gospel.

Hundreds of such teams have gone forth to evangelize heretofore unreached areas. New tribes have been entered and much virgin soil has been broken. Most encouraging reports have been and are being received from this ministry.

At one place more than two hundred young men offered their service during the vacation months to go in gospel teams to large unevangelized areas. After a month's ministry they reported some two thousand people professing Christ as Savior. Mr. Wilfred A. Bellamy gives a vivid portrait of the ministry of these teams in the following article:

It was into this NE corner of Nigeria (Bornu) that, a little under a year ago, New Life For All sent gospel teams. Sixty young men who had volunteered to leave home and family for a month were trained in Jos at NLFA headquarters. They travelled by lorry the 450 miles to Gwosa. From there they were sent out two-by-two to live among people they had never seen before, whose lives and practices were vastly different from their own. They went to reach them for Christ.

Day by day homes were visited, and the simple story of new life in Christ related. An illustrated tract for nonliterates had been especially printed, and this was widely used. Also daily reading classes, with the name "Reading for All" proved popular. Many gathered seeking to understand this mystery for themselves.

It was not long before reports began to filter back to Jos that numbers were turning to Christ. Letters brought details of many converts. In one village a well-known thief, on turning to Christ, packed his belongings and moved to live near to a Christian so that he could be taught how to follow the Lord. In another village for the first time a small church was built, indicating that here was a nucleus of believers who meant business!

However, the opportunity to visit the area did not come until the end of 1967, when the men had been in their Plateau homes for more than six months.

Arriving in the first hill village after a stiff climb (which confirmed that fact that missionaries should keep themselves fit) we were met by an enthusiastic band of men. There were sixteen in all. They gathered around, and after greeting them through an interpreter (who spoke both the language of the hills and Hausa), we sat down to chat with them. We did not imagine that they could all be Christians, and so one by one we asked them: "Do you know Jesus the Son of God? Have you heard the story of new life in Christ?" In each case the reply was without hesitation: "We know Him, He is our Savior!"

There followed an hour of close questioning, and yet this only served to confirm that these men knew the Lord Jesus. How we rejoiced with them that morning. The radiance of some of them outshone the sun. These were our new brethren in Christ; the Holy Spirit left us in no doubt at all.

One young man was asked, "What difference has the Lord Jesus made in your life?" He replied, "The Lord doesn't like anything dirty! I have cleaned up our house, and I bathe every day . . . and let me tell you, I haven't had an ulcer since I became a Christian." Usaman, a very new convert, was listening carefully when his question came: "What difference is there between a Christian and a Muslim?" His answer was quite definite: "The Muslim bows in prayer to the ground as if seeking God, but I know where He is," he said pointing to his heart.

Victory indeed!

High in the hills we met the oldest man of the tribe. Proudly naked, his wizened body spoke of many seasons of hot sunshine and bitter winds. He is now a Christian. "If I fall down dead, and the vultures eat my body, I am not worried. My home is up there," he said with his gnarled finger raised to heaven, "where God is waiting for me." Bear in mind that this is a tribe where of all customs, those which surround the disposal of the body and its preparation for the journey into the "beyond" are surrounded by witchcraft and superstition. Victory indeed!

Certainly there is every evidence that not only is the Spirit at work in the hills, but also across Bornu the traditional centers of Islam are beginning to yield to the gentle pressures of the Gospel. Men and women are seeking the truth.

In one city the bookshop reports more Bibles sold to Muslims last year than to Christians. In another place, while visiting one evening, a Kanuri Muslim came to see us. He calmly announced that he had received Christ as his Savior, and informed us that there are many such in that town. He said: "The time has not yet come for us to declare our faith openly, but it will soon be here." Also a Muslim teacher is now seeking courage to be baptized publicly.[4]

CITY CAMPAIGNS

Other impressive features of the movement were the large and united city campaigns and gospel parades. Mrs. Gerald Swank reports on the meeting in Kaduna, a strong Muslim center.

There were more people on the streets than usual in the capital city of Kaduna that afternoon. Men in white flowing robes were on bicycles and motor bikes, women in colorful dress with babies tied to their backs, hurried along. Buses and motor cars of every description, all loaded to capacity, wound in and out among the crowds that seemed to all to be going in the same direction.

Into the midst of all this stepped 10,000 more people. This group of people was well organized. They had met at church to march together, six abreast, to the Ahmadu Bello Stadium for the final meeting of the New Life For All Crusade. These were zealous Christians of all the participating churches who had united in a campaign to witness to all in Kaduna City that Jesus Christ is "the Way, the Truth, and the Life," and that there is salvation in no other.

This was the climax of a week of evangelistic meetings which were held in the old football stadium with negro evangelist Howard O. Jones as the speaker. Thousands attended the services every night and listened carefully to the Spirit-filled messages. Each time the invitation was given hundreds came forward to receive new life in Christ. Now for the first time, many in the parade were witnessing of their new-found faith in Christ.

Some of us went ahead of the parade to the Ahmadu Bello Stadium. We were surprised to find the grandstand already full—people were even sitting in the aisles. Many were disappointed because they couldn't find seats in the grandstand, but they quickly found seats to the left and to the right. The ushers did a very efficient job in directing people to their seats and keeping order.

The service began promptly at 5:15 P.M. with the singing of the Nigerian national anthem. A local pastor led in prayer, and the meeting was under way. During the service, a request was made for all those who had found new life during the Crusade to stand up. A great multitude of people stood to their feet. This caused everyone to give praise to God for His great power and blessing on the crusade.

The crowd listened attentively as Pastor Jones preached and Malam Dalhatu interpreted the message into the Hausa langauge. When the invitation was given, people were asked to come to the front of the grandstand. There were over 600 who remained behind to be counselled. The counsellors were busy for over two hours.

After the service was over the Minister of Information, who was in the congregation along with many other important personalities, informed the New Life For All team that there were 16,000 in the stadium, which was the largest crowd that had attended Ahmadu Bello Stadium since it had been opened. He also expressed his gratitude for the very interesting program presented. New Life For All is not over in Kaduna. Many have expressed their desire to continue witnessing for Christ. This is the everyday experience that God expects of His children. Some want to have a city crusade every year. Praise the Lord![5]

CHRISTIAN WORKERS' RETREAT TIMETABLE
Theme: Holy Spirit — The Lord of Harvest (Zech. 4:6)

Time	Monday	Tuesday	Wednesday	Thursday	Friday
6:00–7:00		Prayer — Holy Spirit and Prayer: Committee i/c			
8:00–8:45		Message — Holy Spirit and Workers: **NFLA TEAM**			
8:45–10:00		Leaders' Guide Book — Information: **NLFA TEAM**			
Break		Break			
10:15–11:30		Handbook — Instruction: **NLFA TEAM**			
11:30–12:30		Handbook — Discussion in Groups: **Pastors i/c**			
Break		Break			
3:00–3:30	Area Committee meets to plan details of Retreat	Prayer — Specific Requests: Committee i/c			
3:30–4:30		Leaders' Guide Book — Questions — Discussions: **NLFA TEAM**			
4:30–5:30		Committee meetings as necessary			
8:00–9:00		Message — "Holy Spirit and the Church." **NLFA TEAM**			

The Miracle

of

New

Life

Chapter 21

FACTORS IN THE SUCCESS OF NEW LIFE FOR ALL

IN ORDER TO EVALUATE New Life For All it is necessary to penetrate the structured movement to its very heart, to lay bare its ideology, nature and components, and seriously inquire: What is New Life For All at its very core? An analysis of NLFA leads us to recognize several major facts.

First, it is primarily a movement of renewal. It is a serious attempt to awaken the churches and every believer to the fact that they have new life in Christ, a life which can be and must be lived as a witness for Christ in this world. It is a life of fruit-bearing by means of witnessing. This fact is set forth in the NLFA symbol of the corn stalk, which is imprinted on all its literature. It is also vividly portrayed by its tract on the cocoon and the butterfly.

Second, it is a movement of renewal with the definite purpose of making evangelism central in the thrust of the church, and to focus the total life and program of the church on evangelism. In formal and informal preaching of the Gospel to every creature, and by serious attempts to lead people to a decision for Christ, they made evangelism practical in the churches.

Third, it is an organized effort to mobilize every member of the church and every means available to the church within the framework of the local church for an all-out endeavor to accomplish the task, seriously convinced of the fact that total evangelization can be achieved only by total mobilization of men and means within the reach of the church and indigenous to the people and the specific local church. This is well expressed by the equation: total mobilization = total evangelization.

Fourth, it is an organized effort of total evangelism by means of total mobilization of all resources according to:

a. a specific and realizable strategy, a defined geographical area, by united effort and limiting itself to evangelism.

b. a specific schedule (1) of events—preparation, information, instruction, evangelization, consolidation, prayer being continuous and central in emphasis; (2) of calendar — all churches of a given area agree on a calendar, simultaneously engaging in the same effort with everyone doing the same thing at the same time.

c. a specific methodology: the mobilization and training of every believer within the framework of his local church to be an effective witness for Christ, joint evangelistic endeavor, simultaneous church revivals, gospel teams, use of literature and radio, saturation of the community with the Gospel by every means available.

d. a specific organization. From the very beginning the work required a comprehensive, organizational pattern.

e. a specific message. This is a unique feature of NLFA and deserves special attention. While all evangelistic endeavors specialize on preaching the Gospel, I have not found any other movement designing a unique message to be carried by all believers simultaneously into the world about them. NLFA has designed such a message and presented it in spoken as well as in written words. The message is outlined under five captions as follows:

(1) God gave life to man. This was an excellent point of contact and a good starting point. Creation is a truth commonly held by Muslims, pagans and Christians. On this fact they stand united though the interpretation of the fact varies greatly.

(2) Man rejected life. This emphasizes the fall of man, his sinful condition and his guilt before God. At the same time it points to his desperate need of redemption which he cannot achieve by himself.

(3) God provided new life in Christ. Here the story of God's marvelous love comes out and the story of redemption in and through Christ is told.

(4) Man must accept the new life. Here the subjective aspect of salvation is told and the need for repentance and faith are taught. Only as man by faith appropriates what Christ has procured does he come into the possession of new life.

(5) New Life is seen through man. New life is a dynamic in life. It transforms and liberates life in all its relationships. True believers will follow Christ, emulate him and learn from him, and will endeavor to make him known to others. The new life becomes manifested in living and witnessing for Christ.

It is the message rather than any other single factor that cemented the movement into a harmonious unit. It became the dynamic of the program, developed the boldness in the witness, arrested the attention of the hearers, and served to transform the program into a continuing movement. Organization, leadership and schedule formed only a framework within which this dynamic functioned. Few evangelicals have realized the significance of a succinct, dynamic, relative message in an evangelistic movement. This has not been sufficiently explored. This is an untapped dynamic of tremendous importance.

It is noteworthy that this unique and dynamic feature was not in the mind of the organizers on 1 August 1963 when NLFA was founded. It originated in the minds of two national brethren who were made responsible for designing and outlining a manual for training the lay members of the churches to become involved in NLFA. Five chapters in the handbook are devoted to the development of the message. All participants study it in order to carry it into the world about them. It has proven its value in the movement.

Fifth, it is an organized effort of total evangelism by the mobilization of spiritual resources and the cultivation of dependence upon the supernatural. The movement makes the prayer cells central to the whole program, with a strong emphasis upon the Holy Spirit pervading the program. This makes for strong spiritual dynamic.

Six, NLFA as a program has built into it the potential of maturing and enriching the life of the church and every believer. It also has the capacity of transforming itself into an abiding movement integrated into the life of the church as a regular pattern of ongoing service. That such is actually the case the following reports substantiate. These were given at the June, 1968 Council meeting and are the continuation of work begun in 1964.

BUKURU — *M. Cwang Rwang.* Four church groups are co-operating in NLFA. Since our city campaign last year which resulted in about 1,300 being counseled, we continue to have a large monthly meeting in the big cinema at Bukuru. Visitation and gospel teams in our areas have resulted in 278 professions of faith in Christ. The half night of prayer continues monthly in ten places. One hundred and nineteen passed the handbook test.

FOROM — *M. Gyang Jatau.* We sold about 1,200 handbooks and 300 prayer cards. There were 2,000 who took the handbook test. Preaching in the villages resulted in 247 professions in three districts. Several others have not yet reported. We bought and distributed over 5,000 pieces of literature.

DIKO — *M. Sale Abner.* We set aside a week of prayer earlier this year for gospel teams. At the end of the week we asked who would be willing to go. Seventy-six responded to go for one week. Fifty others promised to pray every night for those who went. Twenty people repented. The team preached in 151 villages.

KAGORO — *M. Barnabi Bideth.* Since last year the believers here have set aside time every day to pray for those who are cold, for soldiers, and for return of peace to Nigeria. Many spend time visiting in the villages. A good number have repented. Professions this year are about 300. About 400 have made things right with the Lord in their hearts. Soldiers from here marvel at the answers to prayer.

KWOI—*P. Dawuda Auta*. Through gospel team ministry blessing came to us and our district. They went out to three areas. Altogether there were about 166 professions of faith.

DUTSEN MADA — *M. Dan Taro*. This year we sent out thirty-five men for gospel team work from one to two weeks. There was much blessing. We have about 406 prayer cells, about 150 more than last year. We plan to have courses for gospel teams in three districts next year.

MIANGO — *M. Gado Miango*. The NLFA effort here was not going ahead well. I gave myself to the work. I organized some gospel teams and we went out preaching. As a result we have opened two new churches. Let us pray much for Miango.

WUKARI—*Miss Dorothy Sytsma*. As in the past gospel team work was a great blessing. There was opposition to our preaching in one area. The district head refused us permission to preach. So we made our way by bicycle to Jalingo. It took us two days by bicycle and part of a day by motor before we reached the Central Office. Immediately we were told to go back to our work, and that there was no law to prevent preaching in Nigeria. Taraba district needs preachers to live among the people. We were able to open two new churches. There were about 104 who professed salvation.

ZONKWA—*Pastor Simon Nkom*. Gospel teams were our big work this year. The Lord's people gave money to send out twenty-seven workers to Kufana and Chawai districts. Altogether there were about 900 professions of faith. Our aim now is to try to get preachers from the various churches who will go and strengthen these new converts. We are now praying for funds to send gospel teams into these places next year.[1]

Such in brief is the ideology undergirding NLFA. It is difficult to criticize it from a biblical frame of reference.

PROVIDENCE AND NEW LIFE FOR ALL

With this analysis before us, we turn next to a consideration of the providence of God operating in Africa. Only as we see this providential operation can we understand the success of NLFA. At the outset I state that according to my observations, impressions and factual findings, the program as a whole is a success. It is of high spiritual quality, truly biblical, thoroughly indigenous and sound methodologically. But none of these qualitative factors are sufficient to account for the effect

of NLFA. We must see the hand of God before we see the success
of NLFA. At least four factors appear on the horizon:

First, it is the unanimous finding of researchers that Africa south of
the Sahara, with few exceptions, constitutes a high potential area. Thus
almost any movement succeeds. Africa is not only changing; it is in
a state of convulsion. This, of course, produces a cultural and psychological mood, a sense of uncertainty because of lost moorings and a
spirit of anticipation because of the hoped-for better life and future.
This is fertile soil for the Gospel of God.

Second, the evangelical church has little or no institutional and
structured competition in the field of evangelism. Most of the old
established churches are preoccupied with ecumenism, philanthropy and
social reform, and have neither time, energy nor personnel for biblical
evangelism. Roman Catholicism, as an established system, does not
constitute a formidable threat to evangelism in Africa as it does in
Latin America and parts of Europe. Neither do we face the renaissance of an ancient system of religion as it confronts us in Asia. Africa
almost anywhere is an open and ready continent for the Gospel and aggressive evangelism.

Third, we believe that the Holy Spirit works uniquely in Africa to
stem the inroads of Islam. He blesses the Gospel in a marvelous way
creating response in the hearts of countless numbers of people. God
is calling out His elect from the black race, filling up the quota from
among the nations. Africa must be represented by myriads of people
in the church of Jesus Christ.

Fourth, the program of NLFA is thoroughly biblical and in keeping with the perfect will of God. It is His will that every creature
should know the good news of His gracious and marvelous provision
in His Son Christ Jesus. It is His will that every member of His body,
the church, should be mobilized and be made useful in the vineyard
of the Lord. It is His will that the church should avail herself of the
spiritual resources in the Holy Spirit and claim them by humble, fervent, united prayer in faith. Thus set upon His will, the movement is
bound to succeed. That such a movement as NLFA should make its
appearance "at such a time as this" is to be attributed only to the
gracious providence of God.

Chapter 22

RESULTS OF NEW LIFE FOR ALL

THE RESULTS OF New Life For All can best be highlighted by looking at its spread and also at the benefits derived from it by the churches.

New Life For All has experienced progressive expansion in Nigeria and in Africa as a whole. Its fame was noised about and gradually it has expanded over almost all of Nigeria, except the East because of the war. Though it has not succeeded in permeating the South due to ecclesiastical indifference (there Anglicanism and Methodism are deeply entrenched with a strong Baptist minority), the evangelical churches are putting forth strenuous efforts to mobilize their resources for evangelism. Some of the denominational churches are cooperating, and in Lagos an Anglican is heading the movement.

Outside of Nigeria, workshops and retreats were at first conducted in Niger, Upper Volta, Mali, Sierra Leone and the Ivory Coast. These countries are implementing this program. In response to numerous requests, permission has been granted to as many as twelve different languages to translate NLFA materials. Other requests are under consideration.

In July, 1968, the West African Congress on Evangelism convened on the campus of the University of Nigeria in the city of Ibadan. It was sponsored jointly by the Nigerian Evangelical Fellowship and New Life For All with the Reverend David I. Otalajo as chairman. The congress was called in order that the findings of the Congress on the Church's Worldwide Mission (Wheaton, 1966) and the World Congress on Evangelism (Berlin, 1966) and other related conferences could be implemented in practical ways in Africa, with the hope that it would result in a new impetus to the ministry of evangelism of the continent of Africa. Its purposes were:

1. To define again the gospel message of salvation through faith in Jesus Christ as recorded in the Scriptures.
2. To establish the relevance of this message in meeting the needs of West Africa today.
3. To impress upon West African Christians their responsibility to present this message to all people.
4. To investigate such methods of evangelism as may be most appropriate for West Africa.
5. To provide a medium in which mutual help may be obtained by

115

West African Christians through a sharing of ideas, concerns and ministries.

Some 450 delegates came to the congress from all over the African continent. Most countries had at least two representatives. Here the program of NLFA was presented every afternoon to the general assembly and in workshops. Delegates from the various countries formulated plans for their particular countries. Unanimously and enthusiastically the delegates accepted the principles and methodology of NLFA, with the intention of carrying home their impressions and understanding of the program in order to kindle the fires of evangelism in their home constituencies.

Invitations were received from South, East and Central Africa. In response, the Reverend Wilfred Bellamy and the Reverend Yakubu Yako toured large parts of Africa in November and December of 1968, and shared their experiences and knowledge in retreats and workshops with leaders of eighteen key centers.

NLFA is becoming a pattern of evangelism for large parts of Africa. The NLFA office worked together with the Nairobi office of the Association of Evangelicals in Africa and Madagascar in setting up these conferences. The continent-wide organization has given it its approval and support.

The benefits derived from the movement by the churches have been both quantitative and qualitative.

THE QUANTITATIVE BENEFITS

I can only briefly summarize my findings, that put many of our churches to shame. Here are some positive accomplishments:

1. The penetration of the immediate community with the Gospel. In eight out of twelve meetings I was assured by the pastors of rural areas that there was no village left in their district in which the Gospel had not been preached. In Igbaja I met with eight representatives from fourteen churches surrounded by 100-120 villages. Here I was assured that there was no village left without some kind of gospel witness. In Kwoi I met eight men and a lady representing that area in which more than fifty percent of the population professes Christianity. Here, too, the same assurance was secured. Cities and towns were blanketed with the gospel message, with no home or compound having been omitted.

2. The numerical enlarging of congregations, both in membership and in attendance. Numerous churches are reporting an attendance increase from twenty-five to fifty percent, and baptismal increases from fifteen to thirty-five percent over the year preceding NLFA. Of special interest is the fact of the baptism of older men and women and some numbers of Muslims. The secretary of ECWA (SIM related) churches,

Mr. Kato, informed me that weekly he receives two or three letters requesting help for enlarging of churches, due to the growth of the membership and increased attendance.

This denomination has grown from 918 churches in 1964 to 1,116 churches in 1967, and doubled its membership in these years, rising from 21,000 to 42,000. In these churches the average attendance each Sunday totals between 300,000 and 350,000 individuals.

Scores of new churches and hundreds of preaching centers have been opened wherever NLFA has been conducted. It must be stated, however, that not all churches are recording growth. There are other factors which enter into church growth than the NLFA pattern of evangelism.

Perhaps the greatest success was achieved by the British branch of the Sudan United Mission, as a comparative study seems to indicate. This, of course, prompted me to do some special inquiry into the make-up of this mission. The secret seems to lie in the relationship of the missionaries to the national church. The mission activities and the church have been merged into a healthy union. The marriage is a wonderful success. No doubt, mission-church relationships are a very dynamic factor in church growth.

At the January, 1969, meeting, leaders from evangelical missions and denominations reported that baptisms had doubled and at places trebled. One large body now has an annual growth rate of twenty percent. Another reported an increase of thirty percent.

3. The outward expansion into new villages, areas and tribes by means of gospel teams. These teams were recruited from the ranks of the laymen and dispatched into "unoccupied territory." The teams were composed of groups of from four to eight men, usually on an interdenominational basis, to witness to the Gospel of Christ. A visit to Gani, a village some sixty-five miles from Kano, a bush station of the SIM, convinced us of the impact of such work.

There several teams had spent some months, preaching and witnessing for Christ. These were followed by some evangelists. In our meeting they listed twenty-five villages that had been opened to the Gospel because of the ministry of the teams. In several villages some groups of believers existed, while other villages were asking for teachers to instruct them in the way of God. Such stories can be repeated almost endlessly. Recently about a hundred such villages have been reported to Gerald Swank.

4. It has made Nigeria aware of the presence of a dynamic evangelical Christian movement not content to remain passive and docile. Well did a Muslim teacher of Kaduna express it when he said: "You

Christians have shown us how to make converts. We, too, must get out, work hard. We, too, will make converts."

The united, simultaneous emphases, the invasion of a city by scores of teams of witnesses, the numerous prayer cells throughout the cities to which neighbors were urgently invited, the wide distribution of literature, the united campaigns and parades now and then, the radio and displayed posters—all these awakened Nigeria to the fact that something was happening.

It also marked and distinguished the living, dynamic, functioning church from the capsuled structured church, and a stirring is noticeable within the latter. Divine and spiritual earthquakes have something peculiar in them. Mr. Willis J. Hunking writes:

> I hope Miss Pridham, who is in our Child Evangelism program will be here (Ilorin). She and her two assistants have done by far the greatest job in schools than anyone else I know of in NLFA. They have used our NLFA message. One thing that is interesting is that even though from the Anglican church we haven't gotten much support from the pastors, both the teachers and students are red hot for the whole program in their Anglican schools. The response that they have had there is just tremendous. This is something that I think your friend, Dr. Peters, is going to find interesting. A church is not very interested, but their schools are just crying for the team to come and help them with evangelism. I don't know what the whole thing is going to mean in the future, but at the present time it certainly means that the young people are reaching for something." [1]

An interesting scene developed in Lagos. Here the Anglican Bishop is reported to have said that NLFA was just the movement that Nigeria needs. At a meeting where reports were heard the Archdeacon listened carefully. Overcome by the stories of salvation he heard from simple laymen, he stood to his feet, raised his hand in gratitude to God and called on all to sing the Doxology. There are fringe benefits that are far-reaching and bring about unexpected results.

5. Miracle manifestations. The movement is not devoid of some unique manifestations of the supernatural in the realm of the physical. Divine healings are reported, such as the gradual restoration of sight to a blind woman after prayer for her. A crippled boy of ten years of age was healed. A young girl was instantly cured from a consuming fever. God has proven Himself adequate in physically and spiritually meeting the needs of men, and in establishing His presence and loving care.

The August, 1968, issue of *Africa Now* reports an incident:

> A team member was accosted by a man whose small son was desperately ill. He thrust the unconscious child at him and said, "If your

God is so powerful, have Him heal my son." Shaken, the young man accepted the child and offered a fervent prayer. Almost immediately the child began to regain consciousness, and by morning was completely well. Many in that village turned to Christ." [2]

It must also be mentioned that now and then special answers to prayer were shared with God's people by radio and a circular news-letter to encourage the fainthearted.

THE QUALITATIVE BENEFITS

We stated above that NLFA has built into it the quality of enrich-ing the church and believers and the potential of continuity as a move-ment. This is well-established by the following facts:

1. *Prayer*. There were 7,000 prayer centers in which 50,000 to 60,000 believers met daily. It was the consensus in all twelve conferences with pastors and church leaders that a new spirit of prayer had come upon the churches, and that a new attitude toward prayer had developed in the minds of the people. A marvelous deepening of the prayer life had taken place. Prayer had become a life-reality to the believers. Two factors seemed to account for this transformation.

First, the fact that prayer had been taken out of the churches into the homes had demonstrably taught the people that the home could be made a real place of prayer. Today not only do numerous homes continue prayer cells, but even more are conducting regular family altar. At Igbaja the church bells ring at 5 A.M. to awaken the Chris-tians to a time of family Bible reading and prayer.

Second, the fact that the exercise of faith in prayer has wrought some most remarkable answers to prayer. Many individuals who were on the list of some prayer group suddenly responded favorably to the gospel witness, while others showed up in the prayer cells without special invitation. From one village a most unusual incident is reported.

Several prayer cells agreed to pray for three particular men, only to experience that all three were mightily constrained by the Holy Spirit to seek the pastor's help in one evening. Without knowledge of one another, they met in the pastor's home and surrendered to Christ. God brought honor to His name by answering the prayers of His children.

2. *Witness*. There was general agreement among the pastors that the life of witnessing broke through in the minds of the people for the first time. Whether due to practice or neglect, the fact remains that missions had not succeeded thus far in impressing upon the conscience of the nationals the fact that witnessing is an essential part of the nor-mal Christian life. Even pastors confessed that they had not really expected their people to witness. This was more or less the business of the missionary. The pastor's business was to concern himself with

his flock, while the people as a whole gave little thought to witnessing.

NLFA has revolutionized this attitude and has made witnessing everybody's business. It exempted neither missionary, pastor nor layman, not even the young men, women and children.

3. *Evangelism.* Evangelism has become a new integrated, ongoing and dynamic factor to many pastors and in many churches. As a Methodist district superintendent of Zaria well said, "For years I have preached the Gospel, but I preached it merely as information. Today I preach the same Gospel, but I preach it for decisions for Christ. NLFA did not change my Gospel, but it intensified my motive and transformed my goal." [3]

The status quo and service for service' sake has given way to warmth and zeal in reaching out. Many of the pastors testified that they had professions of faith almost every Sunday. Many of these people had been won to Christ during the week by some church member. On Sunday they were then publicly professing Christ. Others made their decision during the preaching service.

A young evangelist reported the presence of twenty-three converted Muslims in his congregation of fifty people. All had come to know Christ through personal testimony within the last twelve months (June 1967 – June 1968) and had publicly confessed Him before the whole congregation.

Evangelism has become an integral and ongoing part of the church. Writes Miss Cheal (SUM), "My feeling is the NLFA as such has largely been integrated into the normal avenues of the church work and development. In some areas the zeal for visiting and reaching other groups, such as Fulanis, has definitely waned. In some, there is regular effort and we hear good news of what the Lord is doing through them from time to time." [4]

Rev. Thomas Owens writes: "We had another NLFA campaign, just in our own church, 1967 through dry season 1968. But really now it has become so integrated as a normal (we hope) plan of evangelism in the church." [5]

These quotes are two of dozens of assurances that NLFA has become a part of the life of the church, though with fluctuations in degree at various places.

The consciousness of responsibility that has been awakened in the churches has been most wholesome and some districts are doing a repeat of NLFA, feeling that they have not accomplished their maximum value during the first cycle. One district is now in its third cycle, determined to accomplish what it set out to do in the beginning.

4. *Missions.* Sending and being sent has become a new and meaningful part of the church's life. Both mission volunteers and finances

are on the increase. Two factors seem to account for this mission-mindedness.

First, the emphasis that NLFA must be a self-sustaining movement and involve the total mobilization of men and resources. The challenge proved over and over again that even a relatively small church, if burning for God, can make contributions to the cause of God. Illustrations of sacrificial giving inspired others to do likewise. It actually resulted in total or near total mobilization.

The second weightier factor, however, was the sending forth of gospel teams as pioneer missionaries into new and untouched areas and tribes. It can be stated that this has become one of the strong emphases and practices of NLFA. Hundreds of teams of from two to eight have gone forth, in spite of hardship and sacrifice, to pioneer the Gospel in hitherto unreached areas of Nigeria. It is reported that by 1968 about two thousand men and women had already gone out, each giving from four weeks to three months of their time.

Moslem cities, such as Kano, Zaria and others, have been saturated with gospel literature. Street meetings were conducted, and wherever possible, compounds were entered in order to explain the gospel message. Remote villages were visited over a period of several weeks and new tribal areas were reached. A new chapter of missions was begun. It is still continuing even though the teams may be fewer.

The fact, however, is that the national churches have caught the vision of missions. Some team members have actually returned to their former area of witnessing to take up permanent work and continue their ministry. Others are joining some national missionary agency and are making their continued contribution in that way. Church associations ECWA, TEKAS, and UMCA report substantial increases in personnel and finances in their mission project because of the enlarging of the missionary vision and spiritual intensification experienced through NLFA.

5. *Cooperation.* One of the abiding blessings often mentioned by the pastors and church leaders was the fact that they had learned to know and appreciate the church as the body of Christ. Previously, it had been a theory for them, a concept with little or no meaning. But as NLFA had united them in a common task, as they had prayed together in each others' homes, as they had gone out in visitation ministries, as they had witnessed together in city campaigns, they had learned to know and appreciate one another. Christian unity had become a meaningful concept and experience.

When asked whether this experience had in any way weakened their denominational loyalty and appreciation, the pastors affirmed that the opposite had taken place. The cultivated bond of Christian unity had in no way lessened their churches' faithfulness to their own denomination. To the contrary, they felt that their own fellowship had been greatly enriched.

They did not deny the fact that such cooperation was not always easy to maintain. Some difficulties had arisen, but they had been neither serious nor general. The overwhelming majority were happy for the opportunity that had come their way to express before the world that the Christian Gospel unites people across cultures, languages, denominations and tribes. They felt that while they had been greatly enriched, it also had been a marvelous demonstration before the world, torn by tribalism and factionalism.

6. *Instruction.* The concreteness of the instruction by means of the handbook and the material given to the Christians for making known the Gospel had been most helpful. It points up a most significant pedagogical principle in the training of Christian workers and should be of value in the molding of African mentality. It substantiates the fact that too much of our training is ideal and conceptual. This has little meaning to most people. They need something concrete, something simple which they can handle with confidence.

7. *Self-discovery.* The movement called for local and indigenous ingenuity. Though the program was carefully framed, it allowed for sufficient flexibility so that each district could tailor it more or less according to its own needs and available resources. Also, because there were no technical advisers for the program, each area was thrown on its own resources and creative ingenuity, as well as motivation, to make the movement a reality.

The whole program was designed to operate according to general principles handed on by indoctrination rather than by direction of advisers. Homogeneity thus was achieved by pastoral and Christian workers' retreats in which the general principles of NLFA were thoroughly expounded and explored. During the course of the operation literature was prepared and distributed to guide and assist the area committees. Radio releases did their share to give general direction and inspiration to the program. Occasional visits for spiritual ministries by men from headquarters bolstered the motivation within the participating churches. Thus the unity of purpose and sentiment and the spiritual motivation were well-sustained.

In the outworking of the program, however, considerable heterogeneity developed. Mobilization and training of believers and the motivation to make the work progress were local responsibilities. Because the cultural level, the psychological mood and the available resources differed greatly from area to area, the movement became a mosaic of patterns rather than a uniformity in manifestation.

Having been thrown upon their own creative genius and working in perfect freedom, the pace of march differed considerably from district to district and even from church to church. Not all were able to keep to the schedule or work out the complete program. Culturally, psychologically and spiritually this approach has proven itself as a good overall workable principle, though it has manifested some limitations and weaknesses.

8. Bible study and the Christian ministry have gained new meaning. Mr. Farmer, the principal of the Kagoro Bible College (SIM), relates that many more young men are indicating Bible college studies as their first choice, preferring it to general secondary and teachers training college education. This was not so evident before NLFA movement.

Most Bible institutes, conducted in the vernacular, are crowded to capacity and are unable to accommodate the applicants. Similar statements were made by the Rev. Willis J. Hunking (UMS field chairman), and by the Rev. E. H. Smith (SUM missionary and TEKAS executive secretary).

In January, 1969, leaders of evangelical missions and churches made the following two far-reaching decisions:

(1) "We plan to repeat the NLFA program in 1970 throughout the Northern States of Nigeria. A new handbook for instruction of believers will be produced and the Principles and Practices of NLFA, recently published, will provide the guidelines for a total outreach to the 30 millions.

(2) "We are preparing to enter the Midwest State of Southern Nigeria where only a small fraction of the two and one-half million population know the Lord Jesus. . . ." [6]

Chapter 23

POINTS OF WEAKNESS OF NEW LIFE FOR ALL

IN THE LIGHT of all these positive factors it is difficult to come upon some negative aspects of the work. Yet such there are:

1. It is evident that the program was inadequately prepared because of lack of time. The great and radical ideas of NLFA and the preaching of the Gospel to every creature predominantly by a lay movement were new to the Nigerian mentality — pastor, churches and laymen alike.

The reconception of evangelism methodology and Christian service was too revolutionary for most people. While it appealed to them, due perhaps as much to nationalism and present-day African psychological mood as to biblical and spiritual motivation, its deeper dimensions were not truly grasped by the majority of the people. Time should have been allowed for the principles to mature in their minds and to become part of the lives of the pastors and people.

The genius of Western programming is evident on every hand. It sweeps everything along that comes in its way, generating as much emotional enthusiasm as clear intellectual illumination, deep spiritual motivation and abiding convictions. Not a few of the pastors were aware of a pleasant "breeze" and were all for it, but they were not quite sure whence it came or whither it was going. They were happy to be a part of it and moved along enthusiastically, though they did not fully understand the program.

At several sessions with pastors it was expressed to me that they had really not understood the program; they had, however, had full confidence in the men who initiated the program and had been ready to cooperate and march with them. This is praiseworthy, though not the highest level of cooperation.

It is possible that many of the pastors and people would not have grasped the new principles involved in NLFA, no matter how much time they had been given and how diligent the instruction would have been. The African is an activist in religion and not a theorist. Only experience could teach certain lessons and inculcate certain principles. This was the testimony of a number of pastors. The experience itself became their school.

2. The sincere desire for flexibility in the program, indigeneity of the work and confidence in the creative mentality of the individual, denomination, church, and district have resulted in certain weaknesses

and flounderings in the work in some areas. The fear of being suspected of dominating the work and/or lack of personnel have deprived the movement of sufficient, unifying and directive leadership during the time of its formation and initial operation.

It is evident that one brief retreat of three to five days does not provide sufficient time for adequate indoctrination of pastors and workers in *The Leader's Guidebook* and the principles and message of NLFA to work with maximum efficiency. The non-directive approach, while ideal in itself and preferable to the omnipresent adviser, definitely results in weaknesses in the midst of flexibility, creativity and indigeneity.

Deeper indoctrination and saturation along the lines of NLFA principles by means of literature, conferences and personal guidance, and midway sessions of critical evaluation could prove very valuable to the work and would make it more abiding. Yet such a procedure would in no way detract from the opportunity for local leadership, adaptation and creativity.

3. The strong drive, spiritual motivation and united effort to preach the Gospel to every creature are no substitute for clear exposition of the great doctrines of the Gospel as they relate to salvation. The movement betrays lack of doctrinal depth, comprehension, clarity and dynamism. Thousands of hearts have been touched by the testimony of the Christians; they have been awakened from their religious slumber, but many have neither been sufficiently illuminated by the Gospel nor turned by the truth to experience spiritual regeneration. Therefore, they are left in a precarious and nebulous religious condition.

While a sense of readiness has been created, the seed of regeneration is lacking to bring them to the new life intended for them, which attracted them and for which they are longing. The great urgency is for clear and full exposition of the Gospel which is the dynamic of God unto salvation.

4. There seems to be a lack of understanding of the relationship between the cultural upheaval and the turmoil within the soul due to this upheaval on the one hand, and spiritual motivation in conversion on the other. It is evident to any observer that the African's soul, consciously or subconsciously, is experiencing tremendous tensions and conflict. He is being uprooted violently from the traditional past of his ancestors and hurled into an uncertain and unknown future. Dread fills his soul in the midst of a desire for security and belonging.

Into this turmoil comes the testimony of the Christian, songs of praise and prayer, and the message of the Gospel. Almost instinctively the soul turns to it. Such turning, while positive and good, must not be mistaken for conversion. It is an assent to the truth, but not yet a consent to the Savior. It is the first and valuable step toward Christ and salvation.

However, it is not conversion. It is but a preparation for conversion, an expression of readiness to listen and to receive information, perhaps even to decide positively for Christ and His way of life. It must be capitalized on, but it must not be capsuled as a completed experience.

5. The movement is strong in evangelism and witnessing, but it lacks an equal strength, emphasis and program of follow-up. Follow-through work lacks system, enthusiasm and depth. Unless quickly remedied, this will prove fatal to countless souls and disastrous to numerous churches. They will receive large numbers of "converts" into their membership, people who have gone through some awakening experience and instruction but who are not truly born again. The result will be the paganization of the church.

We caution, however, about making it too difficult for people to enter the churches. The half-way station between former paganism and the present church is a most precarious and dangerous position and will lead to catastrophe unless a way to "go on to perfection" (become rightful members of the church) is found much faster than has been evident heretofore.

Half-way citizenship will not do in the long run. Eventually a decision will be made. Half-way citizenship is a most fertile field for Islam, the cults and the rapidly-spreading "messianic" indigenous movements.

CONCLUSION

NLFA as an ideology, methodology and program should not be permitted to wane. It must be encouraged until it infiltrates more fully the bloodstream of the churches, becomes a part of the life of all of them, and spreads throughout the continent.

To be of greatest value, however, an equally strong and equally extensive teaching program must be instituted and systematically carried out either on a denominational or interdenominational level. We must not fail in the second stage. It must be clearly kept in mind that most of the "converts" are awakened souls that need illumination, faith and transformation as well as a church home.

I am deeply impressed by the NLFA program. It is the most complete, dynamic, biblically-oriented, spiritually-motivated and African-adapted movement I have learned to know. I am profoundly moved by its quantitative and qualitative accomplishments under the gracious ministry of the Holy Spirit. It deserves to become an African continental movement.

Chapter 24

LESSONS LEARNED FROM EVANGELISM-IN-DEPTH AND NEW LIFE FOR ALL

MY STUDIES OF Evangelism-in-Depth and New Life For All have been most enriching and rewarding and have led me to several tentative conclusions.

1. *A new age of evangelism has broken in upon the evangelical wing of the church of Jesus Christ.* Evangelism is becoming a primary and determining concern to many Christian leaders, and numerous involved missionaries, churches and organizations. This is evident from the several congresses on evangelism that have been conducted or are being projected — Berlin, 1966; Ibadan, Nigeria, 1968; Singapore, 1968; Minneapolis, 1969; Bogota, Colombia, 1969. This is an unprecedented phenomenon for which we cannot thank God sufficiently. We should also mention the large pastors' conferences World Vision has conducted and the conference on Evangelism-in-Depth the Latin America Mission convened in August 1966.

It is also noteworthy that extensive campaigns have been or are being conducted around the world by the Southern Baptists, with considerable influence and impact for good. The most significant of these were the campaign in Japan in 1963 known as New Life For You and later the Brazil campaign in 1965. Both were most rewarding and led to the Western Hemisphere campaign of 1968–69, the greatest evangelistic undertaking known in the history of the church.

Of interest are the Good News Crusades of the Assemblies of God, concentrating on the larger population centers and which eventually are to reach into every major city of the world.

In 1965 the Korean churches conducted a successful nationwide evangelistic campaign which reached into most areas of South Korea and revived and revitalized the churches in evangelism.

The Asian Evangelists' Commission under the able leadership of Philippine evangelist Greg Tingson has conducted successful crusades in Singapore, Saigon, Colombo, Kuala Lumpur and Surabaja (Indonesia) since its founding in 1964. Korea is the next target.

Overseas Crusades has sponsored large and very successful evangelistic campaigns in several Latin American countries, notably Brazil, Colombia and Mexico. Its evangelistic impact is felt also in Taiwan and the Philippines.

A new organization of considerable vitality has sprung up in South

Africa, known as African Enterprises. Using city and nationwide crusades, university missions, radio, films, literature and other methods of witness, African Enterprise endeavors to reach all sections of African leadership for Christ.

The Latin America Mission is continuing Evangelism-in-Depth efforts in Latin America. It has set up subsidiary offices in Kinshasa, Congo and Singapore. New Life For All is gradually spreading over Africa.

Several similar saturation and mobilization programs are on their way in countries of Europe and Asia, notably Portugal and Japan.

One can attribute this proliferation and intensification of evangelism programs only to a new visitation from above. God is graciously raising up His servants to challenge His people and to channel His forces into world evangelism in a time of unprecedented opportunities. He has stimulated serious, penetrating and practical thinking on the various continents and raised up men of vision and leadership in several countries. While God is operating sovereignly He is also operating mysteriously and generously. He is not limiting Himself to one man, one people, one church, one team or one society. He is present in Latin America, Africa and Asia. We pray that He may also revisit North America and Europe in a new wave of evangelism.

2. *This is an age of great campaigns, and evangelicals ought to capitalize on the present psychological, sociological and spiritual mood.* Great campaigns are evident in many places as we have indicated above. They are sponsored by numerous organizations, each following its pattern and each claiming unique success. No impartial observer will deny that much good is resulting.

God is at work in these campaigns in a marvelous way. They are a tremendous factor in advancing the cause of God. Hundreds of thousands are hearing the Gospel and thousands are coming to know the Lord. However, to compare and evaluate them is a sensitive and difficult matter.

Each believes in his own sanctuary and knows himself divinely guided, scripturally oriented and practically efficient and effective. This is the way it ought to be. He who is not sold on and enthusiastic about his cause will not succeed. Yet, critical and objective evaluations are most essential and should be welcomed. It is evident that no one possesses the sole nor the whole key to success. While each one is a teacher, each one must also remain a learner.

Continuous changes in time and culture demand continuous modifications and adaptations which are not easily accomplished. Movements have a tendency to consolidate and eventually petrify. Initial success blinds to greater possibilities. Present-day research in group movements uncovers new factors of the dynamics of group and multiple-individual movements and thus points the way to greater and richer service. We dare not become static or closed in our patterns and programs. Continuous and creative thinking is demanded to remain fresh, dynamic and up-to-date.

3. *The present-day national, interdenominational and united campaigns are making a tremendous and wholesome impact upon the communities and countries and should not be underrated nor discouraged.* They play a vital part in Christianity and are of great benefit to the churches. They are bringing countless multitudes under the sound of the Gospel, are creating a God-awareness in community after community, and are making the nations conscious of the presence of a dynamic evangelicalism. This is of inestimable significance. Therefore, in no way should such endeavors be discouraged, discounted or limited. They are of God and are instruments in God's purpose and deserve our support.

In their present structure and in present circumstances, however, they are not the most effective nor are they the complete answer to evangelism and church building. They seemingly lack certain elements and need to be supplemented by other services. With the exception of New Life For All, they are not making the contribution to church growth which is generally expected.

This seemingly negative aspect need not be the fault of the evangelism agency as such. It may only point to some defect in the program which should be discovered and could be remedied. It may also indicate a radical weakness in and failure on the part of the churches in the follow-through work. It may be that because of their structure, form and program the churches fail to attract and to hold the converts. It could be a combination of all factors. This fact is at present a subject of diligent and objective research.

As matters stand at present, somewhat smaller, local and denominationally sponsored programs seem to be more effective in bringing converts into the churches, though not necessarily in making more converts. The following accounts, submitted by the Reverend Philip Hogan, executive director of the foreign missions program of the Assemblies of God, presents some stimulating facts on their denominational program, known as Good News Crusades.

The Assemblies of God do not count their gains by professions, or conversions but by churches. This, of course, is a new approach. However, if this is our objective in evangelism, it seems like a sound method. Mr. Hogan points out that some of these are ill-housed, ill-led, ill-organized, and ill-trained. Nevertheless, they are identifiable, local witnessing units of the body of Christ. Such a procedure presents the whole concept of evangelism—planning, preaching, follow-up.

One of the most rewarding successes we have had in recent years has happened in the Republic of Panama. Although we have been in every other country of Latin and Central America, for specific reasons we had not entered Panama. We decided that we would make this a rather classic approach to evangelism and church planting as we see it, and took plenty of time to analyze and prepare the plan.

First of all, we entered the city with an AIM team, which is our program for short-term ministries on the part of college young people. We sowed the city down, door to door, with 50,000 packets of tracts and preparatory literature announcing the coming of the campaign. Before the missionary ever arrived, we had secured radio time and were broadcasting every day on several stations, spot announcements, and other short gospel programs.

When the rainy season was over, we rented a location, put up a tent, and called one of our most experienced evangelists. The crowds were never spectacular but they were consistent. They averaged 500–600 a night, and this happened throughout the duration of the campaign which went on for nine months. This particular evangelist stressed the importance of night to night attendance. As soon as converts began to appear, we separated them in a training class, taught by the missionary, a veteran of two terms already in Latin America. We used a little pamphlet that we widely used over Latin America, which is the prep course for church membership. It is called "Reglamento Local" or "A Standard for Church Doctrine and Practice."

While the campaign went on, the training course grew until by the end of nine months, over 300 people had not only professed salvation but had taken this course. By the time the rains came again and the tent had come down, we had the beginning of a fine church.

Since these people had, among other things, been taught tithing, we put up to them squarely the challenge of securing a location for continuing the effort. The only vacant building we could find in the city was a bankrupt motion picture theater. The cost was $35,000. The mission paid $10,000 in a gift and this local congregation, now organized, borrowed $25,000 and are paying it back at the rate of $650 a month. They have not missed a payment.

The missionary, however, is still the pastor, so that they do not have the responsibility yet of supporting their own pastor. With this coming new season, we went to the other end of the canal to the city of Colon and did almost exactly the same thing, with even more spectacular results. What is even more encouraging is the fact that having gotten the habit of church attendance nightly in order to be established, this congregation prefers to carry on this pattern so that now, over two years and a half, with the exception of a few nights when marshal law was declared during recent political uprisings, they have not missed a night in going to church.

A very elaborate program of visitation and follow-up is now being carried out. A full-time visitation secretary was hired and 100 persons volunteered to make three calls a week on unchurched families. Regular records are kept of these visits and the congregation that went into the theater about 300 strong is now up close to 1,000. What I am seeking to highlight here is that the maturing process began simultaneously with the opening of the campaign and continued throughout, so that it would be difficult to say when the follow-up began and when it finished.

Sometimes, in our urgency to see the work grow, we may try to quickly bring the converts in and identify them with an already ongoing, usually strong, central church. Sometimes, however, this may not be the mind of the Spirit at all, and often real fruitage can develop from organizing small branch developments, cottage prayer meetings, or branch Sunday schools, where the converts first take their fledgling steps in Christian living and witnessing in these small grassroots developments.

In 1956, we had one church in San Salvador. An open air evangelistic campaign was organized and by the middle of the meeting it seemed that there would be too many converts to lead into one big church. The campaign went on from January to April.

The first 5,000 decision cards that came in were therefore sorted according to section of the city. In the beginning, ten places were found and ten workers recruited, most of these with, as yet, very little experience in the formal aspects of the ministry. These workers met every Monday morning to share both blessings and problems. (Incidentally, these same ten workers still meet every Monday morning.) Records were compiled of the statistics every week and comparisons made regularly, so that all would know the work was progressing.

In two years, there were eighteen small groups supporting their own pastors, still very largely in small rented buildings. Branch Sunday school classes were still organized and young people were challenged to go out and conduct these classes. Every pastor had a teachers' training class and taught the next week's lesson.

In the first few years following this organizational concept and the open air campaign, there were eighteen churches with 78 branch Sunday schools and the attendance was from 1,500 to 3,000. In three years, the number of churches had increased to twenty-four, with 225 branch Sunday schools with a total attendance of almost 10,000.

Today there are scores, literally, of these churches. In San Salvador it is estimated that the total attendance equals three percent of the metropolitan population of the city on any given Sunday. All of this from the original church with 60 members, 100 in Sunday school, and five months' open air campaign in 1956.

The genius of this development has been that lay workers have been encouraged and used. They have been trained as they witnessed, but the converts were followed up and hung onto in their local areas without being solicited to go across town and join the large central church.

In Nigeria, our Good News effort was divided into two parts: literature distribution and evangelistic meetings. Follow-up efforts were developed for both phases of this program. Over 200,000 packets of literature, each containing six pieces, were distributed. Among these pieces of literature was an application for Bible correspondence school and an invitation card, in each package, with the address of the local church stamped on it. A free booklet, "Standard of Christian Practice," was offered to any who would submit their card of invitation to the pastor at the close of any one of his services. When this card was submitted, the pastor gave him the book and encouraged him to attend a special class that was meeting on Monday evenings to study that particular book. With the name and address of the individual on the card, workers began to make regular contact.

When the names and addresses of new converts were secured, there was a series of tracts presented in weekly visits. First of all, the tract entitled "Now That I Am a Christian, I Should Be a Witness" was read in its entirety to the new convert. Then the worker had special prayer with the person and encouraged him to attend church next Sunday. One week later, the second tract was taken, entitled "Now That I Am a Christian, I Should Pray," and the same procedure was followed. One week later, the third tract was taken, which was entitled "Now That I Am a Christian, I Should Read the Bible," and the same procedure was followed. One week later, the fourth tract was taken, which was entitled "Now That I Am a Christian, I Should Be Baptized." The same procedure was followed and the new convert was strongly encouraged to enroll in the local baptismal class. This was the final gathering of the net. When possible, the four contacts and presentation of the tracts were made by the same worker. This often developed into a friendship which has been lasting and most meaningful.

In a two-year period, we put into operation three separate Good News efforts in Nigeria. These resulted in the distribution of 4,000,000 pieces of literature, 13,000 recorded decisions coming out of the campaign. The last two of these, however, were pulled off in the middle of the crisis and the last after war itself broke out. Consequently, it was impossible to get the statistics on the last two efforts, which were by far the most organized and the workers better trained.

The following statistics are from the first Good News effort, which was carried out when the staff was still very much in the learning process. Out of 9,000 recorded decisions in the first campaign, there were 2,912 that received the full series of four tracts. Of these, nearly 3,000, we had an increased attendance of 1,000 in the local churches.

Four months later, 254 had completed their baptismal class requirements and had been baptized. You can see, from these figures, that we held about 10 percent of those that made decisions for Christ.[1]

It is too bad that the concluding part of the Nigeria campaign cannot be written. It is impossible to surmise what could have happened. No doubt the response would have been overwhelming, as it is in other parts of Africa. Africa is a continent of great campaigns.

4. *In general the churches in the mission fields are insufficiently equipped for great harvests and plenteous reaping.* Preparation of the churches by missions and sponsoring agencies has been woefully inadequate. Follow-through training should precede the campaign. With few exceptions, neither pastors nor congregations are ready to absorb and care for a large influx of new converts. The spiritual life of many churches is low and the laity untrained. Few churches have the physical facilities to accommodate them, nor has a thorough-going and comprehensive program of follow-up been devised. Thus the losses are abnormal; the casualty rates are out of proportion; only a small portion of people professing faith find their way into the churches.

This is a most crucial area and needs prompt attention and wise action. Something drastic must happen if success is to be assured. It is not sufficient to count professions. Christ has commissioned us to make disciples. We dare not fail Him nor the people who make professions and declare a certain state of readiness. The responsibility is squarely upon the shoulders of the sponsoring agency and the churches need to be prepared as carefully in a follow-up program and in the nurture of the converts as they were taught how to lead them to a profession of faith.

Strengthening should come along several avenues. Pastors should have the opportunity to acquaint themselves with effective methods of follow-up ministries and materials that are available for this purpose. They should also be taught the rudiments of pastoral care and counseling to build and advance converts. This is an art as well as a divine responsibility.

Families should be encouraged to build each other and to assist one another in the faith. The family is the major key to the tremendous problem area. Suitable literature should be provided for this purpose.

Laymen and women should be taught follow-up and follow-through ministries as well as courses in evangelism. The laymen are a vital key in preservation as they are the key in evangelization. Early after the local church campaign the home prayer cells should be converted, at least in part, into Bible class centers to study carefully prepared lessons and assist the converts in their newly found faith and win them for the churches as they have been won for Christ.

A new dimension in the training and in the program must be added if the fruit is to be preserved. It would be well to think of a full-time secretary in follow-up ministry to function in this capacity for at least one year after the campaign is completed. The secretary would co-ordinate and encourage the churches in this ministry. Such an office could also serve as a supply depot and provide suitable literature for new converts. This need not interfere with denominational interests and loyalties. It may curtail some excesses, duplications and other inconveniences.

This is the most difficult problem and the most serious flaw in the programs. Perhaps it is not out of place to restate the effective method of the Reverend Waylon B. Moore, as presented in an article under the title "Evangelism in Depth," a writing we have referred to earlier.

How can we retain the results of our evangelism?

The answer is follow-up; conserve and multiply the fruits of evangelism. It is all that goes into building a soul to spiritual maturity and fruitful witnessing. Follow-up is not giving some material to a new Christian so much as it is sharing personally the life of Christ with another through the Word and prayer.

A babe in Christ must have something better than a class or service where he is a part of the crowd every Sunday and Wednesday and left to himself spiritually the rest of the week. There are certain truths that are vital to the life of a new convert immediately after his decision for Christ. But sometimes he must wait months to study the Bible for himself, or to learn who the Holy Spirit is and what it means to be controlled by the Spirit. No one can live well on one good meal a week. Neither can the average convert thrive on one or two spiritual meals a week. When a baby dies because of starvation and improper diet, we don't blame the baby. The new Christian is a baby and needs to be personally fed, protected, and trained until he can prepare daily food for himself out of the Word of God.

The greatest evangelist, the Apostle Paul, spent more time in follow-up than he did in preaching. In I Thessalonians we find a how-to-do-it lesson from him. He used four major methods in follow-up.

In the first place, he followed up converts by personal contact on a regular basis. He revisited church after church for long periods of time. He earnestly sought to be with the new babes as much as possible (I Thess. 2:17-20).

Second, Paul upheld converts with persistent, believing intercession (I Thess. 1:2; 2:13). He won the battle for their fruitfulness where flesh glories least — in the closet of prayer.

"Send a man" was the third means used by Paul in follow-up. When he was in prison or unable to travel due to sickness, it is recorded many times that he sent a man to visit those new ones in Christ (I Thess. 3:1-6). The man he sent was always one whom he had trained personally and who could continue the work he had started.

Paul's fourth major method in follow-up was writing letters. How glad we are that his love and care are chronicled for us in 13 epistles to individuals and churches.

Two major emphases are given priority in the life of the disciple. First, he has a burning desire to experientially know Christ. He echoes Paul's prayer, "That I may know him and the power of his resurrection and the fellowship of his sufferings." Next, he has a passion for discipling men for the Master. He places time with men next to time with God.

Discipling means getting close to a man or woman and being willing to give your whole life into his or hers. This can hardly be done from a pulpit or before a class. It can best be done individually, man to man. To my knowledge there are as yet no courses in any seminary or Bible school specifically on follow-up. We are strong on what we need to do but weak on the how of doing it.

Paul worked with the Thessalonians for just about a month. He won them, taught them more than a dozen foundational doctrines, and then chose Aristarchus and Secondus to accompany him for more personalized training. He preached first to the masses, and then he discipled individuals so that countless others could be reached.

Does this plan work today?

Where it is used, it always works. When pastors and laymen catch the vision of personally training men and teaching them how to train others also, churches can be revolutionized.

For example, at the First Church of Lakeland, Fla., one deacon was personally discipled for just a short time. During this past year that man has trained over 100 men and women, and they have in turn already won to Christ and begun training 177 others. Many churches, like this one in Florida, are instituting a plan of spiritual adoption for every new member.

Here is a tested prescription for deepening the spiritual life of the thousands who will decide for Christ this year. But follow-up is not something to be tacked on to a church program. It is a process, and it takes time. It must become an integral part of the total program. Do we yet have a *new* soul-winner yearly for every pastor in Texas? Let each pastor covenant before God this year that he will put first his personal work with a few faithful laymen.

Let the pastor take one willing layman visiting with him for a period of time. Let him teach that layman the plan of salvation until he can give it to anyone, anywhere; and until he wins his first soul.

Every church opportunity can be a training opportunity for building up a man. It takes time, but otherwise what guarantee do we ever have of a real break-through where laymen by the thousands will consistently win and build souls?

Next, apply what has been called the "Timothy Adoption Plan." As Paul "adopted" Timothy and reared him to fruitful maturity, let the pastor train the soul-winner to care for the new convert. The soul-winner "adopts" the new convert and visits his home weekly to tutor him in personal Bible study, prayer, and witnessing.

A New Life class for converts taught by the pastor, education director, or experienced soul-winning layman is a minimum for conserving and building future disciples. Time spent with each convert by the pastor-trained layman will do more to guarantee solid church membership and fruitfulness than many sermons.

Association clinics for pastors on how to disciple men should be a part of our program of evangelism. How to follow-up should be a major emphasis of every evangelism conference. Seminars for lay workers in local areas will help also. As pastors and laymen, we can have such a program if we request it. Follow-up must take root in the local church, now.

Such evangelism in depth is the need today; it means multiplication of disciples to the glory of God.[2]

5. *A more radical return to the New Testament in patterns of evangelism; the incorporation of additional principles and emphases; and fuller cultural, sociological and psychological adaptations are demanded than any of the present great movements are manifesting, if genuine, lasting and impressive results are to be achieved, and if justice is to be done to the present overwhelming possibilities in many parts of the world.*

A radical return to the New Testament is not an easy matter to achieve. We are children of time and culture and prefer to move along established ways and familiar patterns. Yet, we must bring our ministry under the judgment of the Bible. Nothing but the uncompromising practice of biblical principles will bring us the fullness of spiritual blessings. The New Testament remains our authoritative corrective and unfailing guide. There we find our orientation and directives. In keeping with the book of Acts, we must enlarge our concept of evangelism to include household and community evangelism that will lead to household and larger unit conversions, whether they be groups of people or multiple-individual professions.

So important is this dimension of evangelism that I have added a third section to this book in order to add and strengthen the movements of saturation evangelism. It is not my intention to weaken what is being done nor to subtract from it. God is honoring the present endeavors. His blessings are evident. The present limited success, however, must not blind us against possibilities of greater accomplishment. My suggestions, therefore, are in part corrections and in part additions, but not subtractions.

The demand of fuller cultural, sociological and psychological adaptations poses both a theological danger and the possibility of greater evangelical advance. There is only one step between adaptations and accommodations which in turn easily lead to syncretism, nativism and Christo-paganism. On the other hand, it also remains a fact that man is a cultural, social and psychological creature who has his life and being in this type of an atmosphere. Here he dwells, here he is at home, here he must be found and won for Christ. The degree of dynamics of any movement depends upon the degree of adaptations to its native environment, as well as other factors of dynamics.

This leads up to the most important question of the dynamics of group movements. Dynamics of group movements must be distinguished from group dynamics. The latter is accelerated, intensified, emotionally-charged personal interaction, a person stimulus-response experience. In the Christian sense it is electrified fellowship.

The former, however, is based upon factors that impel groups of people to deliberate purposeful action. Group dynamics must not be confused with mob psychology. Rather, it is an orderly movement, sustained by definite forces that operate according to definable laws or principles. These principles are incarnated in dynamic leaders and find their point of contact and response in the social, moral, religious and cultural consciousness of the people. Such people movements, while comprehensive and inclusive, are personal, conscious, deliberate and deliberative in their experience. It is not blind action, people merely following a leader or some instinct. It is rational and volitional, and therefore legitimate and biblically sustainable as a principle of action.

We ascribe all credit and honor to the Lord, and do not in the least minimize the direct impact and work of the Holy Spirit. He is the ultimate source of all positive activities. However, the Holy Spirit does not operate in a vacuum. Therefore we need to study the forces behind dynamic movements, factors that generate dynamics of comprehensive action.

As stated before, they are not the ultimate source of spiritual movements. But they are the appropriate channels of the ultimate spiritual sources. We may, therefore, call them secondary sources, that is, sources or factors which channel spiritual power.

To be simple in defining the secondary channels and forces, or to bring them down to one denomination is not always profound. It is as easy to oversimplify as to overgeneralize. The words of Robert Lee are apropos: "The obvious point to be drawn is that no one single explanatory theory of religious growth or decline is sufficient. We do better to look for a cluster or constellation of factors in seeking to understand this complex social situation." [3]

In a similar manner Dr. David B. Barrett, in his comprehensive study of dynamic African movements, repeatedly speaks of "multiple causes," "a whole complex of causes," "the presence together of a number of factors at the same time." He says, "Causation depends on the accumulation of a number of different factors." [4] This we must keep in mind.

We are searching not for one factor only, but for a number of factors with the intention of welding them together into a "complex" or "constellation." It is evident that the more factors we are able to discover and uncover, and the more we can integrate them into a solid dynamically functioning unit, the more dynamic the movement will be.

We do not claim to have discovered all secrets and forces at work in dynamic family, people, multiple-individual or group movements. Neither are all the factors our original finding. Some have been learned and borrowed from other researchers. Studies in dynamics of such movements and larger unit movements are a relatively recent undertaking. However, six factors have come to my attention in these studies, which, if blended, integrated and coordinated according to the specific culture, constitute a mighty dynamic in group and multiple-individual movements.

1. *Relevancy of Message.* The expansion of a Christian movement depends on its ability to make the message of the New Testament relevant to the religious aspirations, anticipations, frustrations, fears and needs of the people as the initial and effective point of contact and departure to the deeper and real needs of the spiritual nature of the life of man.

This principle is most clearly demonstrated at present in the ministry of Wycliffe Bible Translators, who have experienced some remarkable movements among a number of primitive tribes. It has also been very successfully practiced by New Life For All in Nigeria, as I have pointed out above.

2. *Total Mobilization.* The expansion of any movement depends on its success in mobilizing and equipping its total membership in continuous, bold, intelligent and persuasive propagation of its beliefs (R. K. Strachan, *Evangelism-in-Depth,* slightly reworded).

This principle has been practiced through the centuries by groups here and there. At present it is most dynamically applied by the Baptists of Romania (the fastest growing Baptist movement in the world) and the Assemblies of God in several countries, especially in Latin America. It has been integrated into a system of evangelism by Dr. R. K. Strachan, and is most strongly and successfully advocated by Evangelism-in-Depth and New Life For All.

3. *Cultural Adaptation.* The expansion of any movement depends

upon the degree of cultural adaptation it is able to achieve and its ability to harness and mobilize the cultural, social and psychological forces of its native environment, without yielding to compromise in the message and unguided ethical accommodation.

This principle is at present most fully incarnated in the Brethren movements in Spain and Argentina, the Methodist-Pentecostal movement in Chile, and the Assemblies of God in Brazil, El Salvador, Guatemala and in part in Mexico.

This principle may be seen in the Batak movement of the past century in Sumatra, the Karen movement in Burma, the Neuendettelsau Mission in New Guinea, in several fields of The Christian and missionary Alliance and other missions, especially missions to primitive tribes.

4. *Wholesome Relationships.* The expansion of any movement depends upon the depth and breadth of relationships it is able to achieve, whether these relationships are functional or structural.

This is a much neglected and disregarded spiritual and dynamic principle. The unresolved tensions or ill-structured relationships between missions and national churches constitute one of the most serious obstacles in dynamic evangelism and church growth. So, the intermission, interdenominational and interchurch relationships are deep underlying causes for much failure in missions. Evangelical missions have been strangely evasive in this matter. Yet, it is a pressing and urgent cultural and also spiritual issue upon which much depends in the dynamics of missions and church growth.

It is difficult to illustrate the principle. Movements that have come nearest to the biblical ideal are the movements of the Brethren and especially the Swedish Assemblies of God.

5. *Relationship to Traditional Establishment.* The expansion of a movement depends upon the kind and degree of relationship it holds to the traditional and dominant establishment. The qualitative and quantitative degree is determining.

If the attitude of the to-be-reached society is one of appreciation, admiration and aspiration toward the dominant establishment and values, the degree of appeal will depend upon the nearness in ideology and structure of the new movement to the old ways and patterns. The slighter the variation in outer form and appearance and inner function, the less resistance will be encountered in the change. Under such circumstances, all things being equal, the Anglican and Methodist churches should gain most and thrive best in nominally Roman Catholic countries. These churches would come nearest the old establishment. The Baptists should have a limited chance. The Brethren and the Pentecostals should find much resistance and grave difficulties in their advances.

If the attitude of the to-be-reached society is one of apathy, resentment and revolt against the traditional establishments and values, the degree of appeal will depend upon the distance in ideology and structure of the new movement to the old and established ways and patterns. The sharper the contrast and protest, the greater the gulf that is being created, the greater the appeal will be. Thus the reverse order in appeal and growth in the above-listed churches should take place. Pentecostals should lead in their gain and growth, as they do at present.

6. *Spiritual Functionalism.* The expansion of a Christian movement depends on the degree to which the Holy Spirit is permitted to operate freely and unshackled by traditional or idealized structuralism, and allowed to develop a relevant, native and dynamic functionalism with an appropriate but subordinate structuralism. It must be emphasized that functionalism does not become meaningful and purposive without structuralism. There is no pure organism. All organisms function within an organization. The basic question, however, is, Does the organism or the organization dominate?

It remains a fact of history that few factors have obstructed the operation of the Holy Spirit more often than time-worn, traditional and irrelevant structuralism. The Holy Spirit has been quenched and shackled within form, order and organization. It is well to keep in mind that the function of the church is clearly presented in the New Testament. This is not so with the form and structure. Because of this, various forms and structures have grown up in history which the church too often has bound in iron-clad chains.

The principle of functional freedom is best incarnated in in present-day Assemblies of God and in certain places in the Brethren. In general, all of the missions and the churches are struggling with this problem.

Such are some of the factors involved in group and multiple-individual movements that make for the dynamics of such movements. It is possible that no movement embodies all these factors to the same degree, nor is the configuration alike. However, the greater the accumulation of these factors, the greater the dynamic will be. We must strive to integrate, coordinate and weld together as many of these factors as possible.

The triangle may be steep and thus separate the factors vertically. This makes for a less dynamic movement. Or, the triangle may be flatter, making the factors closer to each other. The closer the factors are merged and fused, the greater the dynamics.

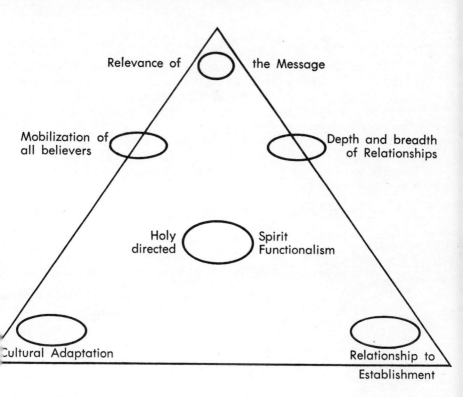

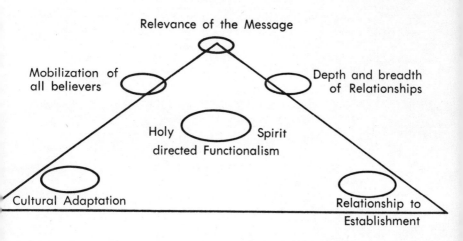

Another consideration is the arrangement of the factors in the triangle. Evangelism-in-Depth has placed first priority on mobilization. New Life For All followed this example. However, in its development New Life For All gave prominence to the relevancy of the message. A shifting of priorities took place.

Brazilian Pentecostalism, according to Dr. Emilio Willems, puts cultural adaptation first.

The second triangle, as I have presented it, represents what I think is the biblical ideal.

FOOTNOTES

PART TWO

CHAPTER 9
[1] *Evangelism-in-Depth,* Latin America Mission (Chicago: Moody Press), p. 19.
[2] *Ibid.,* p. 25.
[3] "International Review of Missions," Vol. 53 (Geneva: International Review of Missions, 1964), p. 194. See also *The Inescapable Calling* by the same author (Grand Rapids: Eerdmans Publishing Co.), p. 108.
[4] Latin America Mission, *Ibid.,* pp. 27-29.

CHAPTER 10
[1] Latin America Mission, *Ibid.,* pp. 30, 31.

CHAPTER 11
[1] *Revolution in Evangelism,* W. Dayton Roberts (Chicago: Moody Press, 1967), p. 84.
[2] *Ibid.,* p. 84.
[3] Correspondence from Rev. Allen Thompson, West Indies Mission, July-August, 1966, p. 6ff.
[4] Private correspondence.
[5][6][7][8][9] Office Information, Latin America Mission, *San Jose,* Costa Rica.

CHAPTER 12
[1] "International Review of Missions," *ibid.,* p. 197.
[2] Oral statement at a Conference on Evangelism-in-Depth, August, 1966, San Jose, Costa Rica.
[3] Mimeographed material, Division of Evangelism, Latin America Mission.
[4] W. Dayton Roberts, *Ibid.,* p. 100.
[5] *Ibid.,* p. 91.
[6] *Ibid.,* p. 87.
[7] Depth in Evangelism, mimeographed material, Division of Evangelism, Latin America Mission, p. 1.
[8] *Ibid.,* p. 1.
[9] W. Dayton Roberts, *Ibid.,* Leighton Ford in Foreword, p. 6.

CHAPTER 13
[1] "The Andean Outlook," Joseph S. McCullough, Andes Evangelical Missions periodical, July, 1968.

CHAPTER 15
[1] Personal correspondence.
[2] Personal correspondence.

CHAPTER 18

  [1] *Marvelous in Our Eyes* (An illustrated pamphlet), Gerald O. Swank (Jos, Nigeria: New Life For All), p. 6.

  [2] *Ibid.*, p. 15.

  [3] Office Records, New Life For All, Jos, Nigeria.

CHAPTER 19

  [1] *Ibid.*

  [2] *Leader's Guide Book* (Jos, Nigeria: New Life For All), p. 9.

  [3] *Ibid.*

CHAPTER 20

  [1] No documentation necessary.

  [2] Office Records, *Ibid.*

  [3] *Ibid.*

  [4] Wilfred Bellamy, Material submitted by Sudan United Mission, London.

  [5] *Marvelous in Our Eyes*, Mrs. Dorothy Swank (Jos, Nigeria: New Life For All).

CHAPTER 21

  [1] Office Records, *Ibid.*

CHAPTER 22

  [1] Personal letter to Rev. Gerald O. Swank.

  [2] Office Records, *Ibid.*

  [3] Personal testimony as recorded by the author.

  [4] Personal correspondence.

  [5] Personal correspondence.

  [6] Office Records.

CHAPTER 24

  [1] Philip Hogan. Report to delegates on "Saturation Evangelism," Leysin, Switzerland, August 28 – September 4, 1969.

  [2] Waylon B. Moore, *Op. cit.*

  [3] *Stranger in the Land*, Robert Lee (London: Lutterworth Press), p. 156.

  [4] *Schism and Renewal in Africa*, David B. Barrett (London: Oxford University Press).

PART THREE

HOUSEHOLD EVANGELISM AND GROUP MOVEMENTS

THE STUDY OF saturation evangelism requires us to examine in detail
the biblical and practical questions of household evangelism and group
movements in missionary outreach around the world. Understanding
how both are treated in Scripture and how they can be utilized in various cultures can provide significant breakthroughs for the Gospel.

We shall define carefully what we mean by these terms, how they
are used in the Bible, and what the requirements are on the mission
field if these movements are to be exploited for God's glory. These are
not gimmicks for a speedy, easy kind of world evangelization, but if
we neglect household evangelism and group movements we are neglecting what are potentially the most fruitful avenues of evangelism God
has given us.

Chapter 25

BIBLICAL AND MISSIONARY PERSPECTIVES ON HOUSEHOLD EVANGELISM

WE HAVE PREVIOUSLY REFERRED to various types and patterns of evangelism. The emphasis must remain upon evangelism, the confrontation of man with the good news of God in Christ Jesus. This is an unalterable principle of revelation. The type or pattern of evangelism is more flexible and is conditioned by culture, society and psychology. No absolutes govern this aspect, except that evangelism must lead to personal faith-appropriation of Christ and commitment to Him.

In view of the fact, however, that the family is not only a universal, social institution but also a divinely-created social unit, and holds a unique place throughout the Bible, household evangelism deserves our closest attention as a biblical priority and ideal.

Household evangelism is not the only pattern of evangelism. The Bible presents numerous illustrations of individuals coming to the Lord. This emphasis must neither be neglected nor minimized. It is present everywhere in the Scriptures. And so is mass evangelism. Christ preached to the masses. So did Peter and Paul. Personal evangelism, individual conversions and mass evangelism are well-established in the Bible and in history. The question, however, remains whether these patterns represent the highest ideal in the New Testament evangelism and a pattern of evangelism that builds the most prospering and effective churches.

The contention of this chapter is that household evangelism and household salvation are the most basic biblical and cultural approaches and expectations, and need revival in our days. Before we can return to family worship, we need to return to family evangelism and household salvation.

With this in mind, we turn to a biblical study of household evangelism and household salvation.

THE PRIORITY OF THE FAMILY

The family did not just happen. It is God-ordained and instituted. Household is a fundamental biblical concept. God willed the family and the home. It is the original, divinely-instituted, natural, social and specific unit; it is essential to the well-being of the human race. It is most significant to note that God created this social institution before the fall of man. It thus belongs to the ideal, though not to the eternal

147

realm of man. Marriage, home and family did not grow out of a derived need because of sin. They were a part of man as he came from the hand of God.

The primacy of the home and family remains intact throughout the Scriptures. Though other institutions are added, or come into being in the course of cultural and social development, the household is never overshadowed, absorbed or superseded by the nation, the people, or any other institution of society. Great sanctity and blessings are attached to it, if preserved according to the pattern of God and lived in His blessed will.

The Bible does not only present to us great heroes of faith and pious men of God. Most often we are also introduced to their parents, or at least to one of them. We know the father of Abraham, the parents of Moses, the father of Joshua, the parents of Samuel. We know something of the relatives of Gideon, David, Isaiah and other prophets of God. We are acquainted with the parents of John the Baptist, the father of Peter and Andrew, as well as the father of James and John. We are introduced to the mother and even the grandmother of Timothy. They share in the honor of their sons, as they also shared in making them into men of God.

THE MEANING OF HOUSEHOLD SALVATION

Before we enter more fully upon the basic thesis of this chapter, permit me to clarify at the outset the meaning of household salvation.

By household salvation we do not understand that each member of the family will be saved because the parents or the father or mother are Christians. We do not find "representative faith" in the Bible operative to the degree that unbelieving members of a family will be saved because the parents are saved.

Certainly, children of believing parents have great advantages in spiritual matters. This is evident from numerous examples in the Bible. It is also clearly implied in the words of Paul when he writes: "For the unbelieving husband is sanctified by the wife, and the unbelieving wife is sanctified by the husband: else were your children unclean; but now are they holy (I Cor. 7:14). A believer brings inestimable blessings into the home. This is especially so if this is the father, as we shall see later.

However, there is nothing automatic about salvation. There is no mechanical or biological carry-over of faith, or the benefits of faith, from parents to children. Faith and salvation are personal matters.

By household salvation we do not mean the covenant idea with its consequent infant baptism, whether baptism is regarded as sacramental affecting regeneration, or covenantal and thus relating the individual uniquely to God for salvation and making him a potential member of the household of God, which in due time he actually becomes.

By household salvation we mean the principle decision on the part of the father and/or parents, and in deliberation with the members of the family, that the household ought to become a Christian family, and that the home ought to become a Christian home. Then, either jointly and simultaneously as a family unit, or individually, each member in personal decision relates himself to Christ as personal Savior. Becoming a Christian thus becomes a family affair and interest, and yet a personal, conscious and volitional act on the part of each member. There is nothing mechanical about it, yet there is something deeply spiritual and social in it. There is a basic, joint, open and deliberative decision on the part of the household, a declaration of readiness and an actual or potential turning from unfaith to faith, from non-Christian to Christian, from being outside of the fold to coming into the fold, from being estranged from God and the commonwealth of God to becoming a member of the household of faith.

The principle features of household salvation are: (1) the family acts in deliberation and unity on the principle issue; (2) the decision is made under the direction and guidance of the parents and/or father; (3) the decision is made consciously, voluntarily and without pressure by the members and with the support of the family.

It is possible, in fact most probable, that upon the principle decision not all members will actually become Christians in the full sense of the word and as understood by the Bible. It is also possible that some children will find it easier to experience full Christian conversion than the parents will. Yet, the principle issue has been decided upon, and each member knows that he has the favor and the support of the household. This is a biblical ideal we must strive for.

It is evident from the above that household salvation must be preceded by thoroughgoing household evangelism, evangelism that penetrates and permeates the depth and relationships of the family and each member. To this we shall turn immediately, seeking to establish this as the biblical order, divine ideal and apostolic norm.

In the light of these principle truths, we should learn to think appreciatively and deeply about household evangelism and household salvation. It must become our consuming evangelistic concern.

The Household in the Old Testament

The student of the Bible soon learns that the family is God's central concern. There are more instructions about the family in the Scriptures than about any other social unit or institution. Husbands are given detailed precepts on how to love their wives and how to relate themselves to them. The wives are given commands on how to behave toward their husbands. The relationship between parents and children is regulated and their mutual behavior is ordered. It is well to study the stringent family requirements for the Christian worker.

The Bible upholds the fact that the family is God's unit of blessings. Early on the pages of the Bible there is the beginning of a beautiful trail that winds through the entire Scriptures.

Noah, being warned of God of things not yet seen, moved with fear, prepared an ark to the saving of his household. Nothing is said of the faith and godliness of the sons of Noah. We know, however, that they were saved with him in the ark.

Abraham, the father of all believing, was a blessing not only to his immediate family but led his extended family, his servants included, into a covenant with God. They all shared in the rich blessings of God. He also obtained the promise: "In thee shall all the families of the earth be blessed."

Moses was faithful with all his household, while Joshua exclaimed: "But as for me and my household, we will serve the Lord."

Rahab, that peculiar (ill-reputed) woman of Jericho, turned to the Lord God of Israel by faith and saved herself and her entire family from destruction. The story continues and climaxes in the New Testament accounts of numerous household salvation experiences, as we shall see later.

It must be stated with equal earnestness and emphasis that the family is often God's unit of judgment. This is evidenced in the experiences of Korah, Dathan and Abiram. These fathers were the cause of their families being buried alive as the earth swallowed up the entire group. Achan, too, perished with his family.

Let it be said in all seriousness that the father is God's key to the blessing and curse that befalls a family.

THE HOUSEHOLD IN THE NEW TESTAMENT

As we turn to the New Testament three facts stand out in relation to households.

1. *The household concept is in no way lowered or weakened.* There is no departure from the original institution and design. The family remains the basic social unit and instructions abound in family relationships.

The glory of the household reached its apex in Christ's relationship to it. It is of great significance that Christ in His incarnation did not by-pass the family, but that He came by way of the home, related Himself to Joseph and Mary as His legal and earthly parents, lived in household relationships with brothers and sisters, and took His place as a regular member in a family until He was thirty years of age. As He hallowed the home and family with His presence and participation, He brought greater sanctity and honor to it than it ever had had before. He knew from experience the value of a home, a family, a household. His appreciation of the home is reflected in His ministry and attitude. Never did He speak critically about it or cast a shadow upon it. Later in His life He repeatedly ministered to households, and dwelled in homes and with families. Often He enjoyed the hospitality in a home, conducted many of His services in homes, and performed many healings in the homes. Christ was as much a friend of the home and the family as He was a man of the public. The home retains its rightful place and honor also in the New Testament.

2. *The New Testament abounds in accounts of household salvation experiences.* These begin with a report from the ministry of Christ. Having met Zacchaeus in the street of Jericho, and having been invited into his house, Christ made the startling and marvelous pronouncement: "This day is salvation come to this house" or household (Luke 19:9). To us this is a surprising statement. Was not Zacchaeus the only believer? Why is there no mention of his family? To the disciples these words brought no astonishment. It seems to have been one of many similar household experiences. A similar experience is related in John 4:46-54. A nobleman is in difficulty. He beseeches the Master to heal his son. As this petition is granted we are informed that he himself believed and his entire household (4:53). Household evangelism and salvation are thus rooted in the exemplary ministry of Christ. The Book of Acts continues with similar reports.

Following the Pentecost experience we read of the believers, "All that believed were together, and had all things common" (Acts 2:44). This has been interpreted erroneously to mean that they all moved together into a common place, forming a community that practiced economic communality. This could not be so, for there was breaking of bread from home to home, or house to house, and the apostles were teaching from home to home (Acts 2:46; 5:42). Later, Paul described his ministry in Ephesus in a similar manner (Acts 20:20). This was not just a program of calling from house to house, or house visitation in the ordinary manner. Neither was this communalism, although the early Christians did share their belongings liberally with other believers.

The fact back of such statements is the unique phenomenon that the numerous households which turned to Christ formed household churches which accommodated other households. So also we must look at Acts 4:4, where it is reported that the number of men was about five thousand. Why are only the men counted and mentioned?

Is it not because they represented that many households? This seems to be implied in the record.

This inference is substantiated when we consider several incidents presented more fully. When Peter came to Caesarea upon an invitation, he found Cornelius waiting for him. However, he was not a solitary person seeking divine guidance and salvation. Cornelius had invited his relatives and friends to be with him. The extended family came together to hear a message from God through Peter. It was to this extended family—the circle of relatives and friends—that Peter spoke. It was upon this extended family unit that the Holy Spirit fell as they heard the Word. It was this extended family that was baptized as they believed. Household salvation was experienced in full because it was anticipated by Cornelius.

At Philippi Paul preached the Gospel at the riverside where prayer was wont to be made (an indication that Philippi had no regular synagogue). There a certain saleswoman from the city of Thyatira, a worshiping woman, heard Paul preach. Strangely the Lord warmed her heart and she believed the message. Upon some instruction (Acts 16: 14), she and her household were baptized.

Somewhat later, Paul and Silas found themselves in the city jail. As they sang praises, God supernaturally intervened and a conversation with the jailer resulted. While the question of the jailer is unexpected, the answer of Paul is startling.

"What must I do to be saved?" was the jailer's inquiry. "Believe on the Lord Jesus Christ, and thou shalt be saved," was the first part of the answer. This would have completely answered the question of the perplexed man. Paul, however, significantly continued: "and thy household" (Acts 16:31, 32).

Believing the promise of Paul in full, the jailer took Paul and Silas to his home, so that they could expound the Gospel to his entire household, with the anticipated result that his household would believe and be saved, as Paul had stated. It really happened. The jailer and his household were saved and were baptized.

Dr. Harry R. Boer says: "How much the effort to effect the conversion and baptism of families was a part of the apostolic method is emphasized by the account of the conversion of the Philippian jailer with its repeated references to his 'house' or 'household.' " [1] It is well to read Acts 16:29-34 and underscore the expressions "house" and "all his."

Household salvation is seen in Acts 18:8, in the case of Crispus, the ruler of the synagogue at Corinth. There also was the household of Stephanas, whom Paul had baptized in Corinth (I Cor. 1:16). Similar references are made to Onesiphorus and his house, and Philemon (II Tim. 1:16; Philem. 2). There were household movements in Jerusalem, in Caesarea, in Asia and in Greece. We find it among Jews, Romans, Samaritans, Greeks. It was not confined just to one people, one place or one culture. It was as universal as the family is universal. The opponents of the Gospel worked in a similar manner and were overthrowing whole houses (Tit. 1:11).

Household evangelism and salvation are not exceptional cases in the New Testament. It is the divine ideal throughout the Scriptures and the apostolic norm. It is biblical and social; only to Western individualism does such a phenomenon seem strange and peculiar.

3. *The New Testament church was made up of basic social units.* Well does Dr. Boer say: "The church (in the N. T.) was not built up of so many individual Christians but of basic social units, of organic wholes, and these units, these wholes, were the fundamental cells of society, namely families." [2]

Again he writes: "It is clearly around this divinely-given social unit that the churches founded by the apostolic witness were built. Families entered the church as units and their integrity was guarded by expresed apostolic concern. The family as a divinely-instituted social unit, and the large attention that is given the family as the only 'natural unit' in the Church forbids us to eliminate it from specifically theological and missionary reflection." [3]

That churches should be built out of family units rather than individual believers seems natural. Yet, this fact has been largely ignored by Western missionaries and church planters, especially by the fundamentalist-type missions.

Our own individualism has been idealized and normalized. At the same time it has dominated our theology of evangelism, missionary strategy, and even ecclesiology. We have become fearful of larger units than the individual and hesitate to deal in larger units. There seem to be three reasons for such fear.

There is, first, an extreme interpretation of the doctrine of election, which has been individualized to the degree that it becomes difficult to think in larger units. There is, second, the narrow concept of a church composed of individually "called out" people. It must be admitted that both of these concepts have some truth to them. The question is how determinative they become in our ministry. There is, however, a third reason for our hesitancy. Christendom and the Volkskirche (state church) have frightened us. We are afraid of falling into the trap our forefathers sought to escape. Thus we hesitate, and we fail in a vital issue.

To substantiate our claim about household churches, let us turn to the New Testament. In no uncertain terms Paul spoke of household churches. Writing to the Romans, he sent greetings to Priscilla and Aquilla and the church in their house (Rom. 16:3-5).

At this occasion these people were in Rome and were busy for the Lord. They had succeeded in founding a church in their home. Sometime earlier, writing to Corinth, Paul sent the Corinthians greetings from the churches in Asia, including the church in the house of Priscilla and Aquilla (I Cor. 16:19). They had had a church in Asia in their home. This was their way of doing missionary work and founding churches.

Nymphas conducted a church in his home in the community of Colossae (Col. 4:15). Philemon, too, had a church in his home (Philem. 2). This fact gives concrete meaning to such expressions describing the practice of the early believers in the book of Acts. The disciples broke bread from house to house and taught in the temple and at home. Paul also taught from house to house (Acts 2:46; 5:42; 20:20). This is not a report of home visitation or of private lessons. This is the record of house churches.

Considering this subject in a booklet entitled *Household Church,* H. L. Ellison concludes:

> It is usually assumed that these household churches mentioned by Paul were merely occasional exceptions to the general picture. In fact they can lay claim to represent the norm for a church in the Apostolic period once it had been properly established.
> The mention of the "school of Tyrannus" (Acts 19:9) is in itself an indication that Paul was able to enjoy unusual facilities in Ephesus — if such lecture halls were frequently at Paul's disposal, Luke would hardly have mentioned it in connection with Ephesus. Normally, as soon as the local synagogue was closed to the preaching of the gospel, every form of set Christian meeting, whether of proclamation or of worship, must have been held in private houses. Buildings specially erected for the purpose cannot be traced further back than the end of the second century, and it seems that they were not officially tolerated for a time until the reign of Severus (222-235). . . . So wherever the message of the gospel found any widespread acceptance, the local church perforce divided into a number of household churches, which must have been very much commoner than the few New Testament references might suggest.[4]

Gustav Warneck and Adolf von Harnack come to similar conclusions in their studies of the church of the apostolic and post-apostolic times.

This is an approach to church planting and church multiplication that is almost entirely overlooked in missions, except by the Plymouth Brethren. Yet, it remains a fact that of all social institutions the Bible puts the family into the center as the fundamental social unit of mankind.

Therefore, it is natural that household salvation should be prominent and emphatic, and that the household as a social unit should form the foundational unit of the local church, the bricks from which the church is built. We must return to this if evangelism is to succeed and the church is to prosper and multiply. Much is being said and written about church planting, church growth, church multiplication. We are concerned about Pauline principles and practices to guide us in building indigenous churches.

In most mission activities, however, we are ignoring God's basic unit, the household, for building growing and indigenous churches. Only churches that are built out of basic social units have true health and the potential of rapid growth and steady expansion. The decisive question in founding a church is not how many people are interested in the project, but rather how many families form the foundation of the church. Churches founded by families have the potential to flourish.

Added Advantages

In addition to the three fundamental thrusts of the New Testament outlined above, there are other significant aspects and advantages to household evangelism and salvation.

1. *It honors in evangelism the social unit that God has created.* We owe respect to a divinely-instituted order; Christian ministries ought to enhance and strengthen this order. Christianity, the gospel, is God's healing and restoring power to counteract the disrupting power of sin. Evangelism is the introduction of this healing and restoring power into the family. Therefore, it ought to strengthen and build the household. This is God's design.

Frequently, however, evangelism approaches and tactics, not necessarily the Gospel, become a disruptive force in the family, creating disharmony rather than peace. Individual members of the family are contacted with the Gospel outside of the home, are drawn out of family relationships, and separated from the divinely-ordained social unit to which they naturally belong. The family fears the intrusion, objects to it at times strenuously, abnormally and even violently, and the household becomes the enemy of the convert and a scene of conflict and war.

In such cases, instead of opening the door into the home, the convert becomes a bar that bolts the entrance solidly for the Gospel, and the household remains closed off. This is most unfortunate and contrary to the design of God.

I grant that in some cases the resentment against the Gospel is so deep that it becomes impossible, from the human point of view, to bridge the gulf and overcome the opposition. In more cases, however, it is not the Gospel as such, but rather the approaches in evangelizing that are the real reason for the animosity.

I do not condemn the evangelizing agent. I realize that the approaches are made in good faith. There is nothing wrong with either the motivation or with the purpose. The problem lies in the methodology, in the way it is being done, and not in the goal.

That serious situations will arise is clearly foretold by our Lord. He informs us, "The brother shall deliver up the brother to death, and the father the child: and the children shall rise up against their parents, and cause them to be put to death." Again, he tells us: "Think not that I am come to send peace on earth: I came not to send peace, but a sword. For I am come to set a man at variance against his father, and the daughter against her mother, and the daughter in law against her mother in law. And a man's foes shall be they of his own household" (Matt. 10:21, 34-36). Similar truths are expressed by Paul in I Corinthians 7:13-15. Unbelief becomes the cause for the disruption of the household.

These are not idle words. They may become awful realities. The Gospel of peace may become the occasion of bitter conflict, and the healing power of the Gospel may be turned into a disruptive force by sinful man. The resistance to the Gospel may be so intense, the enmity against God so deep, the love of sin and darkness so passionate, and the enslavement to sin so complete, that man reacts violently to the presence of all that reminds him of God, the divine and eternity. Let no man minimize the sinfulness of man.

The Christian, therefore, must not be surprised or overwhelmed if his household and community become his foes. Our relationship to Christ may be tremendously costly and painful. There is a price to be paid. For this we must be ready at all times. Thousands of martyrs have died at the hands of men and women who only recently were counted their friends and supporters, yea, members of their own household. Loyalty to Christ and total devotion to him may lead to deep, dark and painful experiences.

However, these experiences must not become regulative in our ministry and normative in our expectation. If they come, they do not take us by surprise. But we do not anticipate them and expect them to happen. We do not permit the principles and patterns of our work to be determined by them. Neither are they an excuse for an indiscriminate and unwise individualistic approach in evangelizing. If we keep in mind that we must win not only a soul but a household to Christ, we will be no less bold but more discriminating and more tactful in our proceedings. Every first member of a family should be considered a God-given opportunity to win the family to the Lord, no matter how difficult the way may seem to accomplish this goal.

I recall meeting Daisaku Ikeda, president of the Soka Gakkai at the headquarters of the movement in Tokyo. Upon my question about what their membership was, he replied in terms of families. When I inquired when they counted a family to be a member of Soka Gakkai, his answer was, "As soon as we have one member of the family. For we will never permit that family to rest until we have won it over to our movement and our cause. The first member is only the gate. The home is our goal. Our mission is incomplete until we have the entire family. This is the Japanese way of life." Should Christians aim lower and be satisfied with less?

Of course, it is somewhat natural for the Westerner to invade a community and draw out whoever he can. Courage, zeal, compassion and a sense of responsibility and urgency combine to constitute a tremendous motive. But we need to ask ourselves the ever-sobering questions: Does it honor the Lord most? Does it accomplish the greatest? Is it the wisest procedure considering the future and the building of a strong, indigenous church? What does divine wisdom dictate?

These are questions to be pondered long and hard. They must be evaluated in the light of the Word of God and the pleasure of God. Is there a more effective way, a more satisfactory way of approach? There must be a nobler way, since God wants to save the household and not disrupt it. Let us honor in evangelism the social unit God Himself has created. Let us not accept defeat but trust God to show us a way into the family. Earnest and united prayer and steadfast expectation will bring many surprises. Beware, lest we accept a lower goal than God desires.

2. *Household evangelism and household salvation serve greatly in the strengthening and preservation of those who believe.* Household evangelism must not be over-simplified. It is a difficult and complicated ministry, requiring much wisdom, patience and perseverance. Neither will household evangelism always result in household salvation to the degree that all members will believe at once or at the same time. While this may be the case, as the author has repeatedly experienced it among the Polish and German people in the homesteading areas of Northern Canada, and as the Bible seemingly implies in a number of reports, it is not always so.

If household evangelism results in household salvation, it is evident that it will be much easier for the individual to stand in the midst of pressures from society, since he finds spiritual and moral support in his home and from his loved ones. If household evangelism has reached the family but has not resulted in household salvation, the believing member may expect tolerance in his family and at least partial understanding and some moral support in his experience and position. This is of tremendous importance in a world of temptations, pressures and animosity.

The stupendous casualty rates in present-day evangelism ought to sober us and drive us into deep probing of our methods in evangelism. We search for effective methods in follow-up of professions and we must continue that search. I am convinced that the most efficient method to preserve professions, and lead them to assurance and stability, is household evangelism. In this we need to specialize.

3. *Household evangelism and household salvation aid greatly in the evangelization of the community.* A saved family has a much greater influence for good upon the community than a group of individuals ever could have, and will serve more readily to win other families to the Lord than individuals could do. Saved households, therefore, bring the greatest evangelizing potential into the community. The presence of a Christian family in a community does make a difference.

Not only does like attract like and family attract family, but the web of relationships is far-flung and flows in many directions. A living canal system has been opened through which the healing waters can flow in many directions.

This is seldom realized and even less utilized in evangelism. The dynamic of living relationships is tragically ignored and numerous possibilities are lost because we think so little in terms of blood relationship and its potential in evangelism and church growth. A church that does not aim at ministering to the family as family is failing at one of its most critical parts and ministries. It must be realized that in the divine order the family antedates the church by millenniums.

I recall a church in Colombia. It began with one father. He heard the Gospel from the lips of a colporteur and, upon reading the New Testament, became a believer. His first convert was his wife, followed by his mother and several brothers and sisters. His father had already died. From here the Gospel followed along the lines of relationship into the community and beyond the community. In 1966 this young country church had three baptismal services of second generation young people, as well as several members of the community. It was most interesting to note the fulfillment of the passage: "Believe on the Lord Jesus Christ, and thou shalt be saved, and thy house." This was an extended household which included the major population of a community.

I am reminded of an experience in Northern Alberta. It was my privilege to dwell with Mr. and Mrs. Wells and their daughter, the only Christian family in a large community. Though simple lay people, they had moved into this rural community from a rather comfortable home and position in Edmonton. They were homesteading with others in order to bring some gospel light to these people. They made it their business to befriend people in the community. Mr. Wells had many friends among the men, Mrs. Wells, among the women, and the daughter of seventeen, among the young people. For about three months it was my privilege to assist them in evangelism in a little country log school house. Because of their friendships with the Wells family, the people came to the services. The Lord graciously blessed the efforts and an evangelical church was born.

Household evangelism and household salvation therefore are of inestimable value in community evangelism, the building of local churches and the kingdom of God upon earth.

Chapter 26

PRINCIPLES OF HOUSEHOLD EVANGELISM

WITH SUCH BIBLICAL directives and support, and the extraordinary advantages that accrue from household evangelism and household salvation, we ask the questions: How can household evangelism become a reality? How can it be done? When can we expect household salvation?

In order to answer these questions properly, it must be stated that household salvation is as much a matter of personal and biblical insight and conviction as it is a matter of methodology and approach. Not only methodology but also theology comes into play. Let us consider some attitudes, conditions and pointers in household evangelism.

1. *The first and foremost condition is the clear realization that household evangelism and household salvation are the biblical ideal and norm in evangelism and salvation.* God wills that the family be one, that it remain a solid and peaceful unit, that the family be evangelized and that the family be saved.

It would be difficult to argue with these propositions. Only as this biblical ideal becomes our ideal and norm, only as this truth permeates our whole being and determines and rules our attitudes, will we be willing to pay the price to toil, to pray, and to wait for God to give us households in salvation.

Of this ideal we have spoken sufficiently. It is a fundamental thrust of both the Old and New Testaments and all dispensations. Let us believe it, claim it and act upon it. If God wills that households be evangelized, and that they as households be led into the salvation of God, then it can be done and it must be done. Let us not surrender the divine ideal for something less, perhaps less difficult, more attractive to us and more dramatic in public. We dare not claim less than households for God. While household evangelism is not the only type of evangelism, it certainly is a major type of evangelism.

2. *We must focus our mission as well as our churches upon households and create a family atmosphere.* There is something about a family church that cannot be explained but which can be felt. Too often our missions and churches are preaching centers or community centers, rather than centers of the household of God—gatherings where God as Father is worshiped and obeyed, and the members experience family relationships. We have a "Mother's Day," we have a "Father's Day," but where is the "Family's Day"? We minister to each member

of the family as an individual, but where is the "family ministry"? We have taken our religion into the church, but where is our family or household church? In how far does our church build our family? This must become a major concern of the church. While preaching must never be neglected, there is a difference whether a church meets as a family unit to be instructed from the Word of God or to be preached at. Only a church with a household atmosphere, sympathy and understanding will attract households into its fold. Perhaps we need to rethink our church concept.

3. *Household evangelism is most successful in homes of the people, the place where the family gathers, where the members are at ease, and where they feel free to ask and to react.* Small and person-related Bible study groups composed of families lend themselves more readily to household evangelism than large and public meetings. It seems psychologically more advantageous and socially more wholesome to go into people's homes than to invite them into our homes for evangelism purposes. In the latter place they feel more reserved and on the defensive than in their own homes.

In this matter we have the noble example of Christ. It will prove profitable to go through the gospels and note how many times Christ went into homes, how often he was with families, how many miracles he performed in homes. There is something about the home even as a place for which there is no substitute. Not even the church building can make up for it.

It is a tragedy that Western Christianity has been taken out of the homes and at present is almost completely confined to the church building. We have programmed Christianity out of the homes into the churches. We need a revival to reverse the trend. Christianity is supremely a household religion and is best propagated to households in family circles and in homes. In this we need to major.

4. *Household evangelism should begin with the parents, and especially with the father, if at all possible.* Though this is not absolutely necessary, nor is it always possible, however, it is highly desirable. Of course, any member of the household, very often a child, may serve as a door or a wedge into the home. Fathers and mothers often have become interested in a ministry that served their children well. The opposite can also be the case. They may consider such service an entrance through the back door that eventually will bring disruption into the family.

The point to be kept in mind is that whatever our service, may it be child evangelism, youth evangelism, women's evangelism, our goal is the family and not the individual member only. We owe to the parents the respect and honor they deserve, according to the Scriptures, and should inform them as much as possible about what is being done. Their consent, approval and cooperation is desirable and should be earnestly solicited. We ought to seek their favor and friendship and honorably serve them. Let me illustrate.

I recall an incident in Japan. A young man made his decision for Christ in a service where he was the only representative of his family and the first member to become a Christian. The missionary knew the relationships of Japanese families and the implications of filial piety. Thus he encouraged the young man to wait because he wanted to accompany him to his home. Having arrived there, the missionary paid due respect to the family and explained to the parents the basic tenets of Christianity. He informed them of the decision of their son, humbly asking their permission.

Though the parents were surprised and pondered the disturbing and disrupting effect this might bring, they appreciated the regard that had been shown to them by the missionary. Not only did they not oppose their son in his change of religion, but they kept their promise to the missionary to accompany the son to the Sunday morning service. Because of the grace of God and the wisdom and tact of the missionary, the door to the family remained open; soon the whole household followed in turning to Christ. A household had been won for the Lord and the church.

It was more than human wisdom that prompted the missionary in his proceedings. He did what is implied in the Scriptures in honoring the parents and God richly rewarded his humility and faithfulness. Household evangelism cannot bypass the parents. If it cannot begin here, it constantly seeks their favor and eventually climaxes in their salvation.

PRACTICAL PLANS IN HOUSEHOLD EVANGELISM

Though the significance and practicability of household evangelism is not generally recognized, some practical plans have been developed. I present in outline two such plans, one from Africa and one from India.

Plan One

In an article in *Church Growth Bulletin,* Mr. Charles Ross of the Presbyterian Church in the Congo describes the establishment of "particular" churches that would be self-dependent and autonomous cells, though closely related to the local presbyteries and General Assembly. He reports:

> The Presbyterian Preachers' School at Luebo, in the Democratic Republic of the Congo, has evolved a simple program for church growth,

and this is applied on week-ends in churched and unchurched villages. There are four parts to the program:

1. Three teams, composed of two students each, visit each house in the village. The evangelist joins one of these teams. If the people visited are Christian, we try to discover *how* each one became Christian; if they are non-Christian, we try to find out what their beliefs are; what has hindered them from becoming Christian; which of his family are Christian; and if he has been influenced by clan members to believe or refuse Christ.

2. Later, the students call the people to a place in the village (not always the church building), where a brief worship service is held. The sermon, previously prepared in class, contains elements of the local religious beliefs and their results in the life of the people; appropriate Bible verses are applied to these beliefs, with the results accruing from a new and different life in Christ. The student preacher asks if anyone would like to empty himself of his beliefs based on fear and sustained by fear, and believe in the courageous Christ. Usually several — up to 30 people — respond.

3. Respondents are separated into two groups; those returning to the Church after having abandoned it, voluntarily or otherwise; and those who are new Christians. The students, now in two teams, call each person individually and spend up to two hours discussing that person's beliefs, what he wants now to do with Christ, and how the new life in Christ is to be lived. We then call in the family of each person — if possible — and talk with them. Are they agreed that a member of their clan, or family, leave the ancestral cult for the Christian faith? How will this conversion affect them? Will their customary beliefs change? If some of the family are already Christian, how have they explained the Christian faith to other members of the family clan, or village? If they have been "silent" Christians, we explain the necessity of the loyalty of the entire family and clan being centered in Christ. We discuss all objections openly and seriously.

4. The evangelist has been present with the students while talking with the converts. By late afternoon, when the discussions have usually terminated, the evangelist and students pause to eat. During the meal they talk of methods of church growth, and the need to concentrate on the family and clan rather than uniquely on the individual. Where there is no pastor, we invite several Christians to join us and inform them of church growth through family evangelism. This part of the program is most difficult, because evangelists have been trained to preach to individuals. Furthermore, because (though reared in their clans) they are now living away from the security and ties of their ancestral groups, the evangelists tend to shun working through a family structure and stress single conversions.

A few months later we return to these villages. The results we find in the church are positive or negative depending on the evangelist's follow-up with the converts and their families. In some villages there has been such strong growth that autonomous churches have resulted.

What is now needed is a program to explain to the Church the potential for church growth in family and clan evangelism. Experience has already shown this to be a valid method in village evangelism, and can be useful in cities as well. It now remains for the Church — in its General Assembly — to appraise the method and its results, accept it and implement it through the area where the Church is established.

I might add that the African Independent Churches — especially the "Apostles" — have been evangelizing through families and clans for some years, and have had phenomenal growth.[1]

Plan Two

A second and very unique plan in family evangelism is practiced by a Bible Institute in Madras, India.

The Institute has prepared a series of ten lessons, printed separately in ten small pamphlets. These lessons are designed to unfold in a progressive manner, and in ten steps they show the spiritual need of man and God's way of salvation for mankind.

In order to penetrate the individual family with the Gospel, a home approach is followed. The idea is penetation and permeation of the entire family with the gospel message, in order to win the family as a unit to the Lord and the church.

According to this plan, the individual student is assigned a specific block of houses for the development of a home evangelism program to be carried through in a systematic and thorough way.

The first responsibility of the student is to discover several homes in his assigned area where an entrance is granted and an interest in the Gospel is found, or a readiness to listen is manifested. He makes an appointment to meet with the family on a weekly basis if possible for studies and deliberations.

In the first meeting the student discusses with the family the lesson of pamphlet number one, reading and studying it with them. Having answered the various questions and satisfied himself that the lesson is understood, at least in part, he leaves pamphlet number one with the family with an encouragement to study it diligently. Before departing, he makes an appointment to meet with the group again at their convenience, preferably within a week.

As the student returns at the time of appointment, he reviews the former lesson, invites questions, discusses objections if there are any, develops a home teaching situation, and engages in friendly dialogue with the people on the issues of the lesson.

Having completed lesson one, he introduces pamphlet number two, discusses the main issues of this lesson, and answers such questions as may arise. Again he leaves the pamphlet with the family with an encouragement to study it carefully and to mark points for discussion or difficulties they may encounter, or even objections they may wish to raise. After he has agreed upon the next appointment, he concludes the visit with a prayer for the family.

This process is followed through ten lessons, in that many visits, over that many weeks.

The students are prepared for the home studies in the classroom, where each lesson is prepared diligently on a weekly basis.

Though the individual student is able to take on only a limited number of families (from three to five), and while not all homes continue in the program (some 25 to 30 percent drop out), the method has proven singularly fruitful in winning entire families to the Lord and bringing them into the churches. The vast majority of families that have received such instructions have become Christians and are active members in some local church.

Both of the outlined methods and approaches have their unique advantages and deserve careful studies and emulation, with some adaptations, on a wide scale throughout the world. Family evangelism could prove a major factor in turning the tide in evangelism and in building stronger and healthier local congregations.

A BIBLICAL REMINDER

We need to be reminded of the stupendous blessings and advantages in winning fathers as heads of the households for the Lord. Let me go back to the early pages of the Bible again.

It was Noah, the family man, and not Mrs. Noah who built the ark for the safety of the family and preached the righteousness of God to his generation and community. Noah received the warning, the command and also the covenant and the promises.

It was Abraham, not Sarah, who built the altars to worship God, who entered into a covenant with God, who received the promises, who inherited the blessings, and who led his extended family into covenant relations with the Almighty. In him the families of the earth were to receive their blessings.

It was to the fathers that God addressed Himself in Egypt. The fathers as heads of the households were ordered to prepare the paschal Lamb for the safety and redemption of the family. The responsibility rested squarely upon their heads, and the Lord suggested no substitutes or any other way to safety. Only as they assumed their reponsibilities were the families safe and secure.

It was Caleb, the father, who received the promise of an inheritance, which he later claimed and with which he blessed his family.

It was the nobleman, a father, who came to the Lord Jesus pleading for the life of his son. And it was a burdened and concerned father who brought his demon-possessed son to the disciples for deliverance and healing.

It was to the fathers, in keeping with the Old Testament order, that God through Moses addressed the solemn words: "And thou shalt love the Lord thy God with all thine heart, and with all thy soul, and with all thy might. And these words, which I command thee this day, shall be in thine heart: And thou shalt teach them diligently unto thy children, and shalt talk of them when thou sittest in thine house, and when thou walkest by the way, and when thou liest down, and when thou risest up. And thou shalt bind them for a sign upon thine hand, and they shall be as frontlets between thine eyes. And thou shalt write them upon the posts of thy house, and on thy gates" (Deut. 6: 5-9).

It was to the fathers that Paul wrote the exhortation: "And, ye fathers, provoke not your children to wrath: but bring them up in the nurture and admonition of the Lord" (Eph. 6:4).

These words neither detract from the privileges nor minimize the influences and responsibilities of the mother and other members of the family. But they do focus on the father and emphasize the fact that the father throughout the Scriptures holds the divinely-bestowed key to the family. The husband and father is the rightful door into the family and to household evangelism. This we must practice. There we must seek to enter, whatever the way, whatever the cost. God's way is the surest way, it is the safest way. And, in the long run, it is the fastest and most fruitful way in evangelism.

Let us reach the fathers that we might honor God's way, preserve the God-ordained social unit, evangelize the families, and realize God's ideal in household salvation.

DETOURS IN EVANGELISM

Missions today present an interesting mosaic of activities and organizations. The question is whether we are in the middle of God's stream of flow. How far we have shifted from the biblical thrust and the ideal of God is evident from a study of mission programs and activities. We have missions to women, to students, to youth, to teens, to boys, to girls, to children, etc. We have global movements such as Child Evangelism Fellowship International, Youth for Christ International, Christian Businessmen's Committee International, and so on. We have developed experts in all these fields and are conducting conferences and workshops to perfect our methodology and approaches in these missions. And, let me emphasize, I would be the last to criticize the efforts. They are good and should be continued and intensified. They are needed and are urgent.

But, where are the experts in household evangelism? Where are the organizations that specialize in household evangelism and know from experience in their work the true meaning, blessings and significance of household salvation, winning families as divinely-ordained units to God and building churches out of family units?

Where are the advocates of household evangelism and salvation as the Bible upholds and portrays them? Where are the conferences and workshops to discover principles that govern successful household evangelism and methodologies that will win families to the Lord, that lead to household salvation? Are we not shifting away from the divine ideal and apostolic norm in our methods and approaches?

Who has blinded us against the divine order that we should so completely neglect it? Who has shifted our base of operation? I am well aware of cultural shift and change; I am not trying to set back the clock. However, are we prepared to say that God's ideal and the apostolic norm are not for our age? Are they outworn? Who is more successful in evangelism and church planting than Paul was in his day? Could we have shifted and drifted from the divine ideal and apostolic norm without realizing it? Have our additions, which are good and legitimate, overshadowed the main stream of God's flow of blessings?

Chapter 27

GROUP EVANGELISM

INTRODUCTION

IT IS EVIDENT that society is not a homogeneous unit. It is a mosaic made up of people who form separate units with their own web of characteristics, interests, needs, and relationships, their own way of thinking, and their own way of behavior. The population of almost every country in the world belongs to different races, tribes, clans and families with different cultural, linguistic and religious backgrounds. Economically and socially we speak of them as ruling and ruled, as professional and nonprofessional, as employees and employers, as progressive and nonprogressive, as liberal and conservative, as urban and rural people, as literate and illiterate, as primitive and civilized.

Society is made up of societies of people, of groups who have certain basics of culture, life and mentality in common, and feel bound one to another in a strong and peculiar way. They are social and cultural units within the population. They are a unique people. Therefore, Webster defines people as "all the members of a group having in common traditional, historical, or cultural ties, as distinct from racial and political unity: as, 'the Jewish *people.*' It may also be the persons belonging to a certain place, community, or class: as, the people of (*place*), or the people of wealth." Numerous factors combine to make a people.

We may illustrate the point by looking at the population of Latin America. The people of Latin America are made up of Indians, Caucasians, Negroes, Mongolians, Mestizoes (offspring of Caucasians and Indians), and Mulattoes (offspring of Caucasians and Negroes). Each of these people are again divided according to cultural background, geographical location, social relationships, economic standing, professional status, tribal and clan origin, religious affiliation, etc. They form different groups with different relationships, and the gap between some of them is greater than the gulf between North American or European and many Latin American groups. There is greater social and cultural distance between Buenos Aires and La Paz than there is between Buenos Aires and New York or London. Therefore, the word *people* may be one of the most general concepts.

It may, however, also take on a specialized form and point to a particular group of persons bound together by a strong sense of belonging and solidarity, whether biological, cultural or geographic. In this specialized form the main characteristics of a people are a sense of communality, solidarity, relatedness, and a people consciousness. Most often marriages take place only within this people and outside marriages are frowned upon.

Though the degree may vary considerably, a people is governed by a group-unit mentality and sentiment in which group authority, loyalty, and interest prevail against self-interest, and the individual regards himself only to a degree as an independent and responsible unit. He knows himself related to a community, to a people which are *his* people and which own him as *their* member. Here he lives in dynamic and meaningful relationships.

Our writing deals with a people in the specialized sense, a group of persons in dynamic, living relationships whom we simply designate as group, people, community, or society, that is, a people in community and not just an aggregation of individuals. Therefore, when we speak of group evangelism we have no distinct gospel in mind, but we do think of a different approach than is common in North America or Europe where individualism is supposed to prevail. In group evangelism we are addressing ourselves to the community of persons, or persons in community, to the group in relationship, to a people that knows itself interrelated, that lives in interresponsibility and in community of life.

In our study of the phenomenon of group evangelism and multiple conversion, we shall consider a definition of multiple conversion, presuppositions to group evangelism, the determining attitudes, and the determining practices conducive to group evangelism and consequent multiple conversions. Finally, we shall consider the dangers and advantages of such an endeavor.

GROUP EVANGELISM AND MULTIPLE CONVERSION DEFINED

Group evangelism should not be thought of as the opposite of individual evangelism. Both concern themselves with the communication and the experience of the Gospel of God. Both are personal and emphasize the personal faith-relationship to Jesus Christ as Savior from sin and condemnation. Both aim at the building up of the individual in his personal faith, personal obedience and personal responsibility.

The difference, however, becomes apparent in the immediate goal, approach, methodology and procedure in the ministry. In group evangelism the immediate goal is multiple, simultaneous personal conversions through a gradual and deliberative procedure. The latter is often spoken of as multiple-individual conversion.

Group evangelism and multiple conversions must not be identified or confused with social evangelism. The latter seeks to "evangelize" the social power structures and organizations, social institutions and cultural patterns in order to "save" society and the individual. According to my insight, this reverses the biblical order and the order of group evangelism and multiple conversions. In the latter the approach is people-centered. It seeks the conversion and regeneration of people and only consequent to that the transformation of the social order and cultural patterns. In group evangelism and multiple conversions it is to be recognized that spiritual and personal regeneration is fundamental to society and culture and not the reverse. Social and cultural change are truly meaningful only where religious transformation of the people has taken place.

The deliberative, simultaneous profession of and accession to Christianity of groups of individuals or groups of people consisting of biologically interrelated or sociologically homogeneous units may be termed multiple, group or community conversions. It should be kept in mind that not all such "professions" will be conversions in the full biblical sense. Only God can discern the heart and know whether actual personal faith has been generated by the preaching of the Gospel. The profession, however, indicates a sense of readiness and a willingness to proceed as additional light comes. It also indicates that there will be group support instead of opposition or ostracism for those who go on to perfection. Such units in decision may consist of families, social units, professional units, closely knit communities, tribes, classes or whatever may make up a certain homogeneous unit or occupy a geographical unit—a people with a sense of belongingness and relatedness, social cohesion and mutual attraction. If such a phenomenon results in a rapid spread of Christianity from person to person, from family to family, from group to group through natural, social or cultural ties (the web of relationships), the phenomenon may be designated as people or community movement.

"Where a Christward movement spreads from person to person in such a fashion that related individuals decide for Christ in consultation with each other, and then spread the light to others in their web of relationship, a people movement to Christ develops. This involves both individual and multi-individual conversion along the lines of family and tribal relationships." [1]

Presuppositions to Group Evangelism

The program of group evangelism and group conversion or multiple individual conversion is based upon certain presuppositions.

1. *It assumes that the evangelist takes the psychology, sociology and culture of the people seriously.* He recognizes the web of relationships, whether biological or social within which the individual lives,

He enlists the established and accepted cultural patterns of relationships, channels of communication, functions of roles and structures of authority for the furtherance of the Gospel. As we seek to utilize the technical and mechanical means of communication in spreading the Gospel, that is, radio, television, newspapers, records, and so on, likewise we should harness the cultural network of relationships for the Gospel.

2. *It presumes that evangelism by confrontation for personal decision will be preceded by careful, patient, gradual and persistent penetration and permeation with the Gospel, a process of saturation of the total group or at least the organizational and functional power structures of the given tribe, society or community.* Only through such permeation will group deliberation and decision become a possibility and be made effective. It is well to keep the process and order before us—presentation, penetration, permeation, confrontation. This makes for sound decisions.

A review of the gospels will quickly reveal that this was the approach and method our Lord employed most extensively. He saturated the soil of Galilee by preaching the Gospel of the kingdom extensively and from village to village. However, He gathered no extensive following around Himself, nor did He establish groups of followers. Through His extensive preaching He saturated the soil with the Gospel and prepared the people for the post-Pentecost decision-preaching of the apostles. Numerous churches soon dotted the lands of Judea, Samaria and Galilee (Acts 9:31).

3. *Group evangelism and multi-individual conversions are possible not only in primitive societies but also in advanced and complex cultures.* Man is a social being and a creature of relationships. Consciously or unconsciously, his life is controlled to a great degree by his yearning for social acceptance and social approval. Even the most rigid individualist dreads "social vacuum" and "aloneness." Man always and everywhere acts more freely when group action takes place. He takes greater risks in groups, he portrays greater courage in groups, he is more "man" in groups than being alone. Conversions may be delayed longer but they go deeper, are more lasting, and are more decisive when experienced in groups.

This has been well established by Bishop J. W. Pickett in his extensive, comprehensive and thorough studies of the mass movements in India. Group evangelism and multiple conversions have great advantages. They are possible at all times, in all climes, and in all cultures. Man is not a mechanical being, nor a creature of aloneness. He is a social being and an organism in relationship. Individualism is not his "native" environment. It is artificial and therefore superficial. It is not essential to his being nor well-being. Subconsciously, he is a group being and in crises acts best and deepest in groups.

Group evangelism and multiple conversions are closely related and should be considered as a unit, one being the cause and the other the effect.

DETERMINING ATTITUDES

It must be stated emphatically and without hesitation that ultimately all movements toward Christianity and Christ are the result of the sovereign and gracious ministry of the Holy Spirit. Man by nature does not incline toward the Savior or God. He is at enmity with God and alienated from the fellowship of God. Thus our dependence is upon the Holy Spirit. We read in Zechariah 4:6, "Not by might nor by power, but by my Spirit, saith the Lord of hosts." Yet, the Holy Spirit works through men and means and according to principles. There are certain factors that must become determining attitudes on the part of Christian worker if he is to be used as an instrument of the Holy Spirit in originating and stimulating such a phenomenon within the group and guiding it to an ever-expanding movement.

We recognize four such attitudes.

1. *There must be a thorough conviction of the biblicity of the pattern of group conversions, the possibility and genuineness of it, a Christian appreciation of the value of such conversions, and a wholesome attitude toward the phenomenon.* This is not "one more" approach to multiply believers. This is a basic, biblical approach.

The Bible is written in concepts of races, nations, churches and households, more so than in terms of individuals. It may well be said that the message of God is personal, but it is neither individual nor private. It calls for personal participation, but not for individual and independent participation. (The difference between personal and individual is explained later.) The divine verdict, "It is not good that man should be alone," affects all areas of life and relationships, and is at enmity with Western individualism, a curse that is spreading over the world. The thoughts of God in the Bible are expressed principally in terms of sociological units and sociological concepts which are different in various cultures. At the minimum, however, and according to the Scriptures, such a unit is the family. It may be the extended family (kinship groups) or the joint family (patriarchal or matriarchal family).

It would be helpful for the reader to study the great revivals of the Old Testament that are recorded for our instruction (Gen. 35:1-15; II Chron. 15:1-15; 23; 24; 29–31; 34; 35; Ezra 5; 6. These should be compared with Hag. 1:1-15; Ezra 8–10; Neh. 8:1–10:39).

A careful study should be made of the book of Jonah and the reports of the revival under the preaching of John the Baptist as recorded in the gospels. As God's judgments fall upon nations, so his gracious blessings may flow down upon the nations. Though such experiences never mean universal salvation or even general conversion, there may be a general turning and the creation of an atmosphere and attitude that makes it possible for the blessings of God to break through and bring seasons of refreshing and salvation to countless individuals within the multitude.

There may be vigorous objections that the Old Testament principle of group or national solidarity does not carry over into the New Testament. In the latter not the group, people or nation, but the individual stands before God in judgment and/or salvation. This sounds logical to the Western mentality and in part it is right. But it is neither the complete truth nor even the most important aspect of the truth.

In the Old Testament the individual, too, stood before God on numerous occasions. So did Moses, Aaron, David and many others. There is a personal aspect to Old Testament religion. This is fully established by the writer of Hebrews in his eleventh chapter. There a list of heroes is presented to us, each standing in a personal faith-relationship to the Lord. Faith is always personal. It sharply contradicts the purely collectivistic approach to Old Testament religion. The personal aspect is not lacking in the Old Testament.

Neither is the group solidarity aspect and approach missing in the New Testament. Christ preached and evangelized villages and cities (Mark 1:38, 39). He pronounced His woes over villages and cities. "Woe unto thee Chorazin! Woe unto thee Bethsaida! And thou, Capernaum . . ." (Matt. 11:20; Luke 19:41-44).

Christ ordered His apostles to disciple all nations (Matt. 28:19) and to preach repentance and forgiveness of sins to all nations (Luke 24: 47).

Paul spoke of his startling command, according to which he was sent to the *people* and to the *nations*. His mission was to open their eyes and to turn *them* from darkness to light and from the power (authority) of Satan to God, that *they* might receive forgiveness of sins. He showed the people of Damascus, of Jerusalem, throughout the coasts of Judea, and then the nations that they should repent and turn to God. "I continue unto this day, witnessing . . . that Christ should suffer, and that he should be the first that should rise from the dead, and should shew light unto the people, and to the Gentiles" (Acts 26:17-23).

Most certainly there is a much broader scope of evangelism than most of us are prepared to recognize. There is an ethnic, or group,

or people approach in evangelism which has been either overlooked
or ignored by the Westerner, not because it is not in the Bible, but
because of his mentality of individualism that determines most of his
ways, colors his attitudes, influences his sentiments and directs his
actions.

The principle of group solidarity and approach in evangelism in the
New Testament is well-illustrated in the record of numerous "household conversions and household churches" (Luke 19:9; Acts 10:2,
44, 47, 48; 11:14; 16:31-34; 18:8; Rom. 16:5, 10, 11; I Cor. 1:16;
16:19; Philem. 2). That is the record of homes, entire families as
units turning to Christ. It is further evident in the *community movements* toward Christ that were experienced.

Peter witnessed the fact that "*all* that dwelt at Lydda and Saron . .
turned to the Lord" and "*many* in Joppa believed in the Lord" (Acts
9:35, 42). Communities turned to Christ. Similar experiences are
recorded by implication of the ministry of Paul (Acts 13:49; 14:31
16:5; 19:10, 17-20, 26, 27). Both Jews and Gentiles became alarmed
because of the dimension of the movements that were witnessed throughout Jerusalem, Palestine and Asia Minor (Acts 5:28; 19:26, 27; 21:28
24:5; 28:22).

Another dimension is added by a careful study of the people movements in apostolic times. Paul's report of the tremendous sweep o
the Gospel among the nations brought joy to the brethren, but they
also perceived that *many myriads* (tens of thousands) *of Jews* were
turning to the Lord (Acts 21:19, 20). This is one of the most startling
and informative passages on the marvelous movements toward Christ
among the Jews in apostolic times. They could be described only by
tens of thousands in numbers.

Earlier, Luke reported that in Jerusalem the work of God increased
. . . the number of the disciples multiplied . . . *a great company o
the priests* were obedient to the faith (Acts 6:7). The wording is sig
nificant. Luke carefully preserved the group solidarity concept in the
singular—a great company, or a great crowd—then added the word
priests in the plural. The priests came in units, preserving their social
and professional solidarity. They moved as a group of people. Similar
statements are found in the gospels. The Pharisees and lawyers (col
lectively) rejected the counsel of God against themselves (Luke 7:30)
whereas the soldiers and publicans (note the plural) came (no doub
in groups) to be baptized of John (Luke 3:12-14). In like manner
the sinners and publicans (as groups) gathered around Jesus to hea
Him (Luke 15:1, 2).

The group solidarity concept is embedded in the New Testament—
the household, a people socially, religiously or professionally bound

together, a society, and the community. This must become a guiding star in our evangelism program. To ignore these and by-pass this group solidarity concept is to ignore a major and effective approach in evangelism, and by-pass multiple conversions that could move multitudes to Christ who will but meagerly respond as individuals.

Radical rethinking and reappraisal of our evangelism approaches in the non-Western world is crucial to the advance of the Gospel. We must return to the scripturally recognized social units — households, communities, people—in our evangelism programs if we are to advance and succeed in the command and plan of God.

The sociological implications of New Testament Christianity are beautifully substantiated by a careful study of the deepest sociological concept of the New Testament, the concept of *koinonia* ("fellowship"). Three facts emerge from a such a study.

First, koinonia is a basic factor of Christianity. Without it the gospel experience is incomplete and the Christian life impossible.

Second, koinonia is a concept of relationship. It relates the subject to the object. As such it is a sociological concept, a group concept. It cannot be lived and experienced on a sociological level in solitude.

Third, koinonia is a common but rich word in the Greek language. It expresses the idea of association, partnership, community. Koinonia is the spirit of generous sharing as contrasted with the spirit of selfish grasping, *pleonexia*. Koinonia also may mean business partnership, marriage partnership, or even express man's relationship with the gods.

It is most significant that the Holy Spirit adopted and adapted this social concept to express one of the richest experiences of the Christian and the deepest and most intimate relationships of the Christian life. It adds divine and social content to the personal salvation experience and crowds individualism out of Christianity. If then the fullness of the Christian life is best experienced in social relationships (koinonia), is it out of order to experience its beginning in a similar relationship? Christianity is not antisocial. It is not individualism. It is partnership, relationship, fellowship.

Christianity thus is a religion of vertical and horizontal relationships and cannot be thought of very well without either dimension. It is divine, personal and social in content, experience and dimension. It thrives within relationships. It is intensely personal, but it is also intensely social. These are not contradictory; these are complementary.

A note needs to be inserted here to distinguish between personal and individual. These terms are not synonymous. *Personal* is a psychological term; *individual,* on the other hand, is a sociological term. There is a vast difference.

Let me illustrate. We all appreciate strong personalities, but we do not like strong individualists. The former indicates the integration of a person and the focusing of it upon an ideal to accomplish a purpose and to experience a relationship. The latter concept refers to a person who is centered upon self. Self is the hub of the wheel in which all spokes are focusing. However, the hub is off center and does not relate itself well to the established and accepted way of life.

Let me illustrate it in another way. Gather a choir of one hundred enthusiastic singers. The choir director integrates them, blends their voices and unifies them into a harmonious unit. The music fills the auditorium and echoes back and forth. Two facts stand out in such music if the harmony is perfect—the voices are blended to the degree that no voice can be singled out. All individualism must be eliminated. And, all present do their part.

A question arises, is the singing less personal because it is in a chorus or group? Is it less meaningful to the singer because it is not individual? A dynamic principle is at work. In order that an experience might be genuinely personal it need not be individual. Group action does not interfere with the personal. In fact, it most often enhances and strengthens the personal. This we need to keep in mind when we think of group evangelism and multiple conversions. Such experience does in no way weaken the personal element in conversion; it heightens and intensifies and enriches it. It brings it to its full fruition.

2. *There must be recognition of the uniqueness of the psychology of the different people.* While all people are essentially alike because all were created in the image of God and all have the same qualitative psychological potential, neither the mold nor the configuration of the human soul are the same. The latter two are not essential to man but are the result of the cultural imprint. The mentality of a people can be molded for dictatorship just as it can be formed for democracy. People can be molded for personal responsibility and they can be shaped for social, economic and religious interdependence. They can be molded into individualism that recognizes little social interdependence and that little appreciates social relationships. They can also be made into group-people, bound together by a group psychology and thus appreciate individualism only to a limited degree.

The same principle operates in meanings and values, tastes and appreciations, and in all other relationships and realms of life. Not all people think in terms of absolutes or in terms of purpose, progress and consummation; not all reason according to principles of Aristotelian logic, because people differ in mentality and emotional experiences.

It remains a fact that most non-Western people are possessed by a group psychology. They think of themselves less as individualized units apart from others. They function as a group closely intertwined and interrelated. All decisions, therefore, are group decisions. Individual decisions may be considered as treason. In many primitive communities a criminal may make atonement for murder by paying a fine. For disloyalty to the clan or tribe, which is treason, there can be no atonement and the penalty must necessarily be banishment or death. Group mentality is all-inclusive and dominates every aspect of life, relationship and decision. Only as we understand these people can we expect a positive response from them. And only as we approach them within the framework of their psychology can we expect to make group evangelism and multiple conversions a reality.

It is well to think of at least *three types of mentality*. They are not totally exclusive of each other; they must not be thought of in absolute compartments. They are basic characteristics.

There is a *causative type of mentality*. Its basic question is Why? Western mentality belongs to this type. It is our great heritage from Aristotle and has led to the great cause and effect scientific inventions and world explorations.

There is an *intuitive type of mentality*. This is the basic characteristic of the East and underlies the great religious movements of Asia. It is often forgotten that all living religions of the world had their source in Asia. The great intuitive mentality of the East is fertile soil for religious activities.

There is the *imaginative type of mentality*. Somehow there is a live and dynamic link between imagination and mentality. Not logic but imagination sets off the spark that motivates the thought process. The rich but little-explored mythology, legends and folklore, and the native ability for drama, in the African culture and soul and among Latin America's primitive Indians are the best embodiments and fullest expressions of this type of mentality.

The difference in mentality plays a tremendous role in communication. Each basic type requires a unique type of literature, if it is to be penetrated.

It is well to keep in mind that the non-Western mentality is different in its characteristics.

(a) It is passive in contrast to being dynamic and inventive. It shuns the new, holds fast to the past, and only slowly adopts the foreign. It is characterized by cultural and religious conservatism.

(b) It is introspective and mystical and thus cares less for the factual and logical. The historical is of lesser importance than the mystical, the awesome, the secretive, the intuitive. The spectacular is attractive and appealing.

(c) It is communal or collective and thus the individual regards himself only to a slight degree as an independent and responsible unit.

He thinks in terms of the family, the clan, the tribe, the people, and now even in terms of the nation. Group authority, loyalty and interest prevail against self-interest. It is a group-unit mentality and sentiment.

(d) It is traditional rather than prophetic. Its golden age lies in the past. It is bound up with its ancestors and history. Change and progress are its enemies. The past is made sacred by their divine ancestors and honored by ancestor worship.

(e) It is exclusive and promotes a strong feeling toward the in-group. It regards its people as a holy community. It is "the people."

(f) It lacks balance and proportion in the triple psychological functions of emotions, cognition and volition, with the first often being dominant and strongly developed.

(g) It is a mentality of continuum. It lives in an inner symbiosis with nature. The gods, man, animals, and nature form one unbroken continuum. They represent a total union of the temporal and eternal, the human and divine, the spiritual and the material in social structures that have been sacralized, a society in which all orders of the status quo possesses divine authority and therefore cannot be challenged.

In contrast to these characteristics, Western mentality has been characterized as being dynamic, factual, causative, inventive, individualistic, universalistic, adaptive and flexible.

Of course, these characteristics must not be accepted as absolute; all of them will not apply everywhere. However, they point up certain basic distinctives and differences that must be taken into consideration if a message is to be communicated effectively and a people is to be interpreted fairly.

3. *There must be respect for the cultural web of relationships within which man has his life and being.* Culture is both his protection and his problem, his strength and his enslavement. It must be kept in mind that culture is not only a part of his environment from which man can separate himself at will. It is part of his very personality and thus without this culture man cannot preserve his selfhood. Man is held captive by a certain biological and also cultural heritage from which he is unable to escape. Man has a past, a history within himself as well as about himself from which he cannot free himself completely.

Man is neither neutral in himself (he is a sinful being), nor is he born into a culturally neutral world. He cannot carve out his own destiny according to some ideal all his own. He comes into a culturally conditioned atmosphere and society that is not of his own making or choosing, but which mercilessly makes him into its patterns and ideals, casting him into a cultural, social and psychological mold that he will never be able to shed without sustaining serious hurt in his self-image. As a being of culture man is, indeed, a captive in a prison house.

It has been well stated, "The chief obstacles to the conversion of large numbers of people are not sins for which they as individuals are wholly or chiefly responsible. They are sins of the group of which they are members, or of the society in which they are enmeshed." [2]

On the other hand, man's decisions, strength, progress, health of personality and effectiveness of life and service are determined largely by his web of cultural and social relationships. He cannot divest himself of that which is part of his life and personality. These are the streams of his life; there is his at-homeness; there his sense of belongingness finds fulfillment; there he makes his contribution; and there his witness counts most as it is also needed most. We must find him in his web of relationships and lead him to the Lord in it, without unnecessarily disturbing this relationship.

Individual man is not only to be rescued, he is to become the doorway into his home and society. None liveth unto himself. This is especially true of the Christian. He needs to remain a member within a web of relationships. As evangelizing agents we must keep in mind that Christ won His disciples in their social and cultural environment and nurtured them to full strength in it. So he also left the Samaritans in their culture. The early Jewish church grew and prospered in the atmosphere of the temple.

Our approaches and methods must become culture-conditioned, though our gospel message is supracultural and absolute. (See Chapter 30, "Cultural Adaptations.")

4. *There must be a conscious and deliberate refocusing of our missionary endeavors and programs of evangelism.* Mission activities have become multiform and evangelistic programs have greatly diversified as they have also multiplied. We dare not become overcritical of honest efforts and serious endeavors. Neither should we give the impression that it is possible to design a blueprint and pattern for effective ministries, covering all cases. It has been well stated, "The abiding temptation of all 'movements' is to bind the Holy Spirit to a method and message which He has used and blessed at a particular moment in history" and, I might add, in a particular place and culture. [3]

This is rather simplistic. Differences and variations there must be, as there are differences in personalities, psychologies and cultures. An evangelistic method producing tremendous results in one area and among one people will not necessarily be the best method for producing equal results in another area and among another people. A certain degree of experimentation and variation will always accompany Christian missions. There will always be some variables and a certain element of unpredictability. We must reckon with these facts. They must not, however, dominate our thinking, nor keep us from planning, evaluating and redesigning our work. If our goal is not clearly defined, our focus will not be clear nor our way steady and progressive, though we may be moving ahead and are exerting great efforts.

Little evangelical work is submitted to rigorous scientific evaluation and tests to measure the actual results and accomplishments of the efforts and sacrifices invested. Evaluations are seldom welcome and much less are the results appreciated. We seemingly fear changes, though we deny we hold to rigid and frozen positions. The well-trodden path, the familiar patterns, the usual way of doing things are mostly uncritically repeated year after year. A science of missions and evangelism, stringent annual evaluations, overall planning and rigid coordination of all means toward a clearly defined goal are scorned by many. These do not fit into their framework of spirituality, a life led by the Holy Spirit, and a ministry performed under His direction.

From the biblical point of view, such a position is theologically indefensible, not matter how honestly motivated and sincerely held. Theologically speaking, this position conceives the mystic, moment-by-moment, individualistic ministry of the Holy Spirit as being superior to the rational (not rationalistic), long-range directive ministry of the Holy Spirit to a group of spiritually-minded men, prayerfully seeking to design a strategy to guide the work in a most effective way to a predefined goal.

The latter position seemingly finds support in the Apostle Paul. He clearly followed a plan in his ministry. He agreed with Peter on the fields of labor. He was able to dispatch his fellow-laborers to prepare the way for him in several cities. He announced to the churches his intended comings and goings. Most certainly, Paul made room for divine interventions and redirections. But he had his plan and his strategy. He had a course that he sought to finish, and when he had completed it, he was conscious of it (Acts 20:24; II Tim. 4:7).

Man seldom achieves more than he aims for; he does not accomplish much more than he is equipped to do. Evangelical missions and evangelism programs thus far have achieved few people movements and community conversions because their missionary thinking did not include these concepts; their ministries were not focused upon such accomplishments. Their programs did not include such movements; their workers were not prepared to handle or initiate such experiences.

A conscious and deliberate refocusing is required if we are to bear more fruit. We must set our goal on winning a people to the Lord—families, communities, tribes, social units, professions, classes, religious units, or whatever may make up a certain homogeneous unit, a people who for all practical purposes function as a unit, carry within them a strong sense of belongingness, practice social cohesion, and experience mutual attraction.

We also must be willing to acquire the spiritual, psychological, sociological and cultural ways, techniques and methods to achieve the goal and tenaciously pursue this purpose without wavering or faltering. It can be done because it is within the plan and purpose of God to win whole groups of people and communities unto Himself.

Chapter 28

DETERMINING PRINCIPLES

MULTIPLE CONVERSIONS are not mere happenings, even though they may seem that way to the casual onlooker. They are determined by definite principles, specific laws of relationship, and regulated practices. This fact places heavy responsibilities upon the Christian worker, seeing that the worker can easily become the main obstacle and obstruction in great movements that could bring multitudes into the Kingdom of God.

An incipient movement may readily be thwarted or paralyzed, not only because of attitudes, but also because the guiding human instrument may be violating or ignoring some determining and dynamic principles. Great wisdom and caution, but also great vision, faith and daring action, are required to see large multitudes move into the Kingdom of God. We must learn to trust the Holy Spirit to equip us and to use us as instruments in guiding and inducing people and communities to move unitedly into the fold of God.

Nothing is impossible with God. As in the days of old, so today he can motivate and mightily draw multitudes unto Himself. Let not Western individualism prejudice us and minimize or obscure the fact of the "multitudes" and "great numbers" in the record of the book of Acts. These are accounts of actual happenings. Multitudes did believe. Communities did move into the fold of God. Churches did multiply daily. These facts are recorded for our encouragement and instruction. They ought to bolster our faith and raise our expectations.

We cannot enter fully into a discussion of the dynamic factors that seem to impel and propel larger and smaller groups of people. These constitute a complex that deserves extensive studies and cannot be presented in one chapter. (*Note:* The author is preparing a separate volume dealing with these factors at length.) However, to assist in group evangelism and multiple conversions, I present four basic principles which, if carefully heeded, will greatly assist in this complex yet fruitful approach in evangelism. These four principles may be stated in four brief headings:

(1) The relevance of the message and group evangelism;
(2) Gospel saturation and group evangelism;
(3) Cultural adaptation and group evangelism;
(4) Mobilization and training of believers and group evangelism.

THE RELEVANCE OF THE MESSAGE AND GROUP EVANGELISM

It is generally agreed that the Christian message must be understood, at least in part, by the people who are to respond to it. Because of this, missionaries learn the language of the people to whom they go. And because of this the Scriptures are being translated into the numerous and at times difficult languages of the people.

While the Gospel strongly appeals to the conscience, it no less appeals to the intellect of man. It is well to note such words as "consider," "remember," "we know" in the New Testament. The message must make sense to the people. It must be intellectually apprehensible, though not necessarily comprehensible. Without such understanding it will remain a mystery that is to be manipulated by some medium. It is no more than magic under Christian names.

There always will be a super-rational aspect to the Gospel, just as Christianity is supernatural. Also, there will be a mystical element which appeals more to the emotions than to cognition. Neither will the will of man remain untouched, unchallenged and uninvolved. However, if it is to accomplish its purpose, the Gospel must become meaningful to the people. It must be relevant, it must appeal to some conscious desire and it must meet some consciously felt need.

All people demand good reasons for changing religion or for embracing Christianity. Therefore, before Christianity will become meaningful, it must discover areas of severe frustrations between aspirations and fulfillment, imbalance between wants and obtainments, tension between the idealized and the realized. In primitive societies such inner strains will most often exist in daily needs of life—food, hunting, fishing, etc.—or in aspirations that have been created in the minds by observing people outside of their own commune, and for which their culture and religion do not make provision—learning to read and to write in order to gain some kind of status or become first-rate citizens.

In more sophisticated civilizations, frustrations and tensions increase because the ideals and aspirations of the people are running ahead of what can be provided to meet such demands. Sad to say, most such ideals are materialistic in nature. How to make the Gospel relevant to such mentality is a most serious question. Yet, if we are to arrest the attention of the people and win a hearing from the masses, we must find some point of attraction.

Besides discovering aspirations, expectations and areas of frustrations, imbalance and tensions as points of departure, the Christian worker must set himself to work in a systematic way, and by teaching and example awaken specific and desired spiritual needs in the minds and hearts of the people he is serving. If he is a true New Testament missionary, he desires nothing more fervently than to see in the people a need for the message of the cross and the risen Savior. Such need, however, is not necessarily present in the conscious mind of the people. It should not be expected to be present as a conscious and defined need. The missionary can, however, assuredly build upon certain undefined, vague feelings, an awareness of God, or a higher spirit, sin and salvation. These concepts are not there in a clearly defined manner. Only the raw and crude material for them is present in man. Such awareness is there because man was created in the image of God, because of the fall of man, and because of the purpose of God for man which includes salvation. Within the very being of man and in the subsoil of man's consciousness, feelings lie buried which by the preaching of the Word can be restored into full consciousness and dynamic forces.

Man carries within himself a dim awareness of guilt and fear for the supernatural and ultimate power, whether that be a person or some object of power. Such subconscious need, dim and undefined, lives on in the soul of man and manifests itself in the sacrificial religious systems, placations, prayers and other rites of the world. These are basically an attempt to placate the gods and the spirits. They are a crude form of atonement. Why such placation should be necessary is not always defined. More often man has projected his guilt and fear and reads malice and caprice into the character of his gods.

In preaching the Gospel to such people, it is well to keep in mind that the cross of Christ gains its saving significance from Sinai, and grace receives its divine glory and urgency from the law, which reveals in part the character and the demands of God. The cross becomes redemptive in experience only where the law has created the image of an ethical God, before whom man stands guilty and condemned. The foundation of New Testament atonement is the Old Testament ethical monotheism.

Too often we are in a hurry to announce the good news of the Gospel of Jesus Christ, without realizing that the Bible sets the Gospel into a unique frame of reference. While in the New Testament the Gospel of God is dominant, which springs from the God of love, light and righteousness, the *leitmotif* of the Old Testament is ethical monotheism. A concept of God who is good and holy, yea, so holy that He cannot behold iniquity, transforms sin into sin as personal transgression, guilt and defilement, so that it separates God and man and condemns man as sinner from the presence of God. Ethical monotheism makes sin more than human weakness, a fault due to environment. It makes sin so sinful that it justly deserves death. Ethical monotheism makes the cross necessary, and gives to the cross soteriological meaning and significance. A right concept of ethical monotheism, therefore, is an essential prerequisite to feel the need of the Gospel of God.

Too often we forget that a right and deep concept of sin does not spring from hammering on sin, but from a right concept of God. Our emphasis in preaching the Gospel, therefore, is not primarily on the sins of the people, but on the concept of the God of the people.

His concept of God is the all-determining factor of man. It will dominate and determine the course and the attitudes and appetites of his life. It will make him into a sinner and into a saint. It will cause him either to flee God or to draw near to God. There is little relevance in the preaching of the cross where there is not a sense of guilt and condemnation. Relevant gospel preaching presupposes a consciousness of sin which springs from a biblical image of God.

The message of the Gospel is of paramount importance. It is the heavenly treasure committed to us, to make it known meaningfully throughout the world. To present it meaningfully, it must be intelligible and related to man in his needs. To discover areas of tension as points of departure, and awaken a need for the Gospel of Jesus Christ will take time and much wisdom. Patience and perseverance are needed; much listening to the people is necessary; diligent and systematic teaching is required in order to win a hearing in the end. The message must "scratch where it itches" if it is to be of value to the individual. The value and practicability of making the message relevant is attested by Christian and non-Christian movements. I have already referred to the message of New Life For All in Nigeria.

Significantly, Dr. Emilio Willems tells us: "If we compare the religious movements of the northeast (Brazil) with the emergence of the Protestant churches as sects, two characteristics seem to be common to all: The followers constitute part of an underprivileged mass of people whose socioeconomic situation has made them susceptible to *the message* of a religious leader. *The message* invariably contains the promise of a better life. Such betterment invariably requires immediate changes, part and parcel of which are the ascetic ways of life." [1] (Italics mine.)

Relevance of message does not mean preaching the Bible in general terms. We begin with emphases of the Gospel that particularly strike home, in order that the truth initially preached might be used as a wedge to open the heart to the total truth of God. No heart, no society, no culture is so completely closed that it becomes impossible to drive a wedge into it, if we but discover the opening, the tensions, frustrations, anticipations, aspirations in that particular society and culture.

> The culture of a nation is an indivisible unity: it is a system of tenets, principles, customs which are all interdependent. That is true, but it is not absolutely true. The culture of a nation tries to become an indivisible unity but it never succeeds. Somewhere in its structure *there is a hidden crack*. The culture of a nation is a product of human work, but there is an untraceable influence in it that cannot be scrutinized because it has its origin in the mercy of God. . . . This mysterious influence cannot be ascribed to man's virtuousness; it is not credited to man's account. It is not man's aptitude or his nobility. It comes from the mercy of God.[2] (Italics mine.)

It is our solemn responsibility to find this "crack" and plant the dynamic of God—the Gospel of God—into it, with the prayer and assured hope that by a sudden explosion or gradual expansion it eventually will open the hearts to the message of God, the Gospel of His salvation.

These facts are well-substantiated by extensive experiences and research. I discussed with Mr. John Beekman of the Wycliffe Bible Translators the several larger tribal movements Wycliffe had experienced. I asked Mr. Beekman to enumerate some of the dynamic factors in such movements. Without hesitation he replied that the most central factor was a relevant message, the message of a Lord who is able to deliver from all evil spirits. Uppermost in the hearts of these people was not a guilt consciousness but the fear of evil spirits. They yearned for a Deliverer. This they found in Christ the Lord. He then recounted several such movements in Mexico and Peru where this had been the case.

Similarly, it has been established that either the Lordship of Christ or the power of the Holy Spirit most appeals to the people of Latin America, especially the lower classes who still hold to a semi-animism, or spiritism, and are plagued by a fear of evil spirits. It is the message which in part constitutes the great appeal of the Pentecostals to the Latin American heart. Here is a message that saves from the fear of evil forces here and now.

The factor of the relevance of the message has been greatly neglected in evangelistic movements and church growth studies. We do not attribute this to an indifference to the message of the Gospel. Rather, it is naively taken for granted that evangelists and evangelicals are always presenting a relevant message because they preach the Bible. However, it is seldom recognized that they do so without concerning themselves with people in their psychological mood, social aspirations, cultural milieu and religious cravings. Therefore, their message may or may not be relevant to the people they seek to reach. Lack of response in evangelism is not always an indication that the people are resistant and unresponsive. It may be because the message does not appear meaningful to the people, either because it is presented in unfamiliar ways or it does not strike home.

Chapter 29

GOSPEL SATURATION

WE HAVE SPOKEN of the relevant message and the intelligible manner of its presentation. Man must at least in part understand the message and he must deem it meaningful if he is to accept it.

There is, however, another dimension to group evangelism. It is difficult for us to grasp how slow man is to realize the value of the Gospel of God. The denseness of the human heart and the dimness of the human mind in spiritual matters are difficult to understand. Yet, such is the case. Paul speaks of it in terms of spiritual blindness. He declared: "If our gospel is hid [veiled], it is hid [veiled] to them that are lost: In whom the god of this world hath blinded the minds of them which believe not, lest the light of the glorious gospel of Christ . . . should shine in" (II Cor. 4:3, 4).

Few people turn to Christ at the first hearing of the good news. It is more general in the history of missions to speak of years of patient and hard toil, mingled with tears and prayers, before visible results can be registered. Recent interviews of some eighty Muslim converts to Christ revealed that the average Muslim had heard the Gospel some two hundred and forty times before it gripped his heart and conscience sufficiently to turn him to Christ. While the response to the Gospel differs greatly, it is wishful thinking to imagine that mankind stands on tiptoes waiting for the gospel messenger to bring the gospel message. In general, resistance is to be expected. At least, we must be prepared for such situations.

I am well aware of the difference in present-day mission areas and peoples. We are surrounded by vast masses of people relatively open to the Gospel, and we speak of them as high potential areas. These areas ought to be occupied and aggressively evangelized at all speed. They will not forever wait for the Gospel. Either they will harden or some other philosophy or movement will capture them. In fact the speedy spread of Communism is in part because of the slowness of the church to move with the Gospel into high potential areas. On the other hand, we have highly resistant people. It is most tragic that missions are so institutionalized that they are unable to take advantage of the open and white harvest fields in the world. However, such emphasis upon the high potential areas should not divert us from the occupation of the resistant fields. The shift into the harvest fields, while absolutely essential, should not come at the expense of the other fields. It should rather come at the cost of the large reserves at home and the untapped masses of national laymen in the various fields. We must never forget that long and tedious labors have preceded the present harvest situation. There is a time for sowing and there is a time for reaping. This is explicitly taught by our Lord, who knows the laws of the natural and the spiritual and is well-acquainted with the fields of the world (John 4:35-38). Not every field is immediately a harvest field.

Because this is so, it is well to think of an orderly and progressive process in gospel saturation before aggressive confrontation in evangelism can begin. This is especially so if we aim at group evangelism with the expected multi-individual or group conversions.

We may analyze the movement of evangelism in previously untouched areas in four progressive steps: (1) presentation, (2) penetration, (3) permeation, and (4) confrontation.

The intelligible communication of the divine message is necessary if it is to be understood sufficiently so as to become meaningful to the people. Slowly it begins to penetrate the hearts of individuals, society and culture. Penetration, as it accumulates through frequent repetition of the same truths, eventually results in permeation.

This process of saturation is difficult to hasten. It takes time to absorb, to digest and to consider the message presented. It all seems so new, so different. Only as individuals, households and other social groupings are saturated by the Gospel can deliberation and consultation about the Gospel take place. To hasten the process may arrest the movement and destroy the goal of multi-individual or group conversions. Only as saturation has reached a certain degree, and deliberation and consultation have taken place, does confrontation become advisable. Saturation is essential to meaningful confrontation and sound decisions.

Much evangelism specializes in confrontation. This is the right emphasis in areas and among people where the groundwork has been laid and the counsel of God has been taught. Confrontation, however, without the necessary saturation is futile. It may result in numerous responses and professions, but in few regenerations and lasting results. Such failure is not because the motivation is not right in the respondent, but simply because the seed of regeneration is not present and the new birth does not take place.

Much is being said about successful follow-up ministries. We have awakened to the fact that many professions do not necessarily mean many converts and potential candidates for church membership. Such emphasis upon follow-up or, perhaps better, follow-through is sound and timely. It cannot be overemphasized. It is, however, not the complete answer. Perhaps not even the main answer, at least not in the so-called mission fields of the world.

Careful preparation in penetration, permeation, and the building of new and biblical concepts of God, sin and moral accountability before confrontation are at least as significant as a sound follow-through program after confrontation. The cultivation of the individual hearts and of the total society to be evangelized by diligent communication, deep penetration and thorough permeation are absolutely necessary if meaningful confrontation and deliberative decisions are to take place.

However, to fail in confrontation when saturation has taken place may become psychologically harmful to society and the individual. Psychological conditioning to the claims of Christ and the Gospel of God may take place. Eventually this makes the message meaningless and impotent. This danger is as real as premature confrontation. This danger is particularly real where much emphasis is placed on Christian education without the appropriate and timely call for decisions. This danger hangs like a dark cloud over many Christian institutions in the mission fields, where the teaching of religion becomes just another subject in the school curriculum. Great wisdom and deep spiritual insight and guidance are required to know just when God's moment has come to confront the people very definitely with the claims of Christ, and lead them to a definite decision for Christ.

We have stated previously that the cross of Christ becomes relevant and subjectively meaningful only where ethical monotheism has laid hold of the mind and conscience of man. It is well to concentrate in the process of saturation on ethical monotheism, in order to give to man a true and biblical image of God. This is an absolute necessity if the sin is to become exceedingly sinful to man, and if the consciousness of personal accountability is to become effective in man. These concepts should be richly illustrated from the Bible and presented from various angles to stamp them indelibly upon the moral consciousness and conscience of man and society. Only as these concepts become alive in man will man see the need for a Savior and call upon His name in repentance and faith.

Many of the moral struggles in the churches of pagan background are the result of an inadequate or distorted concept of the God of holiness and righteousness. In many people this concept is almost totally lacking. Because we have failed in impressing the biblical image of God upon the mind and conscience of man, man has a superficial view of God as love, a love more related to sentimentality than holiness. Consequently, a superficial view of sin and moral accountability has resulted. In the concept of God the battle for regeneration, sanctification and dedication is either lost or won. A clear concept and a deep penetration and permeation of the God of holiness and righteousness will lead to a deep appreciation of atonement and grace and deep repentance from sin. It will become a deep motivation in personal sanctification and dedication. Let us make sure that the foundations of our evangelism programs are deep and lasting, and confrontation is built upon saturation of the right kind.

The principle of gospel saturation by meaningful communication, penetration and permeation is best illustrated in the ministry of our Lord in Galilee and Judea. For three years He faithfully sowed the seed. There was, however, relatively little direct confrontation, though His claims were clearly and emphatically stated and the conditions of discipleship were specific and defined. Neither are incidents lacking in direct confrontation. His repeated, "Follow me!" was direct and specific.

However, in general, Jesus seemingly did not aim at confrontation too strongly. In fact, the Jews accused Him of being insufficiently decisive and holding them in suspense (John 10:24). Whether such accusations were justified must be seriously questioned. It seems more due to their denseness of spiritual discernment than to the indefiniteness of Christ's claims and challenges. However, it seems to indicate that Christ aimed more at saturation than at confrontation. He postponed the latter to the post-Pentecost preaching of the apostles and evangelizing lay people. That they entered into a real harvest field and did not fail in the matter of confrontation is evident from the report of Luke, who reported that the churches in Judea, Samaria and Galilee multiplied (Acts 9:31). A considerable number of churches sprang up soon after Pentecost. They had, indeed, entered into a harvest where they had not sown, but others had sown before them.

A modern demonstration of this principle is Latin America. In no mission field in the world have Bible colporteurs traveled more faithfully and extensively than in Latin America. No modern mission field is blessed with such a number of mission-sponsored radio stations (some twenty-eight are at work) and radio programs sponsored over publicly and privately owned radio stations as Latin America is. The message of God is poured into this continent as into no other continent in the world, with the exception of North America. Communication and penetration aiming at permeation are the daily experience of countless individuals, villages and social groupings. Today Latin America, at least the lower strata of society, beckons for tactful confrontation culturally adapted to the psychology and sociology of Latin America. It calls for a relevant message and a functional dynamism to harvest vast populations of highly potential people.

Japan and certain areas of Africa are rapidly developing into similar situations. Great things are in store for the Christian church in these parts of the world. It should become possible to move households, communities and whole social and professional groupings into the fold of Christ, if only the Christian forces would ready themselves, grasp the principles of group evangelism, apply the principles and practices carefully, adapt themselves culturally, and find ways and means to communicate the Gospel meaningfully within the framework of their cultures and in keeping with their psychology and sociology.

Gospel saturation is of great importance for meaningful gospel confrontation. It becomes absolutely imperative to group evangelism and multi-individual or group conversions. Without it group conversion is impossible. We thus urge diligent work in saturation, without neglecting meaningful confrontation.

In the light of the process—presentation, penetration, permeation and confrontation—the prolonged "Good News Crusades" of the Assemblies of God deserve special research. They seem to be singularly blessed of God in preserving greater percentages of professions than most campaigns result in.

Chapter 30

CULTURAL ADAPTATION

CULTURE IS A STERN REALITY. It is as extensive as man and as comprehensive as his ways, thoughts, sentiments and relationships. It is the all-encompassing nonbiological atmosphere of his being, as well as the institutions that make his life tolerable and mold him into the being he actually is. Without culture man is not truly human, though it is not a part of his essential being. Yet, it is part of us and it is in us. We are not fully aware of its presence, nor can we completely measure it. It is the omnipresent ocean in which we find ourselves and which molds us until it is our way of life. We live our culture. Man is a child and a captive of his culture and in general appreciates it.

Culture is not easy to define. In simplest terms it may be thought of as the nonbiological heritage of man. Basically it consists of:
(1) a body of beliefs;
(2) practices and patterns of behavior directly related to this body of beliefs;
(3) a resultant way of life, social relationships, psychological mood, attitudes, tastes and sentiments, value system, thought forms, patterns and content and life and world view.

We may visualize it in the diagram on the following page.

In order to understand the web of our relationships, we classify culture and then briefly state its rationale.

TYPES OF CULTURE

From the standpoint of social relationships, cultures may be divided into *four different types:*

First, the culture of individualism. In this culture each person is individualized to the degree of individual moral and social responsibility to make his own major decisions of life, know his own accountability, and pursue his own course and goal. Social determinism is at a minimum. (Basically Western.)

Second, the family type of culture. Here the family is a most closely knit unit with the father (or mother) as the deciding voice and ruling authority. Filial piety and family cohesion are the major marks of this culture. (Basically Eastern.)

Third, the community type of culture. Here the community or village is the decisive unit. Though there may be considerable stratification, each class is required to play its role in the community for proper

The Resultant Way of Life
Our Culture, Our Society

Life and World View

Practices and
Patterns
of Behavior Directly
Related to These
Beliefs

BODY OF BELIEFS

communal functioning, progress and security. The community may be geographical or social. (Basically Muslim.)

Fourth, the tribal type of culture. Here society is held together by a network of real or imaginary relationships with almost complete submergence of the individual to the group. The tribe is a people. (Basically African.)

In all of these types, however, culture bears the following *qualities:*

It is man's pragmatic approach to life. It is an adaptive mechanism and as such it is a body of ready-made solutions to the tensions and problems encountered by the group as well as by the individual.

It is man's moral approach to life. It is an embodiment of the sum total of the group's values and value judgments, resulting in the position that my culture is right and the best. It expresses the cumulative wisdom of the ages.

It is man's rational approach to life. It is a structure erected on a set of presuppositions. Every culture is the embodiment of a world and life view. It has subjective meaning and purpose. It is rational, natural and most often sacred to the people.

It is man's social approach to life. It is a common social heritage that makes for cohesion and solidarity to insure the security, harmony and survival of the group life.

It is man's institutional approach to life. It is an institutionalized functional way of life, which though stable is yet dynamic and in continuous tension between adaptation and conservation.

It is man's organismic or functional approach to life. It is an organismic whole in which no part can be understood properly if taken out of its social and cultural context. Any tradition or pattern can be evaluated correctly only in the light of its relation to other elements of the culture. In culture man expresses his desire for comprehensiveness, wholeness, completeness.

It is man's religious approach to life. It is a design of life that relates man to the mystery and forces of nature in order to control them for man's benefit and ward off seeming threats from an unseen yet felt world. It is man's design by which he seeks to relate himself meaningfully to that which seems to him the Ultimate.

Culture cannot be regarded lightly. It is that which makes life possible, tolerable and worthwhile. It gives meaning and purpose to life. It is the social, moral, rational and sacred basis of life, and insures the orderliness and continuity of group life as procreation assures the biological continuity of a people. It is doubly significant among animistic people who believe themselves socially and culturally related to their deceased ancestors who cannot change their way of life in the beyond. We must therefore expect resistance to any form of drastic change.

In view of the above, it is almost unreasonable to expect a people to step out of their culture, as it were, and come and listen to our message delivered within the framework and value system of our culture, even when we use their vocabulary. If we desire the people to move with us into the sphere of Christianity and to find Christ, we must first move into their midst. Cultural adaptations, social identification and religious empathy of the Christian worker must be made as nearly as possible without losing his own identity. All methods, patterns of operation and channels and patterns of communication must be culturally adapted. All strangeness must be removed as far as possible without endangering the message of Christianity. An atmosphere of at-homeness must prevail if Christianity is to attract the people.

The principle of cultural adaptation, social identification and religious empathy was fully embodied in Christ as He lived among men, as He taught and as He performed His miracles. He was not a cultural, social or religious stranger among His people. He lived and moved among them, yet above them to be both their attractive teacher and their Savior. He tells His would-be followers as undershepherds, "A stranger will they [the sheep] not follow, but will flee from him: for they know not the voice of strangers" (John 10:5).

This does not refer only to false theology or false religious leaders. This may also refer to honest missionaries who remain strangers culturally and socially, and often even at heart, to the people they have come to serve. We must disrobe ourselves of our foreignness, as far as humanly possible, and become one with the people until we too can say with Paul: I became all things to all men that by all means I might win some.

Cultural adaptation is of utmost significance. The degree of its achievement will in a great measure determine the degree of the dynamic loosed within a movement and the ease of the flow of communication. Cultural roadblocks and social defense mechanisms may become formidable obstructions to the Gospel. These will be lessened by cultural adaptation and social identification.

We should not deceive ourselves, however, that these techniques will completely erase man's inherent enmity of God and make the cross naturally attractive. This will never be the case. Man's heart is darkened and wicked and at enmity with God. Only the gracious and miraculous ministry of the Holy Spirit is able to break those defenses. Cultural adaptation and social identification should, however, facilitate our approaches to the people and win us a hearing.

It must also be remembered that no culture is absolutely neutral nd is a fit vessel for the Gospel and Christianity. The Gospel and Christianity stand in judgment over all cultures. The cross of Christ manifests itself everywhere. No culture remains intact when Christ moves in. He is the great transformer. Regeneration of heart and culture takes place wherever Christ lives and is enthroned.

CULTURAL ADAPTATION AND CHURCH ORGANIZATION

As cultural adaptation affects the missionary's life and the communiation of the Gospel, so it also affects the organization of the church. This is far more important than it is often realized. In fact, this is one of the reasons for the rapid spread of Pentecostalism in many parts of the world. We consider, therefore, the relationship of church organiation to the existing culture.

The church of Jesus Christ is a living, dynamic functional organism. As the body of Christ it receives its life, unity, function, purpose and dynamic from Christ through the indwelling Holy Spirit. Its life flows along lines of relationships rather than structure. For sure, all organsms are also organized and do exist in a structured form. However, structure is not the fundamental element. While structure belongs to he organism, each living body creates its own form. All organization n the church, therefore, must remain subservient to the purpose of unctionalism. The Bible is not interested in church organization for organization's sake. The organization must enhance, facilitate, strength-n, perfect and channel function, never frustrate it.

In order that organization might serve in this manner it is of utmost mportance that the nature and function of the church be recognized t least to a limited degree. Though difficult to define or describe, we shall attempt to do so briefly.

In simplest terms a church may be described as a *more or less permanent, relatively stable body of believers* (1) in fellowship and worship; (2) bound together in an accepted order and by common xperiences, beliefs, practices, meanings, values, and purposes; (3) according to the Word of God as interpreted by them; (4) rightly related o God through Christ by the Holy Spirit; and (5) rightly related to ach other as members of one community.

Though it is the prerogative of such a group to define its various unctions in detail, certain basics cannot be omitted if it is to be a New Testament church. These minimal functions are four: (1) Fellowship (*koinonia*) for worship of God and the building up of the members of the body of Christ into disciples of Christ. This process will include both training in the Word of God as well as discipline according to the Word of God. (2) Witnessing (*marturion*). This word appears in its several forms 173 times in the New Testament. In many references this concept refers to the experiential aspect of making known the meaning and message of the Gospel of Jesus Christ in the life of the individual believer and the collective life of the church. Witnessing played a tremendous part in the early church. In fact, Christ made His disciples primarily into witnesses. (3) Preaching (*kerugma*). This is the proclamation of the Word of God for the edification of the saints and the exposition of the Gospel for the conversion of sinners. (4) Service (*diakonia*). This is another significant and dynamic word used more than one hundred times in the New Testament. It is these functional, dynamic concepts of fellowship, witnessing, preaching, evangelizing, and service that church organization must enhance. It must facilitate and expedite their unfolding, practice and progress.

Organization which is to serve rather than to dominate, therefore, will bear certain qualifying characteristics. We summarize them under three captions.

It must be functional. As such it will be flexible, adaptable and always purposive. Organization has no self-image. It does not exist for itself. It exists to serve, yea, it is a service agency with no desire of self-perpetuation. It does not seek consistency, except the consistency of being functional and subservient to the organism it serves.

It must be minimal. This will avoid confusing the people and detracting them from the essential, the function of the church. This principle shines through clearly in the ministry of Paul and the churches he established. It is noteworthy that in some churches Paul mentioned only one office, while in another there are two offices. Some would even find three.

Luke reported that when Paul revisited in Pisidia the first churches he planted, he appointed elders in every church. Nothing is said about deacons. In the same manner Titus was instructed to ordain elders in every city. The churches had not yet advanced sufficiently to require two types of servants. This was not so in the churches where Timothy was laboring. There elders as well as deacons were found. The minimal seemingly was Paul's norm and ideal.

It must be natural (indigenous). We must remind ourselves constantly that there is nothing sacred about a certain pattern of organization, be that congregational (communal), presbyterian (councils or elders), or episcopal (chieftainship). The quality, not the quantity or form, is significant.

Organization is culture-related and must be adapted to the culture of a people to be effective. It is possible to be brotherly both in an episcopalian set-up and in a congregational church. And it is as possible to be dictatorial in congregationalism as in episcopalianism. It is possible to practice the priesthood of all believers in any form of church government. This is a matter of spiritual attitude and dynamism and not of pattern of organization. The quality is determined by the attitudes of the heart of man and not necessarily by the pattern of organization. In this matter culture must speak its language.

This is not so with function and relationship. These are revelation-related and determined. They are absolute and abiding. In organization the determining question is which pattern fits best into a given culture without infringing upon the function of the church. Which structure will create an atmosphere of at-homeness and naturalness? Which will lead to the surest and fastest road of self-government and self-administration?

Perhaps no other aspect has created as much prejudice to the spread of the Gospel in the minds of thinking non-Westerners, made for the strangeness of the church in the non-Western world, and cast more rigid shackles upon the new and younger churches than the Western types of church organization. The bondage of organization has often stifled the dynamic of functionalism, and many churches have become copies of the stagnant mother churches. Only here and there has functionalism broken through to liberate dynamism and resulted in a forward thrust of the people of God.

It must also be pointed out that our American emphasis upon the absolute autonomy of the local church is far more causally determined than biblically; it is seriously debatable theologically, just as the hierarchical system is. Most certainly the Bible beautifully balances independence with interdependence. In general the connectional, interdependent churches prosper more in the mission fields than do the strictly independent churches. Whether this is due to a cultural hangover, to a minority feeling that relates people of like experiences, or to a deeper realization of the body of Christ is open for study and discussion. The fact, however, remains that churches in isolation seldom thrive or expand rapidly. Organization seemingly plays a vital part in the expansion of the church if it follows the indigenous lines.

Note: If it is argued that the independent, autonomous Pentecostal churches are growing faster than all others, I merely reply that there is a structural and also a functional interdependence. The former often becomes a snare, the latter usually enhances growth. Pentecostals practice and live in the latter.

Cultural adaptation is a dynamic factor in evangelism. The ability of Christianity to harness and mobilize the cultural, social and psychological forces of the native environment, without yielding to compromise in the message and to unguided ethical accommodation, is of great importance in the evangelization of the masses of people. While great wisdom is required for the process, great reward will flow from such labors and efforts.

Chapter 31

MOBILIZATION AND TRAINING OF BELIEVERS

SERVICE IS AN ESSENTIAL element of Christianity. It arises out of the pattern of Christ as the Suffering Servant of Jehovah, as well as out of the nature of Christianity. Christianity is a religion of worship, fellowship, proclamation, witness and service. Without these ingredients the fullness of Christianity cannot be experienced and expressed.

It is of utmost significance, therefore, that every Christian be instructed and involved in worship, fellowship, proclamation, witnessing and service. This is the divine path that leads to the realization of the divine ideal of being filled with the fullness of God and the joy unspeakable. Christians are not serving because they are mature, but rather that they might mature. They are not serving because they have achieved a certain degree of holiness; they are serving that they might experience progressive sanctification. Service is a divine means as well as a divine purpose.

Yet, service must not be taken for granted. In the life of every believer there is a large and troublesome cultural hangover, as well as innate dullness, sluggishness and sinfulness which make for spiritual lethargy. In view of the fact that many people come out of static cultures and churches, it must not be taken for granted that they will be witnesses and servants simply because they have become Christians. Their cultural hangover will draw them back. They have become psychologically and socially conditioned to react in matters of religion only upon outer motivation which their religion occasionally provided.

In forbearance the church must begin here. A program of volunteers will not prove effective, but only a plan of mobilization with strong motivation will work satisfactorily. Such mobilization should be initiated at a very early stage in the believer's life before the glow of the conversion experience subsides. Mobilization being purposive, it requires, of course, a definite plan of action and a strategy of advance. Without such a plan and preparation mobilization becomes meaningless. It may even be harmful. In any case, mobilization is difficult to achieve. I submit a few guidelines to assist in accomplishing it.

The success of total mobilization depends upon a number of factors.

1. *Information.* Genuine Christian motivation is based upon factual information. While not all knowledge results in activity, action without knowledge is like a flame without fuel.
2. *Energetic leadership.* In general people will respect and follow

energetic and wise leadership. There are far more followers in this world than there are leaders to lead them.

3. *An adequate program.* This must involve every member of the congregation. Group instruction for specific tasks to accomplish specific assignments is very important. Do not make assignments complicated. Give instruction to the degree that confidence is generated within the people that they can accomplish their assignment.

4. *Motivation.* This is given by team ministries under enthusiastic leadership from within the group. Much of the success will depend upon the leadership of the group. If the leader will succeed in winning the confidence in his people, half of the victory is won.

5. *Success reports.* Let them tell and hear what God has done. This is the place Paul used to inspire the churches in mission ministries (Acts 14:27; 15:3, 4, 12; 21:19, 20).

6. *Encourage the people.* Create a sense of success in people.

7. *Adequate and simple literature.* This must be provided to help and guide the people. Much depends upon the confidence created in them by instruction and assistance that they can do it. Simple guidelines and adequate literature are a great help.

All these factors are important and will assist in the mobilization of believers. *Central among these, however, is the factor of one great idea which gives an image to the movement and which becomes a dominant, dynamic, all-absorbing, totally consuming ideal. This in turn finds embodiment or incarnation in one man. God functions through men rather than organizations.*

Let me illustrate. The idea of world evangelism became alive in the hearts of all the apostles. All gave themselves to it. All became missionaries. However, it became something like an obsession with Paul. World evangelism possessed him to the degree that he could do nothing else but give himself totally and unreservedly to the task. This became his singular task. It mobilized all that he had and all he possessed of life, time and goods. As he was totally mobilized in a singular task he was able to mobilize others to the same degree. Through the centuries Paul has continued to mobilize men in missions.

The ideas of "reformation" were circulating for more than a century before Luther came on the scene. Men had been dying for the truth. Luther, however, integrated the ideas (note the plural) into one great idea (note the singular) and embodied this idea. It possessed his total personality to the degree that he could do nothing else but submit his all and risk his all for the idea. The idea became a dynamic, all-absorbing, totally consuming ideal of his life. Only thus was he able to mobilize the electors, noblemen, scholars, warriors and common men to carry forward the banner of the Reformation to a glorious victory.

Similar were the experiences of William Carey, J. Hudson Taylor, Rowland V. Bingham, as well as many other men and women who stood for a cause and realized it. Men of accomplishment have seldom been all-around men. They have been men who have seemed off balance, one-idea men, one-task mentality men, men who have irritated smug organizations and equilibrium-retaining establishments. The embodiment of one great idea and the relentless pursuit of the idea made them appear peculiar. Yet they lived their ideas and ideals in full personal realization and mobilized others with them.

This is the central factor of total mobilization. No effort or scheme at total mobilization will succeed until it finds incarnation in a personality of contagious quality. *At the center of every dynamic movement is a man.*

However, mobilization is only one aspect. It will not be effective in itself. *The Christian requires training to maintain an effective witness, a consistent life to back up his witness and to render useful service.* Our Lord commands to teach them to observe all that He has commanded.

Teaching requires both content and pedagogy. The content is given to us in the Bible. The pedagogy, however, is not thus given by revelation. For sure, our Lord was the master teacher. However, even His teaching methods were psychologically and culturally conditioned. It is well to keep in mind that doctrine and principles are revelation-related; methods and techniques, however, are culture-related.

As to content, Jesus taught the things concerning the kingdom of God (Acts 1:3b). These were not generalities and subjects of general interest. Sound pedagogy demands that beginners be taught specifics. Clearly defined concepts will be of greater value than broad principles.

God sets the example in this matter. Before He gave to Israel the broad interpretations of the moral law through the prophets, He gave to His people a clearly defined law, a law every Israelite could memorize. So did Christ in the Beatitudes and the Sermon on the Mount.

Only specifics will be helpful in the guidance of the Christian conscience; only specifics will establish the believer in his faith and give to him the boldness he needs to be an effective witness for Christ. The Christian mentality of our days is dulled by generalities that pass for principles.

A fine example of training in specifics may be found in Campus Crusade's Four Spiritual Laws. They may seem oversimplified. However, they give confidence to the theologically uneducated layman in witnessing for Christ and explaining the way of salvation to the unsaved. Thousands of people have been won to Christ by this simple but direct and clear way of presenting the Gospel. Similarly, New Life For All in Nigeria has developed a five-point message that every layman can grasp and make known to his friends and neighbors. It is easy to make the Gospel complicated and the way of salvation hazy.

Every Christian who wishes to be effective in the ministry of the Lord and His church must have a clear understanding of at least *four basic biblical concepts. These are the concepts of salvation, the church, the basics of the Christian life, and how to live effectively in the Spirit.* These are fundamental. In these areas we ought to be specific and without apology indoctrinate our converts according to the knowledge God has given to us in Scripture.

As to service, Christ made His followers into disciples, inculcating certain principles that guided them throughout their lives. In their preparation our Lord gave particular attention to the following points:

Note: For the basics of the outline the author is indebted to Alex Rathney Hay and his book: *The New Testament Order for Church and Missionary,* published by New Testament Missionary Union.

1. He paid special attention to their spiritual development and growth. He made full use of all their experiences to teach eternal values. Think of the occasion when the mother of James and John came seeking the highest places for her two sons, and the way Jesus dealt with the difficulties of Peter, Thomas, and Philip, to realize how careful and watchful He was regarding their spiritual condition and progress. Jesus used the everyday experiences, the temptations, the faults and failures of the disciples as the basis for this instruction.

2. He oriented them well in the knowledge and use of the Scriptures. Jesus continually used the Word. All His teaching was based upon the Old Testament. All His reasoning and arguments were derived from the Scriptures. He taught them to love, to revere, to know and to use the Word.

3. He taught them the life and ministry of prayer in the Spirit. How well they learned it is demonstrated in the book of Acts, where seventeen prayer meetings are referred to.

4. He taught them by example and precept to have faith in God to supply all their material and spiritual needs. Jesus had left all to live among men and become the Savior of the world. He looked to God to supply all His needs. They had to learn the lessons with Him, follow Him, and experience God as He did. This accomplished four important lessons: (1) It detached them from the world; (2) It made them exercise faith; (3) It obliged them to walk near to God; (4) It caused them to be living witnesses to God's power and faithfulness.

5. He taught them to live and minister in absolute obedience to the will of God, withholding nothing for self but placing themselves entirely upon the altar.

6. He taught them the supreme task of evangelism. The gospels record their involvement in the work of spreading the good news over the towns and villages of Galilee. Not one of the apostles became a pastor. As their Master had traveled from place to place, so did the disciples.

7. He taught them to minister in the power of the Spirit alone, and not to have recourse to ritual, ceremony, forms of service, programs, emotionalism, sentimentalism, or any other human means to attract or influence people. The ministry according to the book of Acts reveals that they learned their lessons well.

8. He taught them to love the Lord their God with all their heart and their neighbors as themselves. This love was practical and manifested itself in unselfish, sacrificial service, a service unto a violent death for most of them.

9. He taught them the holy art of teamwork. Again, the book of Acts witnesses to their unity in work and in prayer, none seeking preeminence and all serving each other.

As to witnessing, Christ taught His disciples to depend upon the Holy Spirit, who would dwell in them and teach them the things they ought to say. Witnessing, therefore, is not merely rehearsing our experiences. It means to speak of the meaning and value of Christ in our own personal experiences under the anointing of the Holy Spirit. The apostles were uniquely witnesses of the resurrection of the Lord. This they attested with great boldness and consistency. Having saturated them with these mighty and dynamic concepts, they became flaming evangelists.

In His pedagogy our Lord exhibited extraordinary wisdom. *He taught them by practical example as much as by theoretical instruction.* They were both observers and participants of His ministry. Experience was the main classroom. Jesus taught them by a repetition of specific statements and truths until they became a part of their life. (Study the passages on cross-bearing, on following Him, and on the Great Commission of world evangelism in the various gospels. We may well surmise that these are only some examples of His teaching technique.)

Further, *Jesus taught them within their own cultural milieu.* He did not dislocate them culturally. He taught them publicly as much as possible. He did not form a secret or private, secluded society. His followers heard Him daily in public discourses and in private conversations. His disciples remained members of the public and society as such. They did not develop into social separatists under His guidance. For all practical purposes they remained Jewish Galileans, members of the synagogues and devoted to the temple and to their people. These are principles to be pondered and to be followed.

The goal of Christ was to make disciples who would represent Him in this world and who would be able to fellowship, proclaim and serve in His name and for His glory to the good of the world by evangelizing the world. The method to accomplish this goal of evangelization was the mobilization and the training of the believers. Neither from the goal nor the method has He ever departed. We do well to heed this principle and practice. Only to the degree that we preserve the goal and follow His principles will the dynamic of the Holy Spirit manifest itself in a movement or church. Much stagnation and lack of church multiplication is not because of poor theology or a failure to preach the Gospel, but rather because the churches fail to mobilize and train their membership to become effective evangelizing agents of the Gospel.

The practicality of the method of Christ is well-illustrated in the book of Acts where the persecuted believers became the main evangelizing force and carried the Gospel to the various parts of the then known world. How else could myriads of Jews have come to the knowledge of Jesus Christ (Acts 21:20). The workability of it is being demonstrated by movements today. It has become embodied in such movements as Evangelism-in-Depth, New Life For All, and similar organizations. It finds a classic formulation in the theorem of Dr. R. K. Strachan: "The growth of any movement is in direct proportion to the success of that movement in mobilizing its total membership in the constant proclamation of its beliefs." Today it is most fully expressed in the Pentecostal believers around the world. Their astounding multiplication is evidence of its effectiveness and its reward.

Chapter 32

TEN STEPS TO GROUP EVANGELISM

ATTITUDES AND PRINCIPLES are the personal and covert conduits of the flow of dynamics; practices are the overt canals of conveyance and communication. The latter seem far more significant, but they are just the results of the former. Nevertheless, they are important and need careful application.

The Christian worker, interested in community and group evangelism and multiple conversions, needs to keep in mind that fundamentally only Christianity is a *preaching* and evangelizing religion, centering in a message about a Person, the Lord Jesus Christ. Other religions are basically *practicing* religions and are most intimately related to a person as a performer, a mediary. The messenger of the Gospel is more central to the people at the beginning than the message he preaches. They will watch him far more closely than they will listen attentively to his preaching. If he succeeds in winning the people to himself, he most likely will win them also for his message. If he fails in the former, the latter will go unheeded.

In the light of these facts the following factors should guide in the assignment of workers and in the practices in the field:

1. *Assign a Christian worker to a tribe, people or community with permanent responsibilities for this people and/or community.* It is not a matter of a term or a few years, but a work that must be completed. While changes now and then will be inevitable, they should be exceptional and minimal. Frequent changes may not only hamper and retard progress but permanently hinder the work. It must be kept in mind that rapport cannot be demanded. It is a prize gained at great cost of time, prayer and serious effort. Rapport seldom transfers from one person to another person, especially so when the person coming-in is a stranger. Yet, rapport is the absolute prerequisite to win a meaningful hearing and initiate intelligent deliberation which may result in group movements. Rapport, winsomeness and identification are more important than great ability.

2. *Learn the language of the people well.* Language is the fullest symbolic embodiment of culture. In language the mind and the heart expose themselves. Language is the body of the culture-soul. Without it no intelligent communication is possible. A thorough study of the language will be well repaid in later results. However, it must be the

language of the people and not a classical form of it. Neither will a trade language suffice.

3. *Study the culture and the religion of the people well, including the mythology.* A myth is usually based upon a kernel of truth and presents such truth within a special symbolic form. Legends are recitals of presumed historical events and great leaders. Folklore is the recital living only in the imagination; the latter is designed for social entertainment. Folklore is the primitive theater. In these presentations we find a rehearsal of the dreams and aspirations, the hopes and disappointments, the sorrows and the joys, the tragedies and the victories, the fears and the frustrations of the people. They are a display of their life in verbal symbolism and often in drama. In their mythology, legends and folklore the "soul" of the people is laid bare. Here we feel their heartbeat.

Mr. Curtis Cook, a Wycliffe translator and missionary to the Zuni Indians, came into the community of these people only a few years ago. He had been in Zuni land of New Mexico only two years when we visited him there. Several things impressed us when we discussed the Zuni situation and their evangelization.

First, he had come there to begin and complete a ministry. He did not speak in terms of time, short-term or long-term, one term or two terms of service. He had a ministry to perform and whatever time would be required, the ministry was to be completed.

Second, he was learning the language and was determined to master it in order to perform the best possible service and penetrate the heart and mind of the people by means of it. Diligently he labored away in spite of the fact that many Zuni people were bilingual and a regular American grade and high school rendered good services to the young people of the community.

Third, he had gathered an amazing amount of material on the history, genealogies, mythologies, legends and folklore of this people. He was bent on knowing the Zunis, realizing that their past was incarnated in their present and that they were products mainly of these various cultural and religious forces.

But, you ask, does it pay to put all that time and energy into such studies? The short stay in Zuni land at the time of their annual tribal festival and the visit of the mountain gods to the village convinced us that Mr. Cook was on the right track. He experienced the courtesy and enjoyed the confidence of a superstitious and religiously inhibited people. Surprisingly, he was able to explain more fully some of the rites of these people than could be found in books written about them. Especially impressive was the fact that this outsider and Bible translator was asked by the local school board to prepare special lessons in the Zuni language, in order that he might teach the high schoolers the Zuni language using such material as he deemed advisable. This gave Mr. Cook the unique opportunity to take the gospel message directly into the classrooms to a people who have been highly resistant to the Gospel. What will be the results of this unprecedented confidence? Other missions have labored here with very little success for some seventy years.

4. *Study the social structure of the people and community well.* Most societies are held together and are guided by an organizational (decision-making body) and functional (decision-influencing individuals) power structure. These structures may be in tension or they may be complementary to each other. The Christian worker should seek to enlist the favor of both of them in the cause of the Gospel.

5. *Communicate along the culturally-accepted channels of the power structure; avoid all possible offense, and conscious or deliberate violations.* Every people has canals of navigation along which communication flows, with the least obstruction, acceptable and intelligible to the people. To discover these arteries, respect them, and utilize them for the Gospel is a true art of successful communication.

Mr. and Mrs. David Wirsche are teachers in the Fresno, California, school system. During the summer vacation for several years, however, they have spent several weeks among the Indians of Panama in the Darian area. In former years they labored among these people in Choco, Colombia. Later they transferred the base of operation to Panama. Observing them in their teaching, my interest was drawn to the three different classes supervised by Mr. Wirsche and at times taught by him.

Two classes consisted of one person each, one of them taught by Mrs. Dora Wirsche and one by an advanced informant from a neighboring community, Aureliano Sabujara, himself a chief in his community. The third group consisted of twelve to fifteen individuals and was taught by another informant from the nearby village, at times assisted by the Rev. F. Glen Prunty.

"Why make this difference?" I asked. I was informed that Dora Wirsche was teaching the wife of the chief, giving her special lessons in order to keep her somewhat ahead of the other women of the village. The same thing was being done for the chief, who constituted the sole student of the other class and who was taught by the advanced informant. The teaching staff informed me that it was most significant not to minimize or imperil the role of the chief and his wife by the inroads that were being made.

Safeguarding the role would serve at least three purposes: it would maintain the social structure and unity of the people; it would preserve the authority and order of the community; it would assure the good will and cooperation of the chief in the Christian education program of the people and the unhindered turning of the members to the Gospel. Later we witnessed the wisdom of this procedure and the fulfillment of these anticipations. This Christian community is steadily progressing without experiencing social or tribal pressures. In the community of Aureliano Sabujara, he himself is the main evangelist, teacher and church leader. Gradually and progressively he is leading his people to the Lord and into the church. It is hoped that in the latter community the same thing may take place. Thus the natural structure of the people is being utilized to communicate the Gospel and build the church.

6. *Study major interest areas, areas of tension, frustration and imbalance, as well as consciously felt needs and expressed or hidden aspirations, desires and longings.* Become actively involved in the aches and pains, the yearnings and surgings of their hearts and minds. Become a "savior" to them in an area and/or time of special need, tension and anxiety.

The Motiloni Indians of the Colombia-Venezuela border were known for their determination to protect their land against the encroachment of outsiders. The oil companies fared badly in this area and some seventy outsiders lost their lives because of the poisoned arrows of this people. I remember standing with Dr. Jacobsen, looking over vast stretches of jungles inhabited by this tribe. As Dr. Jacobsen related the terror he had seen and the experiences of the oil men with this tribe, I was persuaded to stay out of their territory. I still have a five-foot arrow which Dr. Jacobsen drew out of the chest of an intruder. The latter died during the operation.

Later the challenge to pacify and evangelize this tribe came to a young man, Bruce Olson of Minneapolis. His adventurous story was written up in *The Sunday School Times.* He befriended a medicine man and also the chief of the tribe by becoming a "savior" to them at a time of crisis. At one time he permitted the medicine man to cure an eye disease by using the outsider's eye medicine. This secured him the friendship and good will of the medicine man who could have had him killed at his pleasure.

On another occasion he helped the chief to obtain some seed corn and plant it away from the settlement. Later the corn yielded rich food and enhanced the authority, wisdom and role of the chief. For this and other help the outsider took no credit. The intruder had become a friend to be trusted and consequently he obtained protection and freedom under the direction of the chief. His message found hearing by a people that was known as untamable. Today a peace treaty has been concluded between the chief and the Colombian government, the area is safe and quiet, and the community is open to the Gospel. Someone became a "savior" without taking credit for it and gained the favor and good will of the power structure.

The following is an account of activity undertaken for about two and a half years by Mr. David Bowtree to wedge an opening into a solid Muslim community in Northern Nigeria.

At the beginning our aim was to bring the gospel to these people in a way that they could understand and accept.

On taking up residence in the town of the area we contacted the Emir and his council, explained the purpose of our coming and requested permission to visit in the villages of his area.

This permission was granted readily and all through the time that we remained in the area we had cordial and helpful relations, not only with the Emir and those under him, but with the various departments of local government, i.e., agriculture, health education, etc.

We only spoke a lingua-franca language on coming to the area but slowly learned the main tribal language, as few in the villages knew anything else.

In our visits to the villages we sought to present a gospel for the whole man. Discussions and actions would flow together over one, two spent a lot of time studying the apparent problems and difficulties of the people. This was not easy and it was not until the end of the second year that we began to feel that we were getting to the real root of some things.

Through offering advice about their farms, homes and lives we gradually got to know the people and they got to know us.

Much of our time was spent in sitting down in the villages with the village heads and other men to discuss life in general and theirs in particular. In this way we gradually built up a working relationship of mutual confidence and trust.

In these visits to the villages time could be spent in this way, discussion on the best way to get carrot seed to germinate under a hot sun, showing a householder how to kill and control bedbugs and lice in the home, talking about some aspect of God, man's condition, his needs and God's answer. Spiritual, mental, material — we did not seek divisions. A natural whole is assumed, for God is concerned for the whole man. Discussions and actions would flow together over one, two or three aspects, or all at once.

By the end of the two and a half years about thirty villages had been visited and contact made. About five of these had shown a real interest in Christian matters.

Our aim from there on is to plan a program of maybe one year's duration in each of the five villages, dealing with the faith and beliefs of Christians, agriculture, preventive medicine. In this way we hope that the claims of becoming a Christian will be made clear to a whole village and groups be brought to a living faith in our Lord.[1]

It seems tragic that such a fine beginning and the opening which seemed to result was, at least temporarily, interrupted by reassigning the missionary at work to another location by the respective missionary society.

7. *Work for the closest possible cultural adaptations, social identification and religious empathy without falling into the trap of nativism.* Keep in mind that a leader must be different and ahead of his people, yet no appreciable gulf may be permitted to develop. Cultural, social and psychological distance are tremendous obstacles for successful ministries. On the other hand cultural adaptation, social identification and religious empathy may become very powerful factors in moving people toward Christ.

8. *Study carefully the mentality of the people.* Keep in mind that their psychology is as real to them and as dynamic in them as your particular psychology is to you. Decisions must be made within the framework of their mentality if they are to be genuine and thoroughgoing. Group decision and deliberative decisions after lengthy consultations may be just as personal as individual and impulsive decisions are; and group experiences may be just as genuine as individual experiences.

9. *Make a genuine attempt of evangelism by group penetration and permeation before you attempt evangelism by direct confrontation.* Take time for dialogue and discussion. Do not invade to conquer or to lead people captive. Permeate to persuade. This will assure at least partial understanding of the convert by the group. Work hard for toleration of the convert within the group.

Rev. William Van Tol of the Sudan United Mission describes his evangelism plan this way:

Gashaka, Nigeria, district had no Christian witness prior to 1960. The area has a population of 39,000, 25,000 of which are Jibu, Ndoro and other smaller animistic tribes. The majority of the remainder are town and cattle Fulani who are Muslims. The Fulani have political control and the animistic tribes are severely oppressed.

The first resident missionary (1962-66) worked mainly with the Muslim Fulani. He had no Fulani converts but succeeded in gaining an attitude of tolerance. There were four converts from the Jibu tribe and about twenty-five from the Ndoro tribe.

I came in 1967 and for the last two years have made it my main concern to evangelize the 20,000 Jibu people. There are seven major Jibu towns, each surrounded by a group of villages ranging in number from four to twelve. Our intention is to place an evangelist in each major town with responsibility for it and its villages. These evangelists are now being trained in Serti Bible School.

Part of their training is to evangelize the villages of Serti town under my guidance. Two or three students visit each village once week-ly. I accompany one group.

We began in September, 1968, by visiting the chiefs of seven vil-lages, informing them of our desire to tell them the story of God. All agreed to hear us with their people present. We expanded to fourteen villages in March, 1969.

I prepared a series of nine messages covering the story of salvation from creation to judgment. Each was told twice, a total of eighteen weeks. They were told in the Jibu language by the students after I had spent time discussing and studying the message with them. A simple, applicable Scripture verse was translated and taught with each message. A simple song was also composed and sung with each message.

After eighteen weeks we left them for one month, encouraging them to think about what they had heard. Then we returned and are now presenting a second series of fifteen messages again beginning with creation.

At this point it is difficult to claim concrete results. We have been communicating, penetrating and permeating. We have done no ag-gressive confrontation. We have been careful to always have the chiefs and elders present. The stories have been presented in dialogue form as much as possible.

At first, the majority of men attended, but no women or children. With no overt encouragement, the women and children soon began listening in the background. The number of men gradually declined till about the eighth week when core groups of five to twenty became evident. The chief of each village was among them. After fourteen weeks, the Muslims destroyed our efforts with threats and scare tactics. It took six weeks to regain the confidence of the chiefs. The core groups gradually returned. At present we are near the end of our second series. I feel that two to three villages are nearly ready for confrontation. The remainder need more permeation. Two weeks ago the Muslims initiated another series of threats. The effects remain to be seen.[2]

10. *Do not isolate converts from their cultural context and social interrelationships under the pretense of separation.* Preserve the con-verts within the cultural milieu and the social network. In order to become effective gospel carriers they must retain membership within the group. Do not be hasty in baptizing individuals. Wait, pray and work until a considerable group is ready to follow the Lord in this manner. They can maintain at least a measure of group life and group cohesion which will constitute the basis of Christian fellowship and a church.

These practices are not only for primitive people. With slight modifications they may become general practices in any society.

It should be recognized that preliterate or primitive people are not unique in their manner of behavior. Among them the factors of operation are overt and appear in an exaggerated (perhaps normal) form. In literate and more sophisticated societies the same factors are covert and minimized in the conscious processes. They have been submerged and suppressed. Nevertheless, they are present and dynamic and no less operative and effective. They are the subconscious forces that operate more functionally than in clear and discernible patterns. They color the sentiments and attitudes. Their dynamic is felt, although it is difficult to uncover and define them. Therefore, they go unnoticed and unheeded by many people. However, they form steppingstones or stumbling blocks on the way to progress.

It is wise to reckon with the cultural, social, psychological and religious factors and implications in every community. They are present, operative and dynamic, even though hidden and secret. To enlist their cooperation and to harness their forces is wise (even if not absolutely determining), though not always easy.

It is wise in a patriarchal society where the father is the determining voice, such as in Japan, China, India and other Oriental societies, to respect the men as the head of the family, make our approaches to and through the men, and seek to enlist them first of all in the furtherance of the Gospel. It may be difficult to keep genuinely saved and honestly striving wives back from baptism and church membership before the husbands are won to the Lord. But in the long run, such a trying path for the church and the wife will be rewarded. This has been proven by the churches of the Mennonite Brethren in the Osaka area of Japan. Their churches are thriving and there is no lack of men in the churches.

The same pattern is strong in many European and Latin American countries. It is below the dignity of the husband in certain societies to follow his wife. He either leads or he is out of the game. To win fathers, therefore, must be our supreme effort. We need to engage extensively in men's missions in order to win families and build strong churches.

It may not be easy in Protestant Europe to win the confidence and good will of ecclesiastical authorities and men of communal influence in order that the Gospel might penetrate the community. But what other way would be more rewarding? The church as an ecclesiastical system and structure may mean little spiritually to the average European. He may seldom attend church services. But the church order and religious institutions are part of his cultural heritage in which he prides himself and for which many of his compatriots have laid down their lives. The cathedrals and ecclesiastical authorities, systems and structures are part of his culture and therefore a part of his being and his way of life with its sentiment and relationships. The observer needs to spend only one Sunday at Westminster Abbey in London. Thousands of people tour the place. Yet, the author attended a worship service in the same cathedral with less than one hundred and fifty people present.

The churches and institutions are incorporated in his value system perhaps to a greater degree and with deeper attachment and sentiments than a non-Christian could hold to his religious system and way of life. The battle is seldom won by a frontal attack or by ignoring the existing order as empty and meaningless, even if it seems that way to the outsider. They may actually be meaningless spiritually, but they are meaningful culturally. How to gain the favor without compromising the message; how to evangelize without serious and unnecessary social offenses and disruptions, especially in household relationships; how to win a hearing without arousing unnecessary antagonism and be ostracized as an intruder—these are not easy questions to answer. But answer them we must, if our ministry is to be effective and our efforts are to be lasting. Practices may become lastingly determining.

Perhaps this is why most American missions in Protestant Europe have not been able to get to first base in their operations. By and large they have sought to by-pass both the ecclesiastical order as well as the pietistic groups existing in numerous communities. They have committed a cultural and a spiritual mistake in their approaches. We must find ways to correct these mistakes.

Every society has its value systems, its sentiments, its appreciations, its "role" system, its order, its overt and covert ways of doing things, its relationships, its power structures—organizational and functional— its channels of communications, its traditions and its aspirations. To be effective and to communicate meaningfully, we must experience cultural adaptation, social identification and religious empathy. We must operate within the social and psychological milieu of the people, for "a stranger will they not follow, but will flee from him: for they know not the voice of strangers."

Chapter 33

DANGERS AND ADVANTAGES OF GROUP EVANGELISM

DANGERS OF GROUP EVANGELISM and multiple conversions must neither be overlooked nor too seriously exaggerated. They are real and they are formidable. However, every conversion from unfaith to faith, from a non-Christian religion to Christianity and Christ is a risk. To deny or to belittle the dangers besetting such a ministry is to be blind to the counterfeits Satan is able to create. We must realize the deceitfulness of the human heart and see the inadequacies of our abilities to communicate the Gospel of our Lord Jesus Christ meaningfully. These risks are, of course, multiplied in multiple conversions. This is natural.

However, as we trust the Holy Spirit in the illumination of the mind and animation of the truth in the application of the divine power in the soul conditioned by individualistic psychology, should we trust Him less to do likewise in a soul molded by group psychology? Is He not the wisest and greatest of all psychologists? The danger is increased and/or lessened to the degree that we trust the Holy Spirit to accomplish His sovereign and gracious work in the heart of each.

Nevertheless, there are dangers. They may be stated as three in particular, especially if conversion decision is urged prematurely.

1. *There may develop a superficial conception of conversion.* A two-fold danger besets conversion, especially in first generation Christians, for two reasons:

First, it is not sufficiently recognized that conversion from paganism to Christianity most often takes place in stages or by degrees. There is the experience of turning to the living God from idolatry. This is conversion from polytheism, animism and spiritism to monotheism. People are burning their idols as evidence of their turning away, and in recognition of the only true and living God. This is a tremendous and necessary step forward and a great victory for God.

However, this is not the complete biblical experience of becoming a Christian. These people must recognize their sins in the light of the newly found God, and thus a need and a desire for a divine Savior is created. Upon this they must be led to acknowledge Jesus Christ as Savior and Lord. Only upon such experience, or complex of experiences, can the Christianization of their lives and way of life really be achieved. To lead the people to an acknowledgment of Christ as Savior and Lord will take considerable time. It must also be recognized that the various degrees of their conversion experience will not be as well marked as it may seem on paper. In fact, it may seem more like an extended process than an experience.

Such a complex experience—the turning from idolatry to the living God, the consequent realization of sin and guilt, and the acknowledgment of Christ as Savior and Lord—seems to be implied in the experience of the Thessalonians described by Paul (I Thess. 1:9, 10). Paul follows the same line of reasoning in Acts 17:22-31, preaching first ethical monotheism as revealed in the Old Testament and then salvation in Christ. This order is noteworthy for our ministry and our approach to non-Christian communities.

The danger, however, exists that many people may become arrested in their experience. While they are turning from idolatry to monotheism, they may fall short in their realization of their sinfulness and moral guilt, and not come to know and trust Jesus Christ as Savior and Lord. Their conversion experience remains incomplete, not because of a rejection of the truth, but because of negligence of being taught the whole way of salvation.

The second reason for superficiality in conversion is the fact that it is being viewed as an outer separation from old ways and religious practices and a turning to an outer conformity to the "Christian way" and religious practices. It becomes an exchange of one set of religious beliefs and practices for another set of beliefs and practices, without the realization of a conscious, personal appropriation of the Lord Jesus Christ as Savior and a commitment to Him as Lord. There may even develop group pressure upon the individual to conform to the new way and order of religion. This is understandable especially in the light of the group mentality and the group way of life. Great caution and care need to be exercised to avoid such pitfalls in group movements and multiple conversions.

Group pressure may well develop in our lands as well, especially with children of Christian homes and highly evangelistic Sunday schools and churches. There may take place a yielding to continuous pressures in the home or Sunday school to become a Christian, instead of a deliberate decision out of personal conviction of sin and a deep yearning for salvation. Such dangers, of course, are multiplied in a society with a strong group mentality, or a patriarchal family society where the husband and father makes all the basic decisions without much family consultation; everyone accepts his decisions and authority as natural and right, and unquestionably submits to them.

Actions which seem like pressure must not be interpreted as intention to deceive. Pressures in strong Christian homes, communities and movements become almost unavoidable. Uninstructed people find it difficult to distinguish between natural pressures and Spirit-wrought convictions, between mainly human urgings and divine drawings, between group and personal decisions. Individual and unquestioned submission to group decision is considered a high virtue in many societies, perhaps even part of their religion.

Much wisdom and deep spiritual discernment is required to guide larger group movements. Fear of making mistakes, however, should not keep us back in taking the risks in the name of the Lord and for His glory. We must be dominated by the conviction and faith that He has much people in this city, this community, among this people.

2. *Group evangelism and multiple conversions may overwhelm numerically the Christian forces who may be ill-prepared spiritually, socially, and in their program.* Therefore they are not ready to cope with the situation in an adequate way. They fail (a) to lead the multitudes to a genuine meeting with the Lord Jesus Christ as they turn away from their old religions and practices; (b) to bring them through to a genuine experience of regeneration; (c) to care for their spiritual well-being; and (d) to assist them in their initial stages and experiences of their newly found faith and life. Therefore, there will be stillbirths and people who have been motivated but are not sufficiently illuminated by the Word to find the true way of life. Others are dwarfed in their initial Christian experiences. This seems to be the case in Indonesia, in several countries in East Africa, and also in some sections in Nigeria and the Congo.

The urgency for teachers of the Word is most pressing, teachers who are able to nurture premature and newborn babes in Christ and lead them on in their Christian experience and life. It must be recognized that men who come from pagan backgrounds find themselves in a mesh of cultural entanglements, evil habits and practices, superstitions and fears that make a new beginning most difficult. Only with rare exception does the sun break through the cloud of paganism in brightness and fullness in one great experience. We do not exclude such a possibility. However, this is not the general run of experience. More often it is like a gradual dawning with the fog being dispersed in a gradual way. Continuous teaching and careful nurture, therefore, are of greatest importance, if a healthy Christian life is to result.

Sound church growth takes place best when the following ratios in church attendance are being observed as much as possible and practicable. When the congregation consists of some thirty-five percent or more adult attendants who are not members of the church, it is wise to change from an emphasis on evangelism to a strong teaching emphasis, teaching that should help the people clearly to confess Christ as Savior and find their way into the church. Special lessons on salvation should be taught, richly illustrated from the Scriptures. The need for clear-cut decision should be emphasized without exerting undue pressure for decisions.

The scriptural place, meaning and value of the local church should be made plain. Lessons on baptism should be clearly taught from the Scriptures and in public services. A failure to penetrate and permeate society deeply with the Gospel and the consequent Christian moral standards endangers the whole church and exposes it to Christo-paganism. Superficial evangelism and/or lack of consequent teaching of biblical principles of the Christian life and conduct results in superficial Christians and Christo-paganism in the church.

If, on the other hand, the proportion of adult non-member attendants drops below the twenty-five percent ratio, an intensive and extensive program and emphasis on evangelism should be initiated. This proportion, if disregarded, may lead to a well-taught but stagnant, ingrown, immobile, fat and self-satisfied church. The latter case is as dangerous and obnoxious to the Lord as the former, though it may appear to us in a better condition. A nonevangelistic church has ceased to be a truly New Testament church. It may resemble the church of Ephesus (Rev. 2:1-7). It must be remembered that the Lord warns this church that their candlestick may be removed out of its place.

There always will be a tension between achieving quantitative growth and retaining qualitative growth, between deepening the church life and extending its borders and branches. This tension is healthy and dynamic. It is God-willed and God-ordered. A healthy balance will keep the church both growing and sound.

3. *Group evangelism and multiple conversions easily lead to an unscriptural concept of the church.* It quickly is perceived as a community affair to be governed by community sentiment and standards, rather than accepting it as a divine institution and an assembly of believers in the Lord Jesus Christ which has higher and different standards than the community has. At times it must be opposed to community standards and practices. The Gospel is God's judgment upon man as well as upon his history, culture, religion and community.

Unless the community has been fairly well permeated by the Gospel, and Christian standards of life and conduct have been taught emphatically, community movements may endanger the biblical standards of the church. Paganism may seek to assert itself in various ways and may attempt to dominate the church. This danger is real and should not be minimized.

The danger of creating a Volkskirche (a church of the people) or a tribal church is real. Its evils are at the root of European Christendom, where Volk (people) and church are practically synonymous terms, and where membership in the community is almost identical with church membership. The church has ceased to be a body of gathered believers, a called-out people, a people of God and a people with a mission of God.

To avoid this danger:

(a) There must be very emphatic teaching on salvation as salvation from sin, in contrast to salvation in sin; the church, the Christian life, and ethical, biblical principles of Christianity.

(b) Much time should be taken to clarify the meaning of baptism with a considerable waiting period before *the first* baptism is administered. Clear teaching on baptism is imperative. Such teaching should be given in public that all might know the meaning of it. It is also significant that baptism should be practiced in public, and so also the reception into membership of the church.

(c) Church members should be placed under definite obligation and responsibilities, though not necessarily should special privileges be granted to them. From the very beginning the cost of total dedication and Christian discipleship should become evident in the experience of believers.

While these dangers are real, we must guard against puritanical and legalistic proceedings in church membership requirements. We need to remember that the church is not an institution only for mature Christians. It may be a nursery for infants, spiritually speaking, as well as a hospital for the spiritually ill. It is God's institution to make disciples as well as to mobilize, train and use them.

Thousands of evangelical churches around the world, especially in the lands of the younger churches, are plagued and thwarted in their growth by puritanical and legalistic practices and membership requirements that neither culture, society, the individual conscience nor the Bible justify. They may be a cultural and theological hangover, but they are not biblical realism in practice. Careful studies and, if need be, drastic changes should be instituted to liberate the divine dynamic in the conversion of multitudes and bring them into the church for nurture, fellowship and service.

ADVANTAGES

Over against the dangers there are impressive advantages in group evangelism and multiple conversions that outweigh the dangers by far.

1. *Group evangelism and multiple conversions usually make for greater personal health because the self-image remains unimpaired.* Spiritual vitality, ease of communication, and group dynamics in fellowship and service dispel the impression of the foreignness of

the Gospel and Christianity and make for an at-homeness in the church.

2. *They aid greatly in breaking the non-Christian ways, practices, mental images and psychological molds.* Non-Christian practices are deliberatively abandoned and separation becomes more radical, uniform and clear-cut. It may even become enforced by group pressure or demands.

3. *Group proceedings leave the individual in his web of relationships; he is allowed and encouraged to live a Christian life without fearing social, cultural or economic ostracism or physical persecution.* To the contrary, he not only finds encouragement and fellowship, but he may be of help to those who need him within his own people. By exercising his spiritual gifts and redeeming precious opportunity for service, he becomes a blessing as he shares in the common blessings of the group. This will make for personal, spiritual health as well as group growth.

4. *Group evangelism and multiple conversions will facilitate the social, cultural and spiritual uplift of the people.* Due to the fact that the web of relationships has not been disrupted, the experience of cohesion has not been weakened, and the sense of belongingness and unity has not been invalidated, group motivation remains a possibility. This in turn can lead to group activity in the transformation of society. While the stimulus for advancement and change may need to come from without, the actual uplift will be initiated *with* the people rather than *for* the people. Progress will be greatly facilitated and will be more natural.

5. *Group evangelism and multiple conversions make self-government, self-support and self-propagation not only a possibility but natural from the very beginning of the Christian movement.* Group movements bring with them all the potentials and patterns required for group function and group advancement. Wise guidance, training within the culture and within the group make discipling a possibility, and the establishment and function of the church a reality. Care should be taken, however, that the organization of the church fits into the pattern of the organizational power structure of the people and thus be truly indigenous.

CONCLUSION

It is my deep conviction that group evangelism and multiple conversions are basic patterns of the Bible, both the Old Testament and the New, and must again become a main thrust of world evangelism and world missions, if we are to accomplish the task and evangelize the fast-growing populations of the world. Application of the pattern will need to be modified according to culture, society and psychology. It also will need to be supplemented by additional approaches and methods such as church evangelism and national campaign evangelism movements—Evangelism-in-Depth, New Life For All, Christ For All— and similar endeavors. A return to the fundamental premises of group evangelism and multiple conversions, however, would constitute a more radical return to the New Testament than has been thus far expressed in any movement. It could result in unprecedented New Testament conquests.

FOOTNOTES

PART THREE

CHAPTER 25

[1] *Pentecost and Missions,* Harry R. Boer (Grand Rapids: Eerdmans Publishing Company, 1961), p. 165.

[2] *Ibid.,* p. 176.

[3] *Ibid.*

[4] *Household Church,* H. L. Ellison (Exeter: Paternoster Press), pp. 21, 22.

CHAPTER 26

[1] "Church Growth Bulletin," Vol. IV, No. 6, July, 1968, by Charles Ross, pp. 21, 22.

CHAPTER 27

[1] Donald McGavran — Definition presented at a Church Growth Seminar conducted at Winona Lake, Indiana, September, 1966. (See also *Church Growth in Mexico,* p. 133, by same author.)

[2] *Dynamics of Church Growth,* J. Waskom Pickett (Nashville: Abingdon Press), p. 21.

[3] Max Warren, personal conference.

CHAPTER 28

[1] *Followers of the New Faith,* Emilio Willems (Nashville: Vanderbilt University Press), p. 53.

[2] *The Impact of Christianity on the Non-Christian World,* J. H. Bavinck (Grand Rapids: Eerdmans Publishing Company), p. 77.

CHAPTER 32

[1] Personal correspondence.

[2] Personal correspondence.

SUMMARY

WE BEGAN OUR STUDY with a definition of evangelism and looked in particular at Saturation Evangelism. I presented two contemporary, dynamic movements of this type of evangelism—Evangelism-in-Depth and New Life For All. There is no question that these movements have made tremendous impact upon their respective continents — Latin America and Africa. They also have left an indelible imprint upon present-day evangelism in the world. Neither the impact nor the imprint will ever be fully measured, perhaps nor even readily acknowledged. However, God is able to do most through those men and channels who do not care who gets the credit as long as the cause of the Lord is advanced.

We may anticipate that the two parent movements and all derived programs will undergo considerable modifications and enrichings in the years to come. No doubt, they will endeavor to incorporate additional dynamic factors which have come to light in recent years, add further patterns of evangelism such as household evangelism and group evangelism, learn new lessons from church growth studies and integrate such lessons into their program as the Reverend Malcolm R. Bradshaw is already doing in his project in Southeast Asia, and as they interact, penetrate and permeate even deeper into the functions of the local churches and experience corresponding responses.

Ideally the movements could possibly work themselves as organizations out of the way as they work themselves more deeply into the organism of the churches. This, however, will be so only ideally. There always will be a place and a need for interdenominational service agencies even within the framework of the churches. On the other hand vast areas will continue to challenge evangelism of any kind. As there has always been a need and place for evangelists, so there always will be a place for evangelism agencies and evangelism movements.

Unhesitatingly the author believes that the evangelical forces around the world have at present the potential to evangelize this generation as at no other time. The great need is

for *a Spirit illumined vision* of such possibilities and *a strategy* that will encompass the world, perhaps on a• continent by continent basis,

for *a living faith* that knows itself in the center of God's will and purpose and that claims and appropriates from God all available resources, and for *an orderly, flexible, mobile, dynamic functionalism* which will *integrate* the dynamic factors which behavioral science, history of missions, church growth and evangelism researchers have unearthed in recent years, *mobilize* all knowledge and forces at our disposal, *coordinate* them into a design and *focus* them upon the central purpose of God for our age — the evangelization of our generation not in the days and ages to come but now in the days of grace and unprecedented opportunities.

Yes, the world is an open harvest field, more anxious to hear the Gospel of Jesus Christ than ever before and more anxious than the church is prepared to announce it. Many experiences during our recent ministry in a number of countries in Africa remind us of the report of Luke when he writes: The people pressed upon him to hear the word of God. We need to hear the words of Paul again: "Behold, now is the accepted time [the time of high potentials]; behold, now is the day of salvation."

The above principles can be illustrated from the miracle-parable of our Lord, the feeding of the five thousand. The disciples had *a vision* for the need of the multitude and informed the Lord of it. (No doubt, our Lord had felt this in His own heart before the disciples ever mentioned such need to Him.) Hereupon the Master ordered *an honest evaluation* of all available means. Having received such information, He designed *a strategy* to feed the entire multitude, overfeeding no one and overlooking no one. Next our Lord *mobilized* all available resources in men and means—His disciples and the loaves and fishes, a tiny minority and meager resources. *Prayer* and the conversion of calculating faith into *miracle expecting faith,* plus humble, prompt and *coordinated obedience* and service on the part of the disciples accomplished the otherwise impossible. The multitude went away satisfied, saying: "This is of a truth that prophet that should come into the world" (John 6:14). Who will argue that the Lord cannot and will not again manifest His glory and might to present to the multitude the Bread of Life? The greatness of our Lord, the need of the multitude and our potentialities through the Holy Spirit remain the challenge to our faith.

GENERAL BIBLIOGRAPHY

Allen, Roland. *Missionary Principles* (Eerdmans: Grand Rapids).
————. *Spontaneous Expansion of the Church* (World Dominion Press: London).
Autrey, C. E. *Evangelism in the Acts* (Zondervan: Grand Rapids).
————. *The Theology of Evangelism* (Broadman: Nashville).
Bavinck, J. H. *The Impact of Christianity on the Non-Christian World* (Eerdmans: Grand Rapids).
Boer, Harry R. *Pentecost and Missions* (Eerdmans: Grand Rapids).
Brown, Stanley C. *Evangelism in the Early Church* (Eerdmans: Grand Rapids, 1963).
Bruce, F. F. *The Training of the Twelve* (T. and T. Clark: London).
Coleman, R. E. *The Master Plan of Evangelism* (Revell: Old Tappan, N. J.).
Conant, J. H. *Every Member Evangelism* (Harper & Row: New York).
Dobbins, G. S. *Evangelism According to Christ* (Broadman: Nashville).
Douglas, M. R. *How to Build an Evangelistic Church* (Zondervan: Grand Rapids).
Filson, F. V. *Three Crucial Decades* (John Knox Press: Richmond, 1963).
Ford, Leighton. *The Christian Persuader* (Harper & Row: New York, 1966).
Foster, John. *After the Apostles* (SCM Press Ltd.: London).
Hay, A. R. *The New Testament Order for Church and Missionary* (The N. T. Missionary Union).
Kingsley, Charles W. and Delamarter, George. *Go! Revolutionary New Testament Christianity* (Zondervan: Grand Rapids).
Krupp, Nate. *A World to Win* (Bethany Fellowship: Minneapolis, 1966).
Law, H. W. *Winning a Hearing* (Eerdmans: Grand Rapids, 1968).
Leavell, R. Q. *Evangelism, Christ's Imperative Commission* (Broadman: Nashville, 1952).
Lee, Robert. *Stranger in the Land* (Friendship Press: New York, 1967).
McGavran, D. A. *Church Growth and Christian Mission* (Harper & Row: New York, 1965).
————. *Church Growth in Mexico* (Eerdmans: Grand Rapids).
————. *Bridges of God* (Friendship Press: New York, 1955).
Miller, Paul M. *Group Dynamics in Evangelism* (Herald Press: Scottdale, Pa., 1958).
Moore, Waylon B. *New Testament Follow-up* (Eerdmans: Grand Rapids).
Morgan, G. Campbell. *Evangelism* (Revell: Old Tappan, N. J., 1964).
Mueller, Charles S. *The Strategy of Evangelism* (Concordia: St. Louis, 1955).
Nida, Eugene A. *Message and Mission* (Harper & Row: New York, 1960).
————. *Religions Across Cultures* (Harper & Row: New York, 1968).
Pickett, J. W. *The Dynamics of Church Growth* (Abingdon: Nashville, 1963).
————. *Christian Mass Movements in India* (Abingdon: Nashville).

Schlosser, John H. *Church Planting in Mindanao* (General Missionary Board, Free Methodist Church: Winona Lake, Indiana).

Smith, Asbury. *The Twelve Christ Chose* (Harper & Row: New York, 1958).

Smith, Eugene L. *Mandate for Mission* (Friendship Press: New York, 1968).

Smith, J. Edgar. *Friendship Evangelism* (Warner Press: Anderson, Indiana).

Vicedom, G. F. *Church and People in New Guinea* (Association Press: New York).

Warnshuis, A. L., Singh, G. H., and McGavran, D. A. *Church Growth and Group Conversion* (Lucknow Publishing House: Lucknow U.P. India).

Warren, Max. *Revival, an Enquiry* (SCM Press Ltd.: London).

Webster, Douglas. *What Is Evangelism?* (The Highway Press: London).

Whitesell, F. D. *Basic New Testament Evangelism* (Zondervan: Grand Rapids).

Willems, Emilio. *Followers of the New Faith* (Vanderbilt U. Press: Nashville, 1967).

EVANGELISM-IN-DEPTH

THE ALLIANCE WITNESS

"Peru," *The Alliance Witness*, CII (April 26, 1967), p. 16.

"Evangelism-in-Depth Workshop to Be Held," *The Alliance Witness*, CII (June 7, 1967), p. 11.

Sluyter, Rev. A. Merle. "A Church Is Rising to Serve — Evangelism-in-Depth in Peru," *The Alliance Witness*, CII (July 19, 1967), pp. 14, 15, 18. (4,000 prayer cells, 30 denominations.)

Constance, George S. "A New Day in Colombia," *The Alliance Witness*, CII (August 16, 1967), p. 16.

"Growth Continues in Colombia," *The Alliance Witness*, CII (September 13, 1967), p. 11. (70,803 Prot. Com. Members: an increase of 6,993 over 1966 or increase of 10%.)

"Evangelism-in-Depth Seminar for Appalachia," *The Alliance Witness*, CIII (January 31, 1968), p. 11.

Sluyter, Rev. A. Merle. "Peruvian Christians on the March," *The Alliance Witness*, CIII (June 5, 1968), p. 21. (Final parade of EID in Lima.)

"Evangelism-in-Depth Seminar," *The Alliance Witness*, CIII (July 17, 1968), p. 15. (Short statement of spiritual principle of EID.)

"Evangelism-in-Depth Registered," *The Alliance Witness*, CIII (July 31, 1968), p. 11.

"Visit 25,000 Homes in Colombia," *The Alliance Witness*, CIII (July 31, 1968), p. 13. (First day of visitation, EID.)

"Trouble in Colombia," *The Alliance Witness*, CIII (August 14, 1968), p. 13. (Possible conflict during Eucharistic Congress of Roman Catholic Church in Bogota.)

THE ANDEAN OUTLOOK

Vigus, John. "Evangelism-in-Depth," *The Andean Outlook*, LVII (July-September, 1967), p. 11. (Bolivia, 1965 campaign.)

BIBLICAL MISSIONS

Steele, Irwin W. "An Appraisal of Evangelism-in-Depth Position Papers," *Biblical Missions,* XXXIII (August-September, 1967), pp. 14, 16. (A separatist view of EID — a bitter and unjust attack.)

CHRISTIANITY TODAY

1958

Strachan, R. Kenneth. "Tomorrow's Task in Latin America," *Christianity Today,* III (December 22, 1958), pp. 3-6.

1961

Ford, Leighton. "Review of Evangelism-in-Depth by Latin America Mission," *Christianity Today,* VI (November 10, 1961), p. 59.

1962

"Guatemala for Christ," *Christianity Today,* VI (June 22, 1962), p. 29.

"Evangelism Under Fire," *Christianity Today,* VII (December 21, 1962), p. 33.

1963

Roberts, W. Dayton. "Latin America: Challenge of a New Day," *Christianity Today,* VII (July 19, 1963), pp. 3, 4.

Nelson, Wilton N. "Evangelical Surge in Latin America," *Christianity Today,* VII (July 19, 1963), pp. 5, 6.

"Catholics and Protestants in Latin America," *Christianity Today,* VII (July 19, 1963), p. 8.

"Focus on the Isthmus," *Christianity Today,* VII (July 19, 1963), pp. 10, 11.

"The Caribbean, Paradise or Poorhouse?" *Christianity Today,* VII (July 19, 1963, pp. 12, 13.

"Greater Colombia, Progress Under Persecution," *Christianity Today,* VII (July 19, 1963), pp. 13, 14.

"West Coast Republics: Rome's Last Stronghold," *Christianity Today,* VII (July 19, 1963), pp. 15, 16.

"D-Day for Foreign Missionaries?" *Christianity Today,* VII (July 19, 1963), pp. 24, 25.

Roberts, W. Dayton. "Pentecost South of the Border," *Christianity Today,* VII (July 19, 1963), p. 32.

————. "Latin American Enterprise," *Christianity Today,* VII (August 30, 1963), p. 37.

————. "Christian Coordination, "*Christianity Today,* VII (September 27, 1963), p. 38.

1964

"The Christians' Stake in Appalachia," *Christianity Today,* VIII (March 27, 1964), p. 26.

Rolston, Holmes. "Appalachia Mountains of Poverty," *Christianity Today,* VIII (March 27, 1964), pp. 27, 28.

Fenton, Horace L., Jr. "What Does 'Go Ye' Really Mean?" *Christianity Today,* VIII (July 31, 1964), p. 22.

1965

"Missions on the Academic Frontier," *Christianity Today,* IX (April 9, 1965),

p. 50. (Fuller Seminary dedicates the Grad. School of World Missions in memory of Strachan.)

"Dominican Republic," *Christianity Today,* IX (July 2, 1965), p. 39. (Newsnote on EID in Dominican Republic.)

"Evangelism Around the World," *Christianity Today,* X (December 3, 1965), p. 43. (6,000 conversions so far in Dominican Republic, EID will continue campaign through March, 1966.)

Roberts, W. Dayton. "Solidarity in Bolivia," *Christianity Today,* X (December 17, 1965), p. 34. (20,000 professions during year.)

1966

"The Strachan Memorial," *Christianity Today,* X (March 18, 1966), pp. 23, 24.

"The Revolution in Evangelism," *Christianity Today,* X (April 29, 1966), pp. 38-41. (New emphasis on intensive evangelism in world.)

1967

"Office of World-Wide Evangelism in Depth," *Christianity Today,* XI (March 31, 1967), p. 45.

1968

"Visas for Evangelism-in-Depth in Colombia," *Christianity Today,* XII (March 15, 1968), p. 45.

"Kentucky-in-Depth," *Christianity Today,* XII (April 26, 1968), pp. 40, 41. (Visitation phase of EID begins in Kentucky.)

"Evangelism in Depth Patented," *Christianity Today,* XII (July 5, 1968), p. 47.

CHURCH GROWTH BULLETIN

"Church Growth News," *Church Growth Bulletin,* I (January, 1965), pp. 6-12.

"Books and Articles," *Church Growth Bulletin,* I (March, 1965), p. 14.

"Mission Evaluated by Experts," *Church Growth Bulletin,* II (September, 1966), pp. 7, 8.

"Doubling and Trebling Church Membership," *Church Growth Bulletin,* III (January, 1967), p. 10.

ETERNITY

Roberts, D. "Latin America," *Eternity,* XII (January, 1961), pp. 19, 20. (Evangelism-in-Depth in Nicaragua and Costa Rica.)

"Guatemala Mobilizes for Mass Evangelism," *Eternity,* XIII (August, 1962), p. 33.

Temple, Ruth. "What's Going on in Guatemala?" *Eternity,* XIII (December, 1962), pp. 28, 29.

Roberts, Dayton and Lois Thiessen. "Latin America," *Eternity,* XV (January, 1964), pp. 26, 28. (Survey of 1963.)

Strachan, R. Kenneth. "The Battle of the Long Pants," *Eternity,* XVI (April, 1965), pp. 5, 6. (Editorial by Strachan.)

"Homegoing for a Missionary Statesman," *Eternity,* XVI (April, 1965), p. 5. (Report of Strachan's death.)

Goodwin, John. "Evangelism Goes on Anyway," *Eternity,* XVII (January,

1966), p. 29. (EID in Bolivia and Dominican Republic in spite of uprisings.)

"Civil War Fails to Hinder Bolivian Evangelism," *Eternity*, XVII (April,
1966), p. 32.

EVANGELICAL MISSIONS QUARTERLY

"Climax in Venezuela," *Evangelical Missions Quarterly*, I (Summer, 1964),
pp. 45, 46.

"Evangelism: Climax in Venezuela," *Evangelical Missions Quarterly*, I (Summer, 1965), pp. 45, 46.

Wagner, C. Peter. "Today's Missions in the Latin American Social Revolution," *Evangelical Missions Quarterly*, I (Winter, 1965), pp. 19-27.

"Dominicans Move Forward," *Evangelical Missions Quarterly*, I (Winter,
1965), p. 51.

"Bolivian Rally for Crusade," *Evangelical Missions Quarterly*, II (Spring,
1966), pp. 170, 171.

Peters, G. W. "Church Growth in Colombia," *Evangelical Missions Quarterly*, III (Spring, 1967), pp. 166-170. (Colombia high potential area—
could double church with EID.)

Coggins, Wade T. "Windows in the World," *Evangelical Missions Quarterly*,
III (Spring, 1967), pp. 177-180. (News brief on EID in Guatemala.)

"200 Attend EID Institute," *Evangelical Missions Quarterly*, III (Winter,
1967), pp. 125, 126.

Kenyon, John A. "Hospital," *Evangelical Missions Quarterly*, IV (Summer,
1968), pp. 240, 241. (Bible Clinic closed in San Jose, C. R., for strategic reasons one being LAM's commitment to EID.)

"Consultation Draws Thinkers on Evangelism," *Evangelical Missions Quarterly*, IV (Winter, 1968), pp. 120, 121. (Theological Consultation
sponsored by Office of Worldwide Evangelism in Depth.)

THE INTERNATIONAL REVIEW OF MISSIONS

Newbigin, Leslie. "A Survey of the Year 1962-3," *The International Review
of Missions*, LIII (January, 1964), pp. 3-82.

Strachan, R. Kenneth. "Call to Witness," *The International Review of Missions*, LIII (April, 1964), pp. 191-200.

Hayward, Victor B. W. "Call to Witness," *The International Review of Missions*, LIII (April, 1964), pp. 201-208.

Strachan, R. Kenneth. "A Further Comment," *The International Review of
Missions*, LIII (April, 1964), pp. 209-216.

Barth, Markus. "What Is the Gospel?" *The International Review of Missions*,
LIII (October, 1964), pp. 441-448.

Conway, Martin. "A Permanent Argument?" *The International Review of
Missions*, LIII (October, 1964), pp. 449-451.

Castro, Emilio. "Evangelism in Latin America," *The International Review of
Missions*, LIII (October, 1964), pp. 452-456.

Newbigin, Leslie. "A Survey of the Year 1963-4," *The International Review
of Missions*, LIV (January, 1965), pp. 3-75.

Hayward, Victor E. W. "Call to Witness," *The International Review of Missions,* LIV (April, 1965), pp. 189-192.

Newbigin, Leslie. "A Survey of the Year 1964-5," *The International Review of Missions,* LV (January, 1966), pp. 3-80.

"Survey, South America and Central America," *The International Review of Missions,* LVI (January-March, 1967), pp. 62-67.

"Survey, Latin America," *The International Review of Missions,* LVII (January-March, 1968), pp. 81-98.

LATIN AMERICA EVANGELIST

1961

Melborne, Benton J. "Are We Winning the University Students in Latin America?" *Latin America Evangelist* (January-February, 1961), pp. 2-6.

"Able to Teach Others," *Latin America Evangelist* (March-April, 1961), pp. 15, 16.

"As One Who Serves," *Latin America Evangelist* (March-April, 1961), pp. 20, 21.

"They Shook the Country," *Latin America Evangelist* (March-April, 1961), pp. 3, 4.

"A Vision Becomes Flesh," *Latin America Evangelist* (March-April, 1961), pp. 4, 5.

"Again Comes the Call to Guatemala," *Latin America Evangelist* (July-August, 1961), pp. 7, 8.

Foster, Sabe L. "Diary of an Eyewitness," *Latin America Evangelist* (July-August, 1961), pp. 3-6.

Nelson, Wilton N. "Separation or Cooperation?" *Latin America Evangelist* (September-October, 1961), pp. 6, 7.

Glasser, Arthur F. "New Dimension in Evangelism," *Latin America Evangelist* (November-December, 1961), back cover.

"Latin America News Front," *Latin America Evangelist*

1962

"Evangelism-in-Depth," *Latin America Evangelist* (January-February, 1962), pp. 2-4.

Huegel, John. "Revolution in Evangelism," *Latin America Evangelist* (January-February, 1962), pp. 14, 15.

Strachan, R. Kenneth. "Discipleship Must Cost," *Latin America Evangelist* (March-April, 1962), pp. 1, 2.

————. "Evangelist in a New Age," *Latin America Evangelist* (May-June, 1962), pp. 12, 13. (May be March-April issue.)

Soerheide, Lester J. "Reaching the Inaccessible," *Latin America Evangelist* (November-December, 1962), pp. 14-16.

Thiessen, Lois S. "Reaching Guatemala's Children," *Latin America Evangelist* (November-December, 1962), pp. 16-19.

1963

Strachan, R. Kenneth. "Everybody," *Latin America Evangelist* (January-February, 1963), p. 1.

"Evangelism-in-Depth, Guatemala," *Latin America Evangelist* (March-April, 1963), inside back cover.

Fenton, Horace L., Jr. "Both Here and Abroad — Let the People Rejoice," *Latin America Evangelist* (March-April, 1963), p. 11.

"Forecast: Evangelism-in-Depth for 1963 and 1964," *Latin America Evangelist* (March-April, 1963), pp. 12, 13.

"In-Depth Means In-Breadth Too," *Latin America Evangelist* (March-April, 1963), p. 14.

"The Life-Gate," *Latin America Evangelist* (March-April, 1963), pp. 9ff.

Reapsome, James W. "A Sunday to Remember in Guatemala," *Latin America Evangelist* (March-April, 1963), p. 16

Roberts, W. Dayton. "Is the Job Finished?" *Latin America Evangelist* (March-April, 1963), pp. 1-3.

Strachan, R. Kenneth. "Some Fundamentals," *Latin America Evangelist* (March-April, 1963), inside front cover.

————. "Struggle in the Deep," *Latin America Evangelist* (March-April, 1963), p. 8.

Thor, Christian L. "Personal Witness in Mass Evangelism," *Latin America Evangelist* (March-April, 1963), pp. 6, 7.

"What Has God Done for You and Your Church Through Evangelism-in-Depth?" *Latin America Evangelist* (March-April, 1963), p. 15.

"What Is Evangelism in Depth?" *Latin America Evangelist* (March-April, 1963), pp. 4, 5.

Gonzales, Jonas. "Broadening the Outreach of Evangelism-in-Depth," *Latin America Evangelist* (May-June, 1963), pp. 10, 11

Strachan, R. Kenneth. "1964: The Greatest Challenge," *Latin America Evangelist* (September-October, 1963), pp. 2, 3.

"Honduras," *Latin America Evangelist* (November-December, 1963).

Kenyon, John. "Let's Evangelize Latin America Now!" *Latin America Evangelist* (November-December, 1963), pp. 2, 3.

"Venezuela," *Latin America Evangelist* (November-December, 1963), p. 9.

"What Are Prospects Now for Evangelism in Latin America?" *Latin America Evangelist* (November-December, 1963), pp. 4-7.

1964

(no title), *Latin America Evangelist* (January-February, 1964), back cover.

Cook, William. "Honduras' Hour of Opportunity," *Latin America Evangelist* (March-April, 1964), pp. 5, 6.

"Climactic Events of Evangelism-in-Depth in Honduras," *Latin America Evangelist* (May-June, 1964), p. 14.

"Compassion for the Multitudes," *Latin America Evangelist* (May-June, 1964), pp. 9-12.

"Developments in Evangelism-in-Depth, Venezuela," *Latin America Evangelist* (May-June, 1964), p. 16.

MacDonald, Jack. "It's Campos Instead of Carnival for Venezuela's Young Christians," *Latin America Evangelist* (May-June, 1964), pp. 15, 16.

"Young Christians March in Honduras," *Latin America Evangelist* (May-June, 1964), pp. 13, 14.

"Victory in Honduras," *Latin America Evangelist* (September-October, 1964), pp. 13, 15.

"Evangelism-in-Depth's Gal Friday," *Latin America Evangelist* (November-December, 1964), pp. 13, 14.

Flory, Dorothy. "Bolivia," *Latin America Evangelist* (November-December, 1964), pp. 15, 16.

Gonzales, Jonas. "God's Miraculous Hand Is on Venezuela Today," *Latin America Evangelist* (November-December, 1964), pp. 6-8.

1965

"Evangelism-in-Depth: Triumphs and Plans," *Latin America Evangelist* (January-February, 1965), pp. 17, 18.

"Perspective," *Latin America Evangelist* (January-February, 1965), p. 19.

Fenton, Horace L., Jr. "What Is Our Message?" *Latin America Evangelist* (March-April, 1965), inside front cover-4.

Flory, Dorothy. "Dominican Republic," *Latin America Evangelist* (March-April, 1965), pp. 8, 9.

"Honduras . . . Six Months Later," *Latin America Evangelist* (March-April, 1965), p. 14.

Kenyon, John. "Can Anybody Save Bolivia?" *Latin America Evangelist* (March-April, 1965), pp. 12, 13.

"Like a Mighty Army," *Latin America Evangelist* (March-April, 1965), pp. 10, 11.

"Why Has Evangelism-in-Depth Fired the Interest of Mission Leaders Worldwide?" *Latin America Evangelist* (March-April, 1965), back cover.

Fenton, Horace L., Jr. "Unfinished Business," *Latin America Evangelist* (May-June, 1965), p. 16.

————, et al. "What Kenneth Strachan Meant to Me," *Latin America Evangelist* (May-June, 1965), pp. 5-8.

Glasser, Arthur F., et al. "Our Esteemed Brother, and Our Friend," *Latin America Evangelist* (May-June, 1965), pp. 13-15.

"A Life Known and Read of All Men," *Latin America Evangelist* (May-June, 1965), pp. 9-12.

"The R. Kenneth Strachan Memorial Fund for World Evangelism," *Latin America Evangelist* (May-June, 1965), back cover.

Strachan, R. Kenneth. "For This Cause, I," *Latin America Evangelist* (May-June, 1965), pp. 1-3.

————. "Other Writings of Kenneth Strachan Reveal His Faith, Vision and Passion," *Latin America Evangelist* (May-June, 1965), pp. 3, 4.

Fenton, Horace L., Jr. "Here We Stand," *Latin America Evangelist* (September-October, 1965), pp. 20, 21.

Kenyon, John. "Meet the General Director," *Latin America Evangelist* (September-October, 1965), pp. 4, 5.

————. "Preaching Out of Season," *Latin America Evangelist* (September-October, 1965), inside front cover-3.

Roberts, W. Dayton. "New Dimensions in Evangelism," *Latin America Evangelist* (November-December, 1965), pp. 13-15.
"Toward Finale in Bolivia, Past Midpoint in Dominican Republic," *Latin America Evangelist* (November-December, 1965), pp. 10-12.

1966

"Bolivia, A Country Shaken by the Gospel," *Latin America Evangelist* (January-February, 1966), inside cover-4.
"Latin America Mission Evangelism-in-Depth Activities in 1966," *Latin America Evangelist* (January-February, 1966), p. 16.
Roberts, W. Dayton. "How Did the Tiny Minority Turn Bolivia Upside Down?" *Latin America Evangelist* (January-February, 1966), pp. 5-7.
"Interest in Evangelism-in-Depth," *Latin America Evangelist* (March-April, 1966), p. 17.
"In the Dominican Republic," *Latin America Evangelist* (March-April, 1966), p. 17.
Cook, William. "Turning Point in Santo Domingo," *Latin America Evangelist* (March-April, 1966), inside cover-3.
Roberts, W. Dayton. "God's Calm Reigned in Santo Domingo for the Evangelism-in-Depth Finale," *Latin America Evangelist* (May-June, 1966), p. 17.
"Toward the Climax in Santo Domingo," *Latin America Evangelist* (May-June, 1966), inside cover-1.
Roberts, W. Dayton. "Global Interest in Evangelism-in-Depth," *Latin America Evangelist* (September-October, 1966), pp. 4-7.
Young, Gwen. "History Making in Peru," *Latin America Evangelist* (September-October, 1966), pp. 14, 15.
"Evangelism Workshop, 1966," *Latin America Evangelist* (November-December, 1966), pp. 6-8.

1967

"Growing Interest in Evangelism-in-Depth," *Latin America Evangelist* (January-February, 1967), p. 7.
Baltodano, Rafael. "Evangelism-in-Depth Begins With Blessing in Peru," *Latin America Evangelist* (March-April, 1967), inside cover-1.
"Evangelism-in-Depth," *Latin America Evangelist* (March-April, 1967), p. 17. (Deals with follow-up in Nicaragua.)
"In Peru," *Latin America Evangelist* (March-April, 1967), p. 17.
"Evangelism-in-Depth Around the World: Actual Programs and Widespread Interest," *Latin America Evangelist* (May-June, 1967), pp. 2, 3.
"Evangelism-in-Depth Goes Worldwide — LAM Announces New Global Task Force," *Latin America Evangelist* (May-June, 1967), inside cover-1.
"Evangelism-in-Depth in Eastern Nicaragua Reaches Final Phase," *Latin America Evangelist* (May-June, 1967), p. 5.
"Vincente Coral: One Man's Vision for Peru," *Latin America Evangelist* (May-June, 1967), pp. 4, 5.
Boss, Richard G. "Colombia: Christian Forces Gird for Nationwide Evan-

gelism in 1968," *Latin America Evangelist* (September-October, 1967),
pp. 12-14.

Franklin, Garland. "Evangelizing Yesterday's People," *Latin America Evangelist* (September-October, 1967), pp. 15, 16.

"In Peru," *Latin America Evangelist* (September-October, 1967), p. 17.

Voelkel, Mary Anne. "The Harvest Rolls on in Peru," *Latin America Evangelist* (September-October, 1967), p. 11.

1968

"Peru Has Heard," *Latin America Evangelist,* 48 (March-April, 1968), pp. 1-6. (Survey of EID in Peru.)

"Colombia," *Latin America Evangelist,* 48 (March-April, 1968), p. 16. (Report of preliminary work of EID.)

"Appalachia to Africa," *Latin America Evangelist,* 48 (March-April, 1968), p. 16. (Activities of Office of World Wide EID.)

Fenton, Horace L., Jr., "Shaping the Future of a Mission," *Latin America Evangelist,* 48 (May-June, 1968), p. 1. (Future hopes of Evangelism in LAM.)

"Colombia," *Latin America Evangelist,* 48 (May-June, 1968), pp. 2, 3.

"Latin American News Front," *Latin America Evangelist,* 48 (May-June, 1968), pp. 15, 16, 18. (News briefs on EID.)

Howard, David M. "Colombia's Growing Church Is on the March," *Latin America Evangelist,* 48 (July-August, 1968), p. 5. (Mobilization for EID).

"Appalachia 'in-depth' Seminar," *Latin America Evangelist,* 48 (July-August, 1968), p. 12.

Roberts, W. Dayton. "Evangelism and Social Structures," *Latin America Evangelist,* 48 (July-August, 1968), pp. 13-15.

"Latin American News Front," *Latin America Evangelist,* 48 (July-August, 1968), p. 16.

"Lima Crusade, God Comes to Man," *Latin America Evangelist,* 48 (January-February, 1968), pp. 15, 16.

"Evangelism-in-Depth Orientation," *Latin America Evangelist,* 48 (January-February, 1968), p. 17. (EID theory for British evangelicals.)

"Theological Consultation," *Latin America Evangelist,* 48 (January-February, 1968), p. 17. (Discussions on evangelism sponsored by EID.)

Voelkel, Mary Anne. "Colombia: Those Who Sowed With Tears Are Reaping With Joy," *Latin America Evangelist,* 48 (September-October, 1968), pp. 1-3.

"Latin America News Front," *Latin America Evangelist,* 48 (September-October, 1968), p. 14. (News briefs on EID in Colombia, possible use in British Isles, plans for use in Portugal, Ecuador and seminars around the world.)

Fenton, Horace L., Jr. "False Economy," *Latin America Evangelist,* 48 (September-October, 1968), pp. 18, 21. (Abundant reaping requires abundant sowing.)

LATIN AMERICAN LUTHERAN

Latin American Luthern, Vols. L-LXXVIII. Geneva, Switzerland: The Commission on Latin America of the Lutheran World Federation, 1952-1966.

MOODY MONTHLY

"Surge of Evangelical Activity in Latin America," *Moody Monthly*, LXII January, 1962), p. 5. (EID in Nicaragua and Costa Rica.)

"Evangelism in Depth," *Moody Monthly*, LXII (July-August, 1962), p. 8. (News Brief EID in Guatemala.)

"Evangelism in Depth," *Moody Monthly*, LXIII (November, 1962), p. 8. (News brief EID Guatemala final campaign, Oct. 29 - Nov. 25.)

"Guatemala's Year of Decision," *Moody Monthly*, LXIII (January, 1963), pp. 22-24.

"Guatemala Rally Held in Spite of Revolt," *Moody Monthly*, LXIII (February, 1963). p. 6.

"Secrets of Success," *Moody Monthly*, LXIII (March, 1963), p. 8. (Statistics on Nicaragua, Costa Rica, Guatemala.)

"In Depth, Honduras," *Moody Monthly*, LXIV (October, 1963), p. 8.

Landrum, Phil. "New Push in Latin America," *Moody Monthly*, LXIV (February, 1964), pp. 20, 21. (EID schedule, 1960-1964.)

"La Paz, Bolivia," *Moody Monthly*, LXIV (December, 1964), p. 8. (EID plans continuation in spite of revolution.)

"In-Depth," *Moody Monthly*, LXV (April, 1965), p. 11. (17,000 added to church in Venezuela by EID.)

"Dominican Republic," *Moody Monthly*, LXV (July-August, 1965), p. 50. (EID plans begin, news brief.)

"Cochabamba, Bolivia," *Moody Monthly*, LXVI (September, 1965), news.

"Evangelism-in-Depth," *Moody Monthly*, LXVI (June, 1966), news. (EID ended in Dominican Republic.)

"Evangelism-in-Depth," *Moody Monthly*, LXVII (September, 1966), p. 10.

"Evangelism-in-Depth, Peru," *Moody Monthly*, LXVII (January, 1967), p. 16.

"In-Depth Evangelism," *Moody Monthly*, LXVII (May, 1967), p. 16.

"Evangelism, Appalachia," *Moody Monthly*, LXVII (June, 1967), p. 13, news.

"Rubén Lores," *Moody Monthly*, LXVIII (September, 1967), p. 13, news.

"The Gospel in Appalachia," *Moody Monthly*, LXVIII (November, 1967), p. 12, news.

"Emphasis on Evangelism," *Moody Monthly*, LXVIII (January, 1968), p. 10, news.

"Evangelism in Depth Expands," *Moody Monthly*, LXVIII (April, 1968), p. 10, news.
news.

"Counter Attack in Colombia," *Moody Monthly*, LXVIII (July-August, 1968), p. 10, news. (Possible conflict wtih Eucharistic Congress.)

Constable, Robert L. "Discovery in Nicaragua," *Moody Monthly* (July, 1960), pp. 14, 15.

OCCASIONAL BULLETIN

Clemmer, Myrtle M., and Rycroft, W. Stanley. "A Statistical Study of Latin America," *Occasional Bulletin,* XIII (May, 1962), pp. 1-17.

THE SUNDAY SCHOOL TIMES

Strachan, R. Kenneth. "A Great Workers' Conference in Nicaragua," *The Sunday School Times,* CII (March 19, 1960), p. 7. (Preparation for EID.)

Fenton, Horace L., Jr. "A New Thing in Latin America," *The Sunday School Times,* CII (August 6, 1960), pp. 5, 6. (Full report on EID in Nicaragua.)

"Evangelism in Depth, Costa Rica," *The Sunday School Times,* CIII (February 4, 1961), p. 4, news.

"More Is Said Than Done," *The Sunday School Times,* CIII (February 25, 1961), p. 5. (Editorial on EID in Nicaragua and Costa Rica.)

"Evangelism-in-Depth, Costa Rica," *The Sunday School Times,* CIII (May 13, 1961), p. 4, news.

"News Report, Costa Rica," *The Sunday School Times,* CIII (September 23, 1961), p. 4. (EID in Guatemala postponed.)

"News Report — Evangelism-in-Depth Rescheduled," CIII (December 30, 1961), p. 4. (New dates for Guatemala campaign.)

Reapsome, James W. "Guatemala, A Nation Evangelized," *The Sunday School Times,* CIV (December 29, 1962), p. 1. (Editor's report on EID.)

————. "Will EID Work in My Church?" *The Sunday School Times,* CV (January 26, 1963).

————. "Latin America: Collapse or Breakthrough?" *The Sunday School Times,* CV (February 9, 1963). (Survey of Latin America.)

"Evangelism Strategy for Latin America," *The Sunday School Times,* CV (August 24, 1963), p. 2. (EID host to evangelists in Costa Rica.)

"Nationwide Evangelism in Honduras," *The Sunday School Times,* CVI (June 22, 1964), p. 3.

"Evangelistic Offensive in Venezuela," *The Sunday School Times,* CVI (October 10, 1964), p. 3.

"Ken Strachan's Vision," *The Sunday School Times,* CVII (March 13, 1965).

"Bolivia's Evangelism-in-Depth," *The Sunday School Times,* CVII (July 26, 1965), news brief.

"Cochabamba, Bolivia Evangelism-in-Depth," *The Sunday School Times,* CVII (October 9, 1965), p. 14, news brief.

"La Paz, Bolivia, Evangelism in Depth," *The Sunday School Times,* CVII (December 11, 1965), p. 4, news brief.

"Two Revolutions Touch the Dominican Republic," *The Sunday School Times,* CVIII (January 15, 1966).

"Christians in Dominican Republic Conclude EID," *The Sunday School Times,* CVIII (May 7, 1966), news.

"Costa Rica EID Institute," *The Sunday School Times,* CVIII (September 10, 1966), news.

"Campaign Launched in Congo," *The Sunday School Times*, CVIII (Octob 29, 1966). ('New Life For All' similar to EID.)

WORLD VISION MAGAZINE

Mackay, John A. "Christ or Religion?" *World Vision*, IX (July-Augus 1965), pp. 4 ff.

Seamands, John T. "Marvel of Multiplication," *World Vision*, IX (Jul August, 1965), pp. 6 ff.

Howard, David. "Colombia: Where the Bible Was Poison," *World Visio* (June, 1967), pp. 2-5.

Jones, Bill. "Evangelism-in-Depth Begins in Appalachia," *World Vision* (Se tember, 1967), pp. 2-5. (Gives statistics for all previous campaign Nicaragua, Costa Rica, Guatemala, Venezuela, Bolivia, Dominican R public, and Peru.)

Strachan, R. Kenneth. "What Your Church Was Meant to Be," *Worl Vision Magazine*, 12 (June, 1968), pp. 10-13.

"He's in Touch With Today," *World Vision Magazine*, 12 (July-Augus 1968), p. 34. (Personality profile of Horace L. Fenton, Jr.)

ALLIANCE WITNESS
1968

"Evangelism-in-Depth Still Alive in Peru," *Alliance Witness*, CIII (Novem ber 6, 1968), p. 13. (News brief on follow-up.)

CHRISTIANITY TODAY
1968

Sywulka, Stephen. "Colombia: An Illegal March," *Christianity Today*, XI (November 22, 1968), p. 45. (EID parade violated concordat with Rome

EVANGELICAL MISSIONS QUARTERLY
1968

Lores, Rubén. "The Mission of Missions," *Evangelical Missions Quarterl* IV (Spring, 1968), pp 140-147. (Missions-National Church relations.

LATIN AMERICA EVANGELIST
1968

Kenyon, John. "What Is Evangelism-in-Depth?" *Latin America Evangelis* XLVIII (November-December, 1968), pp. 1-5. (Principles, goals, brie history, and key men.)

"Latin America: First Proving Ground for Evangelism-in-Depth," *Lati America Evangelist*, XLVIII (November-December, 1968), pp. 6, 7 (Chronology of campaigns in Latin America.)

"In-Depth Evangelism Around the World," *Latin America Evangelist*, XLVII (November-December, 1968), pp. 8, 9. (Chronology and plans for cam paigns around the world.)

Sluyter, A. Merle. "Peru: The Church Has Been Activated," *Latin Americ Evangelist*, XLVIII (November-December, 1968), pp. 10, 11.

"Latin America News Front," *Latin America Evangelist*, XLVIII November-December, 1968), pp. 10a, 10b. (News briefs on Colombia.)

"What I've Learned Through Evangelism-in-Depth," *Latin America Evangelist*, XLVIII (November-December, 1968), pp. 12-15. (Testimonies by members of LAM advisory team.)

Braun, Willys K. "Congo: A Campaign Becomes a Movement," *Latin America Evangelist*, XLVIII (November-December, 1968), pp. 16, 17. (Congo campaign patterned after Evangelism-in-Depth.)

"Here's More Information on Evangelism-in-Depth," *Latin America Evangelist*, XLVIII (November-December, 1968), p. 19. (Books and audio-visuals available on EID.)

Hocard, David M. "A Calling That Is Inescapable," *Latin America Evangelist*, XLVIII (November-December, 1968), p. 19. (Book review of *The Inescapable Calling* by R. K. Strachan.)

Fenton, Horace L., Jr. "A Hard Question," *Latin America Evangelist*, XLVIII (November-December, 1968), pp. 20, 21. (Editorial on priorities for LAM.)

"What Does Evangelism-in-Depth Cost?" *Latin America Evangelist*, XLVIII (November-December, 1968), p. 22. (Cost figures on Latin American campaigns.)

Moody Monthly
1968

"Evangelism Takes the World," *Moody Monthly*, LXIX (December, 1968), p. 6. (News report on IFMA-EFMA meeting at Winona Lake; Dr. G. W. Peters' evaluation of EID.)

New Life For All

Marvellous in Our Eyes, Headquarters, NLFA.

New Life For All, Leader's Guide Book, Headquarters, P.O. Box 77, Jos, N. Nigeria.

New Life For All, Handbook for all Christians who desire to help others find New Life in Christ.

Pamphlets: *New Life For All; The Miracle of New Life; Steps to New Life.*